America's Best Recipes

A 1994 HOMETOWN COLLECTION

America's Best Recipes

Oxmoor House

ISBN: 0-8487-1163-7
ISSN: 0898-9982

Manufactured in the United States of America
First Printing 1994

Editor-in-Chief: Nancy J. Fitzpatrick
Senior Foods Editor: Susan Carlisle Payne
Senior Editor, Editorial Services: Olivia Kindig Wells
Art Director: James Boone

America's Best Recipes: A 1994 Hometown Collection

Editor: Janice Krahn Hanby
Copy Editor: Donna Baldone
Editorial Assistants: Kelly E. Hooper, Whitney Wheeler
Director, Test Kitchens: Vanessa Taylor Johnson
Assistant Director, Test Kitchens: Gayle Hays Sadler
Test Kitchens Home Economists: Susan Hall Bellows,
    Beth Floyd, Michele Brown Fuller, Elizabeth Tyler Luckett,
    Christina A. Pieroni, Kathleen Royal, Angie Neskaug Sinclair,
    Jan A. Smith
Senior Photographer: Jim Bathie
Senior Photo Stylist: Kay E. Clarke
Senior Production Designer: Larry Hunter
Indexer: Mary Ann Laurens
Associate Production Manager: Theresa L. Beste
Production Assistant: Marianne Jordan

Project Consultants: Meryle Evans, Audrey P. Stehle

Cover: *Discover the uniqueness of America's regional cuisines
and celebrate the bounty of the land in every recipe included in*
America's Best Recipes.

Preceding Page: *Cherished family recipes are sometimes given a
modern twist, like the addition of orange-flavored liqueur to a
traditional apple pie in New-Fashioned Apple Pie (page 210).*

Contents

Introduction

Outstanding recipes and regional charm distinguish community cookbooks published across the country each year. *America's Best Recipes: A 1994 Hometown Collection* contains over 400 of the very best recipes from these fund-raising cookbooks. Each year in our kitchens, we test hundreds of recipes from these sources, and only those getting the highest ratings are included in our collection. In the latest volume—our seventh—we feature cherished recipes from some of America's best cooks.

This year in response to the demands of today's busy cooks for quicker recipes, we offer a special chapter, "Quick and Easy Recipes," beginning on page 7. It includes the following:

- Over 60 quick and easy recipes—from appetizers to desserts.
- Recipes that call for a minimal number of commonly used ingredients, including high-quality convenience products.
- Recipes that take you from your pantry to your table in just 45 minutes or less or that can be totally prepared ahead of time.
- Valuable tips (page 8) such as organizing your kitchen, shopping with savvy, and preparing quick and easy meals.
- A handy ingredient substitution chart (page 9) to help prevent a last-minute dash to the grocery store.

The cookbooks we feature offer a glimpse into your communities and your regional food traditions. They also provide a means to generate funds that help the nonprofit organizations meet a variety of local needs. For example, some of the sponsoring organizations fund programs and services to help senior citizens, renovate a landmark theater, support a local food bank, provide trained dogs for the handicapped, buy a new fire truck, and protect a historic lighthouse from eroding cliffs.

As we applaud the organizations' generous efforts, we offer an alphabetical listing of each cookbook and the mailing address in the Acknowledgments (page 320). When you order any of the cookbooks, you'll receive not only terrific recipes, but also the satisfaction that comes from knowing you are contributing to the fund-raising successes of the volunteer groups that *America's Best Recipes* salutes each year.

The Editors

Quick & Easy Recipes

Cooks from across America share their best timesaving recipes and cooking strategies in this special quick and easy recipe chapter.

Stir-Fry Beef, page 18

Quick and Easy Cooking

Everyone loves good food, but today's fast-paced schedules hardly allow enough time to eat a good meal—much less prepare one. So what can you make in a hurry that tastes great?

You'll find delicious answers in this chapter of quick and easy recipes from some of America's best cooks. All of the recipes have a short ingredient list and skillfully use quality convenience products. As a result, you'll find the recipes are truly time-savers!

The key to quick and easy cooking is being ORGANIZED. These tips will help you make the most of your time in the kitchen and prepare great food fast.

Smart Shopping Shortcuts
- Think and plan ahead so you'll have to shop only once a week.
- Make a list following the aisle layout of the grocery store. Jot down what you need for meals and for restocking your pantry.
- Shop during off hours, if possible, to avoid the crowds.

Timesaving Kitchen Tips
- Organize your kitchen so that utensils are at your fingertips.
- Keep knives well sharpened and in a safe and convenient holder.
- Stock your pantry with staple items. Group similar items together, and rotate older items to the front to use first.

Quick and Easy Cooking Strategies
- Read the recipe before you start cooking to avoid last-minute surprises. If you run out of an ingredient, you may be able to substitute (see chart on facing page).
- Gather ingredients and utensils before you begin cooking.
- When making several recipes, think about the preparation order. Use the cooking time of one recipe to work on another.

Work-Saving Cleanup Tips
- Measure dry ingredients first and then reuse the measuring spoons for any wet ingredients.
- Wipe out skillets or pans for immediate reuse.
- Line the bottom of the broiler pan with foil for easy cleanup.

INGREDIENT SUBSTITUTION CHART

Ingredient Needed   *Substitution*

Baking Products:

1 cup powdered sugar | 1 cup sugar plus 1 tablespoon cornstarch, processed in food processor

1 cup honey | 1¼ cups sugar plus ¼ cup water

1 teaspoon baking powder | ⅓ teaspoon baking soda plus ½ teaspoon cream of tartar

Dairy Products:

1 cup milk | ½ cup evaporated milk plus ½ cup water

1 cup whipping cream | ¾ cup milk plus ⅓ cup melted butter (for baking only; will not whip)

1 cup sour cream | 1 cup yogurt plus 3 tablespoons melted butter or 1 cup yogurt plus 1 tablespoon cornstarch

Vegetables:

1 pound fresh mushrooms, sliced | 1 (8-ounce) can sliced mushrooms, drained, or 3 ounces dried mushrooms, rehydrated

1 small onion, chopped | 1 tablespoon instant minced onion or 1 teaspoon onion powder

3 tablespoons chopped sweet red pepper | 2 tablespoons chopped pimiento

3 tablespoons chopped shallots | 2 tablespoons chopped onion plus 1 tablespoon chopped garlic

Seasonings:

1 clove garlic | ⅛ teaspoon garlic powder or minced dried garlic

1 tablespoon chopped chives | 1 tablespoon chopped green onion tops

1 tablespoon grated gingerroot | ⅛ teaspoon ground ginger

1 (1-inch) vanilla bean | 1 teaspoon vanilla extract

1 teaspoon garlic salt | ⅛ teaspoon garlic powder plus ⅞ teaspoon salt

1 teaspoon dry mustard | 1 tablespoon prepared mustard

Miscellaneous Products:

¼ cup Marsala | ¼ cup dry white wine plus 1 teaspoon brandy

1 tablespoon brandy | ¼ teaspoon brandy extract plus 1 tablespoon water

½ cup balsamic vinegar | ½ cup red wine vinegar (slight flavor difference)

2 cups tomato sauce | ¾ cup tomato paste plus 1 cup water

Caramel Dip

For an attractive presentation, try serving this sweet, creamy dip ringed with a colorful variety of apple slices—Granny Smith, Red Delicious, and Golden Delicious.

1 (8-ounce) package cream
  cheese, softened

½ cup commercial caramel
  sauce

Beat cream cheese in a mixing bowl at medium speed of an electric mixer until creamy. Add caramel sauce, and mix well. Spoon into a serving bowl. Serve at room temperature with apple slices or pretzels. Yield: about 1½ cups.   Ann Berling

Cooking in Ohio, The Heart of It All
41st National Square Dance Convention
Cincinnati, Ohio

Karla's Bean Dip

When company's coming, serve this easy three-ingredient dip from a small chafing dish to keep it warm.

1 (11¼-ounce) can chili beef
  with beans soup, undiluted
1 (11-ounce) can Cheddar
  cheese soup, undiluted

1 (4-ounce) can chopped green
  chiles, undrained

Combine all ingredients in a medium saucepan, stirring well. Cook over medium heat 8 to 10 minutes or until thoroughly heated, stirring occasionally. Serve dip with tortilla chips. Yield: about 3 cups.   Karla Payne

Kailua Cooks
Le Jardin Academy
Kailua, Hawaii

Hot Onion Soufflé

This onion dip is really not a soufflé because it does not puff or contain beaten egg white, but it mimics the light, delicate texture of a soufflé.

4 cups frozen chopped onion, thawed

3 (8-ounce) packages cream cheese, softened

2 cups grated Parmesan cheese

½ cup mayonnaise

Press onion between layers of paper towels to remove excess moisture. Combine onion and remaining ingredients in a medium bowl; stir well. Spoon into a lightly greased 2-quart soufflé dish. Bake, uncovered, at 425° for 15 to 17 minutes or until golden. Serve warm with corn chips or assorted crackers. Yield: 6 cups.

Heart & Soul
The Junior League of Memphis, Tennessee

Tasty Roll-Ups

1 (8-ounce) can refrigerated crescent dinner rolls

1 (3-ounce) package cream cheese, softened

½ cup (2 ounces) shredded Cheddar cheese

2 tablespoons chopped ripe olives

2 tablespoons chopped green chiles

1 teaspoon instant minced onion

1 to 5 drops of hot sauce

Separate crescent roll dough into 4 rectangles. Press perforations to seal. Combine cream cheese and remaining ingredients in a small bowl; stir well. Spread cream cheese mixture evenly over rectangles. Roll up rectangles, starting at long side; pinch seams to seal. Cut each roll into 10 slices; place slices, cut side down, on greased baking sheets. Bake at 400° for 10 to 12 minutes or until golden. Serve warm. Yield: 40 appetizers.   Melita Vickter

A Jewish Family Cookbook
Valley Beth Shalom Nursery School
Encino, California

Tangy Kielbasa

When serving this simple yet satisfying appetizer, provide decorative party picks for your guests to spear the slices of sausage.

1 (10-ounce) jar red currant jelly

1¼ pounds fully cooked kielbasa sausage, thinly sliced

Cook jelly in a large saucepan over medium heat, stirring constantly, until jelly melts. Add sausage; stir well. Bring to a boil; cover, reduce heat, and simmer 30 minutes. Serve warm. Yield: 10 to 12 appetizer servings. Karin Grenier

Family Cookbook: A Collection of Favorite Recipes
Women's Ministries of Trinity Assembly of God
Derry, New Hampshire

Apricot Punch

Chill the apricot nectar and seltzer before making this punch to keep the sherbet from melting too quickly when you combine the ingredients.

1 quart orange sherbet, softened
1 (46-ounce) can apricot nectar, chilled

1 (1-liter) bottle seltzer or ginger ale, chilled

Scoop sherbet into a punch bowl. Combine apricot nectar and seltzer; pour over sherbet. Yield: 3½ quarts. Carolyn Small

From the Prince's Pantry
The Friends of Prince Memorial Library
Cumberland, Maine

Iced Tea Punch

If you don't have family-size tea bags, substitute 9 regular-size tea bags.

3 quarts boiling water
3 family-size tea bags
½ cup sugar
1 (12-ounce) can frozen
  lemonade concentrate,
  thawed and undiluted

1 (1-liter) bottle ginger ale,
  chilled

Pour boiling water over tea bags; cover and let stand 5 minutes. Remove tea bags, squeezing gently. Add sugar and lemonade concentrate, stirring until sugar dissolves. Chill. Gently stir in ginger ale just before serving. Serve over crushed ice. Yield: 1 gallon.

Under the Mulberry Tree
United Methodist Women of Mulberry Street
United Methodist Church
Macon, Georgia

Breakfast

1 pound mild bulk pork sausage
1 (8-ounce) can refrigerated
  crescent dinner rolls
2 cups (8 ounces) shredded
  mozzarella or Monterey Jack
  cheese

4 large eggs, beaten
¾ cup milk
¼ teaspoon salt
⅛ teaspoon pepper

Brown sausage in a skillet, stirring until it crumbles; drain. Place crescent roll dough in bottom of a greased 13- x 9- x 2-inch baking dish; press perforations and pinch seams to seal. Sprinkle reserved sausage and cheese over dough. Combine eggs and remaining ingredients; pour over mixture in dish. Bake, uncovered, at 425° for 15 minutes or until set. Let stand 5 minutes before serving. Yield: 8 servings.

Roaring Springs Recipes & Memories
Roaring Springs Volunteer Organization
Roaring Springs, Texas

Grilled Catfish with Dijon Sauce

If you prefer broiled fish, you can place the catfish fillets on rack in a broiler pan and broil them 5½ inches from heat (with electric oven door partially opened) 10 to 12 minutes or until fish flakes easily when tested with a fork.

4 (8-ounce) farm-raised catfish
  fillets
3 tablespoons butter or
  margarine, melted
1 teaspoon lemon-pepper
  seasoning

1 teaspoon Worcestershire
  sauce
Garnish: lemon twists
Dijon Sauce

Rinse fillets with cold water, and pat dry. Combine butter, lemon-pepper seasoning, and Worcestershire sauce in a small bowl; stir well. Brush butter mixture over fillets.

Grill fillets, covered, over medium-hot coals (350° to 400°) 5 to 6 minutes on each side or until fish flakes easily when tested with a fork. Remove fillets to a serving platter. Garnish, if desired. Serve immediately with warm Dijon Sauce. Yield: 4 servings.

Dijon Sauce

½ cup sour cream
1 tablespoon Dijon mustard

1 teaspoon Worcestershire
  sauce

Combine all ingredients in a small saucepan; cook over medium-low heat, stirring constantly, until mixture is thoroughly heated. Yield: ½ cup.

Phillip Sherman, Jr.

Impressions: A Palette of Fine Memphis Dining
Auxiliary to the Memphis Dental Society
Memphis, Tennessee

Baked Orange Roughy

1½ pounds orange roughy
  fillets
2 egg whites

¾ cup mayonnaise
1 teaspoon curry powder

Place fillets in a lightly greased 13- x 9- x 2-inch baking dish, and set aside.

Beat egg whites at high speed of an electric mixer until stiff peaks form. Gently fold in mayonnaise and curry powder; spread mixture evenly over fillets. Bake at 350° for 25 to 30 minutes or until fish flakes easily when tested with a fork. Serve immediately. Yield: 4 servings.

Jean Eisenhuth

American Heritage Cookbook
Brownsville General Hospital Auxiliary
Brownsville, Pennsylvania

Sugar-Grilled Salmon

Grill the salmon steaks in a grill basket that's been coated with vegetable cooking spray to keep the fish from sticking to the grill and basket.

½ cup firmly packed brown
  sugar
¼ cup butter or margarine,
  melted

2 tablespoons dry sherry
2 tablespoons soy sauce
4 (6-ounce) salmon steaks, 1
  inch thick

Combine first 4 ingredients in a small bowl, stirring until sugar dissolves. Place steaks in a large shallow dish. Pour marinade mixture over steaks; cover and marinate in refrigerator 15 minutes, turning once.

Drain steaks, reserving marinade. Grill, covered, over medium-hot coals (350° to 400°) 5 minutes on each side or until fish flakes easily when tested with a fork, basting frequently with reserved marinade. Yield: 4 servings.

Family & Company
The Junior League of Binghamton, New York

Scallops with Balsamic Vinegar and Basil

For a change of pace, try serving this shellfish meal for two over fine egg noodles instead of rice.

1 shallot, minced
1 clove garlic, minced
2 tablespoons butter or
  margarine, melted
14 ounces bay scallops
1½ tablespoons finely
  chopped fresh basil

1 tablespoon balsamic vinegar
⅛ teaspoon salt
Dash of pepper
Hot cooked rice

Sauté shallot and garlic in butter in a large skillet over medium-high heat, stirring constantly, until tender. Add scallops and basil, and sauté 2 minutes. Add vinegar, salt, and pepper, and sauté an additional 3 minutes or until scallops are opaque. Serve immediately over rice. Yield: 2 servings.   Beatrice Gaydos

What's Cooking in Nutley!
The Friends of the Nutley Public Library
Nutley, New Jersey

Shrimp with Asparagus

Buy shrimp that has been peeled and deveined, and you'll net great savings in preparation time for this recipe.

1½ pounds fresh asparagus
1 pound peeled and deveined
  medium-size fresh shrimp
¼ cup butter or margarine,
  melted
1 large clove garlic, crushed

2 teaspoons grated lemon rind
1½ tablespoons fresh lemon
  juice
¼ teaspoon salt
6 lemon slices
Hot cooked rice

Snap off tough ends of asparagus. Remove scales from stalks with a knife or vegetable peeler, if desired. Cut asparagus into 2-inch pieces. Arrange asparagus in a vegetable steamer over boiling water. Cover and steam 3 minutes. Rinse with cold water; drain.

Arrange asparagus in a lightly greased 11- x 7- x 1½-inch baking dish. Place shrimp over asparagus; set aside.

Combine butter and next 4 ingredients; stir well. Drizzle butter mixture over shrimp and asparagus; top with lemon slices. Cover and bake at 400° for 15 to 20 minutes or until shrimp turn pink. Serve over rice. Yield: 4 to 6 servings.   Laurie Guy

Cooking with Class, A Second Helping
Charlotte Latin School
Charlotte, North Carolina

Speedy Stroganoff

Partially freezing the porterhouse steak makes it easier to cut the meat diagonally across the grain into thin strips. Slicing the meat diagonally helps tenderize it and makes the strips of meat appear larger.

1 (1-pound) porterhouse steak	3 tablespoons water
3 tablespoons all-purpose flour	1 (1-ounce) envelope onion
¼ cup butter or margarine,	soup mix
melted	1 (8-ounce) carton sour cream
1 (3-ounce) can sliced	Hot cooked fine egg noodles
mushrooms, undrained	or rice

Slice steak diagonally across grain into thin strips; toss with flour. Brown steak in butter in a large skillet over medium heat; add mushrooms, mushroom liquid, and water. Stir in soup mix. Bring to a boil; reduce heat, and stir in sour cream. Cook, uncovered, until thoroughly heated (do not boil). Serve over noodles. Yield: 4 servings.   Edith Smith

A Taste of Paradise
Anna Maria Island Community Center
Anna Maria, Florida

Stir-Fry Beef

This beef stir-fry is terrific—and hot! For a milder version, reduce the amount of dried crushed red pepper by half.

2 pounds boneless sirloin steak
2 large sweet red peppers, coarsely chopped
¼ cup vegetable oil, divided
2 medium onions, cut into wedges
4 cloves garlic, minced
2 small yellow squash, cut into ½-inch cubes
3 tablespoons soy sauce
2 tablespoons dried crushed red pepper
1 teaspoon black pepper
Hot cooked rice
Garnish: green onion strips

Trim excess fat from steak; slice steak diagonally across grain into thin strips. Set aside.

Place sweet red peppers in container of an electric blender or food processor; cover and process until smooth, stopping frequently to scrape down sides. Set aside.

Pour 2 tablespoons oil around top of preheated wok or large skillet, coating sides; heat at medium-high (375°) for 2 minutes. Add onion and garlic, and stir-fry 2 minutes. Add squash, and stir-fry 1 to 2 minutes or until crisp-tender. Remove vegetables from wok, and set aside.

Pour 1 tablespoon oil into wok; add half of reserved steak strips, and stir-fry 2 to 3 minutes or until browned. Remove steak from wok, and set aside. Pour remaining 1 tablespoon oil into wok; add remaining steak strips, and stir-fry 2 to 3 minutes or until browned. Combine soy sauce, crushed red pepper, and black pepper. Add soy sauce mixture, reserved sweet red pepper puree, reserved vegetable mixture, and reserved steak strips to wok; stir-fry until thoroughly heated. Serve over rice. Garnish, if desired. Yield: 6 servings.

Plain & Elegant: A Georgia Heritage
West Georgia Medical Center Auxiliary
LaGrange, Georgia

Grand-Style Ground Beef

1½ pounds ground beef
1 cup chopped onion
1 (10¾-ounce) can cream of
  mushroom soup, undiluted
1 (8-ounce) package cream
  cheese, softened

¼ cup milk
¼ cup catsup
1 teaspoon salt
1 (10-ounce) can refrigerated
  biscuits

Brown ground beef and onion in a large skillet, stirring until meat crumbles; drain and set aside.

Combine soup and next 4 ingredients in a large bowl; stir well. Add reserved ground beef mixture, and stir well. Place in a lightly greased 2-quart casserole. Bake, uncovered, at 375° for 10 minutes. Separate biscuits, and arrange on top of ground beef mixture. Bake an additional 15 to 20 minutes or until biscuits are golden. Yield: 6 servings.   Randy Marrs

More, Please!
St. Thomas More Catholic School
Baton Rouge, Louisiana

Hamburger Quiche

1 pound ground beef
2 large eggs, lightly beaten
½ cup mayonnaise or salad
  dressing
½ cup milk

1 cup (4 ounces) shredded
  sharp Cheddar cheese
⅓ cup finely chopped onion
1 unbaked 9-inch pastry shell

Brown ground beef in a large skillet, stirring until it crumbles; drain and set aside.

Combine eggs, mayonnaise, and milk in a large bowl; stir well. Stir in reserved ground beef, cheese, and onion. Pour mixture into pastry shell. Bake, uncovered, at 350° for 30 to 35 minutes or until set and lightly browned. Let stand 5 minutes before serving. Yield: one 9-inch quiche.   Marilyn Fontayne

Our Favorite Recipes
Unity Truth Center
Port Richey, Florida

Garden Taco Rice

By substituting 1 pound of fresh ground turkey for the ground beef, you'll create a simple, low-fat variation of this colorful rice dish.

1 pound ground beef
½ cup chopped onion
1 (14½-ounce) can stewed
   tomatoes, undrained and
   chopped
1½ cups thinly sliced zucchini
1½ cups water

1 cup frozen whole kernel
   corn
1½ cups instant rice, uncooked
1 cup (4 ounces) shredded
   Cheddar cheese
Garnish: cherry tomatoes

Brown ground beef and onion in a large skillet, stirring until meat crumbles; drain well. Return meat mixture to skillet; stir in tomatoes and next 3 ingredients. Bring to a boil; stir in rice. Cover, reduce heat, and simmer 5 to 7 minutes or until rice is tender and liquid is absorbed. Remove from heat, and sprinkle with cheese. Cover and let stand 3 minutes or until cheese melts. Garnish, if desired. Yield: 6 servings.

Fiddlers Canyon Ward Cookbook
Fiddlers Canyon Ward Relief Society
Cedar City, Utah

Pork Medaillons Dijon

Crushed black peppercorns fire up the flavor of this entrée. The popular spice is actually a berry that grows on the pepper plant. It's harvested when not quite ripe and then dried.

1 (1-pound) pork tenderloin
¼ cup all-purpose flour
3 tablespoons butter or
   margarine, melted

⅓ cup white vinegar
8 black peppercorns, crushed
2 cups whipping cream
⅓ cup Dijon mustard

Cut tenderloin into ½-inch-thick slices. Dredge tenderloin slices in flour. Brown tenderloin slices in melted butter in a large skillet over medium-high heat 3 to 4 minutes on each side. Remove tenderloin slices to a serving platter, reserving drippings in skillet. Set tenderloin slices aside, and keep warm.

Add vinegar and crushed peppercorns to drippings. Cook over medium-high heat until liquid is reduced to 2 tablespoons. Reduce heat to medium. Add whipping cream; cook 15 minutes or until mixture is reduced to 1½ cups, stirring occasionally. Remove from heat, and stir in mustard. Serve reserved tenderloin slices with warm sauce. Yield: 4 servings. Martha Jones

Cooking with Grace
Grace Episcopal Church
Kirkwood, Missouri

Stir-Fried Pork with Broccoli and Sesame

Using a high cooking temperature and small pieces of food make stir-frying a quick and easy cooking method.

1 (14½-ounce) can ready-to-
  serve chicken broth
4 green onions, chopped
2 tablespoons cornstarch
1 tablespoon soy sauce
1½ pounds fresh broccoli

2 tablespoons vegetable oil
1 (1-pound) pork tenderloin,
  cut into 1-inch cubes
1 clove garlic, crushed
2 tablespoons sesame seeds,
  toasted

Combine first 4 ingredients in a small bowl; stir well. Set aside.
Trim off large leaves of broccoli; remove tough ends of stalks. Wash broccoli thoroughly; cut into 1-inch pieces. Set aside.
Pour oil around top of preheated wok, coating sides; heat at medium high (375°) for 1 minute. Add tenderloin and garlic, and stir-fry 5 minutes. Remove tenderloin and garlic from wok; set aside. Add reserved broth mixture and reserved broccoli, and stir-fry 6 minutes or until broccoli is crisp-tender. Add reserved tenderloin, and stir-fry until thoroughly heated. Sprinkle with sesame seeds. Yield: 4 to 6 servings. Phyllis Tuggle

The Summerhouse Sampler
Wynnton Elementary School PTA
Columbus, Georgia

Impossible Ham 'n' Swiss Pie

Green onions add flecks of color and flavor to this entrée, but the same amount of yellow or white onions can be substituted.

¾ pound cooked ham, chopped
1 cup (4 ounces) shredded Swiss cheese

⅓ cup chopped green onions
2 cups milk
4 large eggs, beaten
1 cup biscuit mix

Combine ham, cheese, and green onions in a greased 10-inch pieplate. Set aside.

Combine milk and eggs; stir well. Gradually add milk mixture to biscuit mix; beat at medium speed of an electric mixer until smooth. Pour batter over ham mixture. Bake, uncovered, at 400° for 35 to 40 minutes or until set and lightly browned. Let stand 5 minutes before serving. Yield: 6 servings.   June Coltharp

Incredible Edibles
The Salvation Army Women's Auxiliary
Baltimore, Maryland

Smoked Sausage and Rice Jambalaya

When you're in a hurry, use 1 pound of smoked cocktail sausages instead of cutting up a large smoked sausage into 2-inch pieces.

Butter-flavored vegetable cooking spray
1 pound smoked sausage, cut into 2-inch pieces
½ cup chopped onion
½ cup sliced celery
½ cup chopped green pepper
1 (28-ounce) can whole tomatoes, undrained and chopped

3 cups cooked rice
½ teaspoon garlic powder
½ teaspoon ground red pepper
½ teaspoon dried thyme

Coat a large skillet with cooking spray. Sauté sausage, onion, celery, and green pepper in skillet over medium heat, stirring constantly, until sausage is browned and vegetables are tender. Stir in tomatoes and remaining ingredients. Cook an additional 5 minutes or until mixture is thoroughly heated, stirring frequently. Serve immediately. Yield: 6 servings.   Fannie Mae Jones

Golden Goodies: Favorite Recipes from Positive Maturity
Positive Maturity
Birmingham, Alabama

Broccoli Lasagna au Gratin

To save time, use the paper-thin, precooked lasagna noodles. This convenience product is available in the dried pasta section of most grocery stores.

2 (10-ounce) packages frozen chopped broccoli, thawed and drained
2 cups small-curd cottage cheese
2 large eggs, lightly beaten
1 (26-ounce) jar spaghetti sauce
9 cooked lasagna noodles
2 cups (8 ounces) shredded mozzarella cheese
½ cup grated Parmesan cheese

Combine broccoli, cottage cheese, and eggs in a medium bowl; stir well. Set aside.

Spoon ⅓ cup spaghetti sauce into bottom of a lightly greased 13- x 9- x 2-inch baking dish; spread evenly. Arrange 3 cooked lasagna noodles on top of sauce. Layer one-third reserved broccoli mixture over noodles; top with one-third each of remaining spaghetti sauce, mozzarella cheese, and Parmesan cheese. Repeat layers twice. Bake, uncovered, at 350° for 30 to 35 minutes or until hot and bubbly. Let stand 10 minutes before serving. Yield: 8 to 10 servings.   Carolyn M. Parker

Food for Family, Friends and Fellowship
Covenant Women Ministries of Forest Park Covenant Church
Muskegon, Michigan

15-Minute Creamy Fettuccine Alfredo

Freshly grated Parmesan cheese will offer maximum flavor in this dish. For convenience, buy it in the cheese section of your grocery store.

8 ounces fettuccine, uncooked
1 (8-ounce) package cream
   cheese, cubed

¾ cup grated Parmesan cheese
½ cup butter or margarine
½ cup milk

Cook fettuccine according to package directions; drain. Place fettuccine in a serving bowl. Set aside, and keep warm.

Combine cream cheese and remaining ingredients in a saucepan. Cook over low heat until cheeses and butter melt, stirring frequently. Add cheese mixture to reserved fettuccine; toss to coat. Serve immediately. Yield: 4 servings. Alison Foye

A Taste of Twin Pines
Twin Pines Alumni of Twin Pines Cooperative House
West Lafayette, Indiana

Orzo with Parmesan and Basil

To keep freshly grated Parmesan cheese on hand at all times, freeze it. Freezing the cheese up to two months doesn't result in significant loss of flavor.

1½ cups orzo, uncooked
3 tablespoons butter or
   margarine, melted
3 cups chicken broth
½ cup grated Parmesan cheese

¼ cup plus 2 tablespoons
   julienne-sliced fresh basil
Salt and freshly ground pepper
   to taste
Garnish: fresh basil sprigs

Sauté orzo in butter in a large skillet over medium-high heat, stirring constantly, until golden. Add broth; bring to a boil. Cover, reduce heat, and simmer 20 minutes or until orzo is tender (liquid will be absorbed). Stir in Parmesan cheese, julienne-sliced basil, and salt and pepper to taste. Garnish, if desired. Serve immediately. Yield: 4 cups. Elizabeth H. Catlin

June Fete Fare
The Women's Board of Abington Memorial Hospital
Abington, Pennsylvania

Apricot-Dijon Mustard Chicken

Dijon mustard is a mixture of brown mustard seeds, white wine, unfermented grape juice, and seasonings. Originally made in Dijon, France, the mustard is known for its sharp flavor.

2¼ cups chicken broth
1 (10-ounce) package couscous
1 (12-ounce) can apricot nectar
3 tablespoons Dijon mustard
6 skinned and boned chicken
   breast halves

2 tablespoons minced fresh
   basil
Garnishes: lime wedges, fresh
   basil sprigs

Bring chicken broth to a boil in a medium saucepan; stir in couscous. Cover, remove from heat, and let stand 5 minutes or until liquid is absorbed. Remove couscous to a serving platter; set aside, and keep warm.

Combine apricot nectar and mustard in a large skillet; bring to a boil. Add chicken; cover, reduce heat, and simmer 10 minutes. Turn chicken; cover and simmer an additional 5 to 8 minutes or until done.

Remove chicken from skillet, reserving liquid in skillet. Place chicken on top of reserved couscous; set aside, and keep warm. Bring liquid to a boil; cook, uncovered, 10 minutes or until reduced to 1 cup. Spoon sauce over chicken; sprinkle with minced basil. Garnish, if desired. Yield: 6 servings.

Leslie Wills

From the Hearts and Homes of Bellingham Covenant Church
Covenant Women's Ministries of Bellingham Covenant Church
Bellingham, Washington

Chicken in Mustard Sauce

4 skinned and boned chicken
  breast halves, cut into
  1½-inch pieces
1 tablespoon vegetable oil
⅓ cup Chablis or other dry
  white wine
½ cup whipping cream

1 tablespoon Dijon mustard
1 tablespoon lemon juice
½ teaspoon salt
¼ teaspoon pepper
¼ teaspoon dried tarragon
Dash of ground red pepper

Brown chicken in oil in a large skillet over medium-high heat 4 minutes or until done, turning occasionally. Remove chicken from skillet, reserving drippings in skillet. Set chicken aside; keep warm.

Add wine to drippings; cook over high heat, deglazing pan by scraping particles that cling to bottom. Reduce heat to medium. Stir in whipping cream and remaining ingredients. Cook, uncovered, until mixture is thick enough to coat a spoon, stirring occasionally. Add reserved chicken. Bring to a boil; cover, reduce heat, and simmer 5 minutes. Yield: 4 servings.

Desert Treasures
The Junior League of Phoenix, Arizona

Lemon-Broccoli Chicken

4 skinned and boned chicken
  breast halves
1 tablespoon vegetable oil
1 (10¾-ounce) can cream of
  broccoli soup, undiluted

¼ cup milk
2 teaspoons lemon juice
⅛ teaspoon pepper
4 lemon slices

Brown chicken in oil in a large skillet over medium heat 5 minutes on each side.

Combine soup and next 3 ingredients; stir well. Pour soup mixture over chicken. Top each piece of chicken with a lemon slice. Cover, reduce heat, and simmer 5 minutes or until chicken is done. Yield: 4 servings.
Wayne McHatton

M.D. Anderson Volunteers Cooking for Fun
University of Texas M.D. Anderson Cancer Center
Houston, Texas

Chicken with Lime Butter

6 skinned and boned chicken
  breast halves
½ teaspoon salt
½ teaspoon pepper
⅓ cup vegetable oil

Juice of 1 medium lime
½ cup butter or margarine
½ teaspoon freeze-dried chives
½ teaspoon dried dillweed

Sprinkle chicken with salt and pepper. Brown in oil in a skillet over medium heat 7 minutes on each side or until done. Remove chicken from skillet; set aside, and keep warm. Wipe drippings from skillet. Add lime juice; bring to a boil over medium heat. Add butter; cook, stirring constantly, until butter melts. Stir in chives and dillweed. Spoon sauce over chicken. Yield: 6 servings.

The Best of Sunset Boulevard
University Synagogue Sisterhood
Los Angeles, California

Chicken Livers with Mushrooms

¼ cup all-purpose flour, divided
1 teaspoon salt
1 pound chicken livers
1 small onion, chopped
1 (4-ounce) can mushroom
  stems and pieces, drained

¼ cup butter, melted
1 (10¾-ounce) can cream of
  chicken soup, undiluted
¾ cup milk
¼ teaspoon pepper
Buttered toast

Combine 2 tablespoons flour and salt; dredge livers in flour mixture. Cook livers, onion, and mushrooms in butter in a skillet over medium heat 5 to 6 minutes, turning occasionally. Remove livers from skillet, reserving vegetables and drippings in skillet. Set aside; keep warm. Reduce heat to low. Stir in remaining 2 tablespoons flour; cook, stirring constantly, 1 minute. Gradually add soup, milk, and pepper; cook, stirring constantly, until thickened and bubbly. Add livers; cook until thoroughly heated. Serve over toast. Yield: 4 to 6 servings.   Grace Cothern

Enon's Best Kept Secret II
Enon Baptist Church
Jayess, Mississippi

Turkey Breast Marsala

8 (½-inch-thick) slices cooked
turkey breast, about 1½
pounds
¼ cup butter or margarine,
melted
⅛ teaspoon pepper
8 slices prosciutto (about ¼
pound)

8 (1-ounce) slices Monterey
Jack cheese
½ cup Marsala
Garnish: chopped fresh
parsley

Brown turkey in butter in a large skillet over medium-high heat 2 minutes on each side. Sprinkle with pepper. Place 1 slice of prosciutto and 1 slice of cheese on top of each slice of turkey. Pour Marsala over cheese. Cover, reduce heat to medium-low, and cook until cheese melts. Garnish, if desired. Yield: 8 servings.

Celebrate!
The Junior League of Sacramento, California

Quick Soup

No cooking is required for this soup. Just blend the ingredients together, and chill thoroughly to allow flavors to blend.

1 (46-ounce) can vegetable
juice
1 (8-ounce) carton sour cream
1 teaspoon dried onion flakes

1 teaspoon Worcestershire
sauce
Salt and pepper to taste
Garnish: chopped fresh chives

Combine all ingredients except chives in a large bowl; stir well. Transfer half of vegetable juice mixture to container of an electric blender; cover and process until smooth, stopping once to scrape down sides. Repeat procedure with remaining vegetable juice mixture. Cover and chill thoroughly.

To serve, ladle soup into individual soup bowls. Garnish, if desired. Yield: 8 cups.

Virginia Celebrates
The Council of the Virginia Museum of Fine Arts
Richmond, Virginia

Speedy Spinach Soup

1 (10-ounce) package frozen chopped spinach, thawed
1 (8-ounce) package cream cheese
1 (14½-ounce) can ready-to-serve chicken broth, divided

Press spinach between layers of paper towels to remove excess moisture. Combine spinach and cream cheese in a medium saucepan. Cook over medium-low heat until cheese melts, stirring frequently. Remove from heat; stir in half of broth.

Transfer spinach mixture to container of an electric blender; cover and process on high speed 1 minute or until smooth, stopping once to scrape down sides. Return mixture to saucepan; stir in remaining broth. Cook over medium heat until thoroughly heated, stirring frequently. Yield: 3½ cups.

Steamboat Entertains
Steamboat Springs Winter Sports Club
Steamboat Springs, Colorado

Old Homesteader Main-Dish Soup

1 pound ground beef
½ cup julienne-sliced green pepper
½ cup chopped onion
2 tablespoons chili powder
2 (11¼-ounce) cans chili beef soup, undiluted
1 (16-ounce) can whole tomatoes, undrained and chopped
1 (16-ounce) can kidney beans, undrained
½ cup water

Brown ground beef in a large skillet, stirring until it crumbles; drain. Return ground beef to skillet; add green pepper, onion, and chili powder. Cook, uncovered, over medium heat until vegetables are tender, stirring occasionally. Add soup and remaining ingredients. Bring to a boil; reduce heat, and simmer, uncovered, 15 minutes, stirring frequently. Yield: 8 cups.   Karen Ellis

Treasured Recipes
Morton County Hospital Auxiliary
Elkhart, Kansas

Bean-Bacon Chowder

6 slices bacon, chopped
1 cup chopped onion
2 tablespoons all-purpose flour
3 cups milk
2 medium baking potatoes,
    peeled and diced

1 teaspoon salt
¼ teaspoon dried thyme
⅛ teaspoon pepper
1 (21-ounce) can pork and
    beans in tomato sauce
¼ cup chopped fresh parsley

Sauté bacon and onion in a Dutch oven over medium heat, stirring constantly, until onion is tender. Reduce heat to low. Add flour; cook 1 minute, stirring constantly. Gradually add milk; cook over medium heat, stirring constantly, until thickened and bubbly. Stir in potato, salt, thyme, and pepper. Bring to a boil; cover, reduce heat, and simmer 15 to 20 minutes or until potato is tender. Stir in beans; cover and cook until thoroughly heated. Sprinkle with parsley. Yield: 7 cups.   Tondi Tillman

Family Style Cookbook
Northern Door Child Care Center
Sister Bay, Wisconsin

Ham-Vegetable Chowder

1 (10¾-ounce) can cream of
    tomato soup, undiluted
1½ cups water
1 cup chopped celery
½ cup chopped onion
1 (10-ounce) package frozen
    mixed vegetables

1 (10¾-ounce) can cream of
    potato soup, undiluted
1¼ cups milk
1 cup chopped cooked ham
1 tablespoon dried parsley
    flakes

Combine tomato soup and water in a Dutch oven; add celery and onion. Bring to a boil; reduce heat, and simmer 5 minutes. Add mixed vegetables. Bring to a boil; reduce heat, and simmer, uncovered, 10 minutes or until tender. Add potato soup and remaining ingredients; bring just to a boil. Yield: 7 cups.   Phyllis Camper

Country Church Favorites
St. John's United Church of Christ
Genoa, Ohio

Fast Clam Chowder

The term chowder originates from the French word chaudière, a caldron in which fishermen prepared their stews using freshly caught seafood.

1 medium onion, chopped
2 tablespoons butter or
  margarine, melted
1⅓ cups milk

1 (10¾-ounce) can cream of
  potato soup, undiluted
1 (6-ounce) can minced clams,
  undrained

Sauté onion in melted butter in a large saucepan over medium heat, stirring constantly, until onion is tender. Add milk and remaining ingredients, stirring until blended. Bring to a boil over medium heat; reduce heat, and simmer, uncovered, 10 minutes. Yield: 4 cups.

Shirley Beringer

Pride of Gaithersburg
Gaithersburg Lioness Club
Gaithersburg, Maryland

Corn-Crab Chowder

¼ cup chopped green onions
1 clove garlic, minced
⅛ teaspoon ground red
  pepper
1 tablespoon butter or
  margarine, melted
2 (10¾-ounce) cans cream of
  potato soup, undiluted

2 cups milk
1 (15¼-ounce) can golden
  kernel corn, undrained
1 (8-ounce) package cream
  cheese, cubed and softened
1 (6-ounce) can crabmeat,
  drained

Sauté green onions, garlic, and red pepper in butter in a large saucepan over medium heat, stirring constantly, until tender.

Combine soup and milk, stirring well. Add soup mixture, corn, and remaining ingredients to saucepan. Reduce heat to medium-low; cook, stirring constantly, just until cheese melts. Serve immediately. Yield: 8 cups.

Deena Shealy

Starlight and Moonbeams
Babies' Alumni of Hilton Head Hospital
Hilton Head Island, South Carolina

Fast and Easy Italian Green Beans

Canned vegetables are always quick to prepare, yet here they take on a new flair in this colorful side-dish recipe.

½ cup chopped onion
½ cup chopped green pepper
1 tablespoon butter or
  margarine, melted
1 (16-ounce) can whole new
  potatoes, drained and sliced

1 (14½-ounce) can stewed
  tomatoes, undrained
1 (16-ounce) can cut Italian
  green beans, drained
¼ cup grated Parmesan cheese

Sauté onion and green pepper in butter in a large skillet over medium heat, stirring constantly, until tender. Add potatoes, and sauté an additional 2 minutes. Add stewed tomatoes and beans, and cook until thoroughly heated. Sprinkle with cheese. Serve immediately. Yield: 10 servings.

Thymely Treasures
Hubbard Historical Society
Hubbard, Ohio

Sicilian Broccoli

2½ cups fresh broccoli
  flowerets
2 cloves garlic, minced
2 tablespoons butter or
  margarine, melted

2 tablespoons olive oil
¼ cup sliced ripe olives
⅓ cup grated Parmesan cheese
Garnish: lemon wedges

Arrange broccoli in a vegetable steamer over boiling water. Cover and steam 8 to 10 minutes or until crisp-tender. Arrange broccoli on a serving platter; set aside, and keep warm.

Sauté garlic in butter and oil in a small saucepan over medium heat, stirring constantly, 2 to 3 minutes or until golden. Stir in olives. Pour mixture over reserved broccoli; sprinkle with cheese. Garnish, if desired. Serve immediately. Yield: 4 servings.

Catawba Seasons
Catawba Memorial Hospital Auxiliary
Hickory, North Carolina

Scalloped Tomatoes with Cheese

1 (16-ounce) can whole
   tomatoes, undrained and
   coarsely chopped
1½ cups plain croutons
4 ounces mozzarella cheese,
   cut into ½-inch cubes

4 ounces Cheddar cheese, cut
   into ½-inch cubes
1 tablespoon minced onion
½ teaspoon salt
½ teaspoon pepper

Combine all ingredients in a large bowl, and stir well. Spoon tomato mixture into a greased 13- x 9- x 2-inch baking dish, spreading evenly. Bake, uncovered, at 375° for 20 minutes or until cheeses melt and tomato mixture is thoroughly heated. Serve immediately. Yield: 6 to 8 servings.   William Godbey

Our Cherished Recipes, Second Edition
First Presbyterian Church
Skagway, Alaska

Fresh Tomato Sauce with Basil

Substitute 2 teaspoons dried basil if you don't have the fresh herb on hand.

1 to 3 cloves garlic, minced
2 tablespoons finely chopped
   onion
2 tablespoons olive oil
2 large tomatoes or 10 plum
   tomatoes, coarsely chopped
2 tablespoons chopped fresh
   basil

Salt and pepper to taste
1 teaspoon dried parsley flakes
   (optional)
¼ teaspoon dried oregano
   (optional)
⅛ teaspoon dried thyme
   (optional)
Hot cooked pasta

Sauté garlic and onion in oil in a large skillet over medium-high heat, stirring constantly, until lightly browned. Add tomato; cook over low heat 10 minutes, stirring occasionally. Stir in basil, salt and pepper to taste, and, if desired, parsley, oregano, and thyme. Serve sauce over pasta. Yield: 1½ cups.   Eve Marcus

California Kosher
Women's League of Adat Ari El Synagogue
North Hollywood, California

Cherry Salad

You can get up to a month's head start with this sweet freezer salad. Just be sure to wrap the salad so that it's airtight to preserve its freshness.

1 (21-ounce) can cherry pie
   filling
1 (14-ounce) can sweetened
   condensed milk
1 (5¼-ounce) can crushed
   pineapple, drained

1 (8-ounce) container frozen
   whipped topping, thawed
Garnishes: whipped topping,
   maraschino cherries

Combine first 3 ingredients in a large bowl; stir well. Fold in thawed whipped topping. Spread mixture evenly in a 13- x 9- x 2-inch pan. Cover and freeze at least 8 hours.

Remove from freezer, and let stand at room temperature 5 minutes. Cut into squares. Garnish, if desired. Serve immediately. Yield: 15 servings.   Adela Kisker, Marie Pinckard

Idalia Community Cookbook
Women's Fellowship of St. John United Church of Christ
Idalia, Colorado

Carrot Salad with Lemon-Dill Dressing

Substitute 2 teaspoons dried dillweed if fresh dill isn't available.

½ cup vegetable oil
¼ cup lemon juice
2 tablespoons minced fresh
   dill

1 teaspoon salt
2 (16-ounce) packages frozen
   crinkle-cut carrots, thawed

Combine first 4 ingredients in a large bowl; stir with a wire whisk until blended. Add carrots, and stir gently to coat. Cover and chill. Yield: 12 servings.   Florence Keuler

Grazing Across Wisconsin, Book II
Telephone Pioneers of America, Wisconsin Chapter 4
Milwaukee, Wisconsin

Peas and Smoked Almond Salad

1 (16-ounce) package frozen
English peas, thawed
1 (6-ounce) can whole smoked
almonds

3 green onions, thinly sliced
½ cup mayonnaise
1½ tablespoons curry powder

Combine peas, almonds, and green onions in a large bowl, and toss gently.

Combine mayonnaise and curry powder; stir well. Add mayonnaise mixture to pea mixture; toss gently. Cover and chill at least 8 hours. Yield: 6 to 8 servings.   Joan Turcotte

Georgia Land
Medical Association of Georgia Alliance
Atlanta, Georgia

Herbed Biscuits

With an investment of just a few minutes, you can add these savory herb-flavored biscuits to your next dinner.

3 tablespoons butter or
margarine, melted
1 tablespoon instant minced
onion
1 teaspoon dried dillweed

1 teaspoon poppy seeds
¼ cup grated Parmesan cheese
1 (10-ounce) can refrigerated
buttermilk biscuits

Pour melted butter into an 8-inch round cakepan. Sprinkle onion, dillweed, and poppy seeds evenly over butter. Set aside.

Place Parmesan cheese in a large heavy-duty, zip-top plastic bag. Cut each biscuit into 4 pieces; add biscuit pieces to bag, and shake to coat. Arrange coated biscuit pieces in prepared pan; sprinkle with any remaining Parmesan cheese. Bake at 400° for 14 to 16 minutes or until golden. Serve immediately. Yield: 4 servings.

A Cleveland Collection
The Junior League of Cleveland, Ohio

Ham and Cheese Muffins

2 cups self-rising flour
½ teaspoon baking soda
1 cup milk
½ cup finely chopped cooked
  ham

½ cup (2 ounces) shredded
  Cheddar cheese
½ cup mayonnaise

Combine flour and baking soda in a medium bowl; make a well in center of mixture. Combine milk and remaining ingredients; add to dry ingredients, stirring just until dry ingredients are moistened. Spoon batter into greased muffin pans, filling two-thirds full. Bake at 425° for 25 to 28 minutes. Remove muffins from pans immediately. Yield: 1 dozen.   Joan H. McDaniel

Home Cooking with SMRMC
Southwest Mississippi Regional Medical Center Auxiliary
McComb, Mississippi

Honey-Lemon Cheese Danish

1 (8-ounce) package cream
  cheese, softened
⅓ cup sifted powdered sugar
¾ teaspoon grated lemon rind,
  divided

1 (8-ounce) can refrigerated
  crescent dinner rolls
2 tablespoons honey

Combine cheese, sugar, and ½ teaspoon lemon rind; set aside.
Separate crescent roll dough into 4 rectangles. Press perforations to seal. Press each into an 8- x 4-inch rectangle. Cut in half to form 8 squares. Place 1 inch apart on ungreased baking sheets.
Spoon 1 rounded tablespoon reserved cream cheese mixture into center of each square. Fold the corners of each square to the center, and lightly press into cream cheese mixture. Bake at 350° for 15 to 18 minutes or until golden. Combine honey and remaining ¼ teaspoon lemon rind; drizzle over warm rolls. Serve immediately. Yield: 8 servings.

We're Really Cookin' Now!
Epsilon Sigma Alpha of Oklahoma
McAlester, Oklahoma

Fastest Cake in the West

2 cups all-purpose flour
1½ teaspoons baking soda
½ teaspoon salt
1½ cups sugar
1 teaspoon ground cinnamon

1 (21-ounce) can cherry or
  apricot pie filling
¾ cup vegetable oil
3 large eggs, lightly beaten
Powdered sugar (optional)

Combine all ingredients except powdered sugar; stir well. Pour batter into an ungreased 13- x 9- x 2-inch pan. Bake at 350° for 35 to 40 minutes or until a wooden pick inserted in center comes out clean. Let cool completely in pan on a wire rack. Sprinkle with powdered sugar, if desired. Yield: 15 servings.   Billie Dunkin

Cooking with PRIDE, Volume 2
Alton Community PRIDE
Alton, Kansas

Molly's Gooey Butter Cake

1 (18.25-ounce) package yellow
  cake mix
½ cup butter or margarine,
  melted
2 large eggs
1 (8-ounce) package cream
  cheese, softened

1 (16-ounce) package
  powdered sugar, sifted
2 large eggs
Powdered sugar

Combine first 3 ingredients in a large mixing bowl; beat at medium speed of an electric mixer until blended. Pour batter into a greased and floured 13- x 9- x 2-inch pan; set aside.

Beat cream cheese until creamy. Gradually add sifted powdered sugar, beating well. Add eggs, one at a time, beating after each addition. Pour cream cheese mixture evenly over batter. Bake at 350° for 30 minutes or until golden. Let cool completely in pan on a wire rack. Sprinkle with additional powdered sugar. Yield: 15 servings.   Molly Moritz

Favorite Recipes by the Students and Staff of St. John's School
St. John's Home and School Association
Beloit, Kansas

Marguerite Cookie Delite

Biscuit mix is the key ingredient to making these cookies in record time.

4 large eggs, lightly beaten
1 (16-ounce) package light
  brown sugar

2 cups biscuit mix
1 cup flaked coconut
1 cup chopped pecans

Combine eggs and brown sugar in a large mixing bowl; beat at medium speed of an electric mixer until blended. Add biscuit mix, and beat until smooth. Stir in coconut and pecans. Spread evenly in 2 greased and floured 8-inch square pans. Bake at 350° for 30 to 35 minutes. Cool completely in pans on wire racks. Cut into 2-inch squares. Yield: 32 cookies.   Marguerite Sherman

A Collection of Favorite Recipes
Po'okela Church
Makawao, Hawaii

Unbelievables

Although you may think we've forgotten to add the flour in this recipe, we haven't. Unbelievably, these super-simple cookies are made with only three ingredients—peanut butter, eggs, and sugar!

1 (16-ounce) jar crunchy
  peanut butter

2 small eggs
1½ cups sugar

Combine all ingredients in a medium mixing bowl; beat at medium speed of an electric mixer until blended. Drop by rounded teaspoonfuls onto ungreased cookie sheets. Flatten cookies in a crisscross pattern with a fork. Bake at 375° for 8 to 10 minutes or until edges are golden. Cool 5 minutes on cookie sheets; remove cookies to wire racks, and let cool completely. Yield: 3 dozen.   Stella Pollock

A Taste of Honey
Cranston-Warwick Hadassah
Warwick, Rhode Island

Judy's Crazy Christmas Candy

Two ingredients are all it takes to make this sweet holiday treat—a great Christmas gift idea when packaged in pretty tins, boxes, or gift bags.

1 (24-ounce) package vanilla-flavored candy coating

10 peppermint candy canes, crushed (about 4 ounces)

Line a 15- x 10- x 1-inch jellyroll pan with wax paper; set aside.

Place candy coating in top of a double boiler; bring water to a boil. Reduce heat to low; cook until candy coating melts, stirring occasionally. Remove from heat; stir in crushed candy canes.

Spread mixture thinly and evenly in prepared pan. Let cool completely; break into pieces. Yield: 1½ pounds.

Lambda Chi Alpha Brothers', Mothers' Christmas Recipes
Lambda Chi Alpha, Hanover College
Hanover, Indiana

Diamond Fudge

Here's a melt-in-your-mouth fudge that couldn't be easier—simply melt three ingredients together, stir in a fourth, and chill until firm.

1 (6-ounce) package semisweet chocolate morsels
1 cup creamy peanut butter

½ cup butter or margarine
1 cup sifted powdered sugar

Combine first 3 ingredients in a medium saucepan. Cook over low heat, stirring constantly, until smooth. Remove from heat. Add powdered sugar, stirring until smooth.

Spoon fudge mixture into a buttered 8-inch square pan, spreading evenly; chill until firm. Let stand about 10 minutes at room temperature before cutting into squares. Store fudge in refrigerator. Yield: 1⅓ pounds.

Mary Belle Liggett

A Centennial Sampler
The American Association of University Women, Elkins Branch
Elkins, West Virginia

Apricot Fool

This old-fashioned English dessert is traditionally made with gooseberries, though today, any pureed fruit, such as apricots, can be used.

1 (8¾-ounce) can apricot
  halves, drained
1½ teaspoons lemon juice
¼ teaspoon almond extract

1 cup whipping cream
2 tablespoons powdered sugar
2 tablespoons sliced almonds,
  toasted

Combine apricot halves, lemon juice, and almond extract in container of an electric blender; cover and process until smooth, stopping once to scrape down sides. Set aside.

Beat whipping cream until foamy; gradually add sugar, beating until soft peaks form. Gently fold whipped cream mixture into apricot mixture to create a marbled effect. Spoon into dessert dishes. Sprinkle with almonds. Serve immediately. Yield: 4 servings.

Cooking Good Eating Better
Sisterhood Israel Center of Hillcrest Manor
Flushing, New York

Banana Split Pudding

3 bananas, thinly sliced
1 cup fresh strawberries,
  hulled and sliced
1 cup whipping cream

¼ cup commercial fudge sauce
2 tablespoons crunchy peanut
  butter

Reserve 4 banana slices and 8 strawberry slices for garnish. Beat remaining banana in a mixing bowl at medium speed of an electric mixer until smooth. Add whipping cream; beat until soft peaks form (mixture will not beat to stiff peaks).

Combine fudge sauce and peanut butter; fold into whipped cream mixture. Gently fold in strawberry slices. Spoon evenly into four 8-ounce parfait glasses. Top with reserved fruit slices. Serve immediately. Yield: 4 servings.　　　　　Norma Nemphos

Cooking with Love, Second Edition
Brevard Hospice
Rockledge, Florida

English Trifle

1 (3-ounce) package vanilla
   instant pudding mix
1 (10¾-ounce) pound cake
1 (10-ounce) package frozen
   sliced strawberries in light
   syrup, thawed

2 medium bananas, sliced
1 (12-ounce) container frozen
   whipped topping, thawed

Prepare pudding according to package directions; set aside. Cut cake into 10 slices. Layer half of cake in a 12-cup trifle bowl. Spoon half of strawberries and syrup over cake; top with half each of banana, pudding, and topping. Repeat layers. Cover and chill at least 8 hours. Yield: 10 servings.   Margaret Koessl

Taste & Share the Goodness of Door County
St. Rosalia's Ladies Sodality of St. Rosalia's Catholic Church
Sister Bay, Wisconsin

10-Minute German Sweet Chocolate Cream Pie

1 (4-ounce) package sweet
   baking chocolate
⅓ cup milk, divided
1 (3-ounce) package cream
   cheese, softened

2 tablespoons sugar
1 (8-ounce) container frozen
   whipped topping, thawed
1 (9-inch) graham cracker crust
Garnish: chocolate curls

Combine chocolate and 2 tablespoons milk in top of a double boiler; bring water to a boil. Reduce heat to low; cook until chocolate melts. Set aside.

Beat cream cheese at high speed of an electric mixer until creamy. Gradually add sugar; beat well. Add chocolate mixture and remaining 3 tablespoons plus 1 teaspoon milk; beat until smooth. Fold in topping; spoon into crust. Garnish, if desired. Cover and chill at least 8 hours. Yield: one 9-inch pie.   Carol Piganelli

Our Daily Bread
Women's Club of Our Lady of Mt. Carmel
Carmel, Indiana

Coffee Ice Cream Quickie

Walnuts, sugar, and coffee granules patted into a commercial pastry shell add a special touch to this frozen coffee ice cream pie.

½ cup finely chopped walnuts, divided
1 tablespoon sugar
1 teaspoon instant coffee granules

1 unbaked 9-inch pastry shell
3 pints coffee ice cream, softened

Combine ¼ cup chopped walnuts, sugar, and coffee granules; stir well. Pat mixture into bottom of pastry shell. Bake at 450° for 9 to 11 minutes or until lightly browned. Let cool completely on a wire rack.

Spoon ice cream into prepared crust, spreading evenly. Sprinkle with remaining ¼ cup walnuts. Cover and freeze until firm. Let stand at room temperature 5 minutes before serving. Yield: one 9-inch pie.

Mrs. Loren Fletcher Cole

The Garden Club Cooks
The Garden Club of Palm Beach, Florida

Grasshopper Pie

You can use white crème de menthe in this pie filling, but the green crème de menthe adds a striking color contrast to the dark chocolate cookie crust.

32 cream-filled chocolate sandwich cookies, divided
¼ cup butter or margarine, melted

1 (7-ounce) jar marshmallow cream
¼ cup green crème de menthe
2 cups whipping cream

Finely crush 24 cookies. Combine cookie crumbs and butter in a medium bowl; stir well. Firmly press crumb mixture in bottom and up sides of a 9½-inch deep-dish pieplate. Set aside.

Combine marshmallow cream and green crème de menthe in a large mixing bowl; beat at medium speed of an electric mixer until mixture is smooth. Beat whipping cream at high speed until soft peaks form. Gently fold whipped cream into marshmallow cream mixture. Pour whipped cream mixture into prepared crust.

Crush remaining 8 cookies; sprinkle on top of pie. Cover and freeze until firm. Let stand at room temperature 5 minutes before serving. Yield: one 9½-inch pie.   Eric Anderson

The Happy Cooker
Safeway, Inc.
Oakland, California

Orange Sherbet Pie

1 (7-ounce) can flaked coconut
½ cup butter or margarine,
  melted
½ gallon orange sherbet,
  softened
2 tablespoons Triple Sec or
  other orange-flavored
  liqueur

Garnishes: fresh mint leaves,
  mandarin oranges, orange
  rind knots

Sauté coconut in butter in a large skillet over medium heat, stirring constantly, 6 to 7 minutes or until lightly browned. Reserve 2 tablespoons browned coconut for topping. Firmly press remaining browned coconut in bottom and up sides of a 9-inch pieplate. Freeze 10 minutes.

Spoon half of sherbet into prepared crust, spreading evenly; drizzle with liqueur. Top with remaining sherbet, spreading evenly. Sprinkle with reserved coconut. Cover and freeze until firm. Let stand at room temperature 5 minutes before serving. Garnish, if desired. Yield: one 9-inch pie.   Ginny Slick

From Zion's Kitchen
The Semper Fidelis Sunday School Class of Zion Lutheran
Evangelical Church
Williamsport, Maryland

Creamy Dutch Apple Dessert

1½ cups graham cracker
crumbs
¼ cup butter or margarine,
melted
1 (14-ounce) can sweetened
condensed milk

1 (8-ounce) carton sour cream
¼ cup lemon juice
1 (21-ounce) can apple pie
filling
¼ cup chopped walnuts
½ teaspoon ground cinnamon

Combine cracker crumbs and butter in a small bowl; stir well. Firmly press crumb mixture on bottom of an ungreased 11- x 7- x 1½-inch baking dish. Combine condensed milk, sour cream, and lemon juice; spread evenly over crumbs. Spoon pie filling evenly over sour cream layer. Bake, uncovered, at 350° for 25 to 30 minutes or until set. Let cool slightly.

Combine walnuts and cinnamon; stir well. Sprinkle over dessert. Serve warm. Yield: 6 servings.   Deb Feste

Feeding the Flock
Ellsborough Lutheran Church
Lake Wilson, Minnesota

Washington Quick Apple Crisp

1 (21-ounce) can apple pie
filling
½ (11-ounce) package pie
crust mix
½ cup firmly packed brown
sugar

¼ teaspoon ground nutmeg
¼ teaspoon ground cinnamon
Vanilla ice cream or whipped
cream (optional)

Spoon pie filling into a greased 8-inch round cakepan. Combine pie crust mix, sugar, nutmeg, and cinnamon in a medium bowl; stir well. Sprinkle pie crust mixture evenly over pie filling. Bake, uncovered, at 375° for 20 to 25 minutes or until lightly browned. Serve warm. If desired, serve with vanilla ice cream or whipped cream. Yield: 6 servings.   Debra R. Jacobs

We the People . . . have the right to eat Good Food!
Fifth Grade Classes of Milwaukie Elementary School
Milwaukie, Oregon

Appetizers & Beverages

*From tangy dips to icy fruit punches, the recipes
on these pages will have conversation flowing and appetites
soaring at your next party.*

Sun-Dried Tomato and Roasted Red Pepper Dip, page 48

Mexican Hummus

5 cloves garlic
2 (15-ounce) cans garbanzo
  beans (chick-peas), drained
⅓ cup tahini (sesame seed
  paste)

¼ cup lemon juice
¼ teaspoon ground cumin
5 drops of hot sauce

Position knife blade in food processor bowl. Drop garlic through food chute with processor running; process 3 seconds or until garlic is minced. Add garbanzo beans and remaining ingredients; cover and process until smooth, stopping once to scrape down sides. Transfer dip to a serving bowl. Serve with pita bread chips. Yield: 3 cups.

Sister Mercita Pipp

Franciscan Centennial Cookbook
Franciscan Sisters
Little Falls, Minnesota

Bell Pepper Dip

You can vary the look of this creamy dip by simply changing the color of the sweet pepper you use.

2 large eggs, beaten
2 tablespoons sugar
2 tablespoons butter or
  margarine, melted
2 tablespoons white vinegar

2 (3-ounce) packages cream
  cheese, softened
½ cup chopped onion
½ cup chopped green pepper

Combine first 4 ingredients in a small saucepan; stir well. Cook over medium-low heat, stirring constantly with a wire whisk, until mixture is thickened (do not boil). Remove from heat; let cool.

Beat cream cheese in a small mixing bowl at high speed of an electric mixer until creamy; stir in egg mixture. Add onion and green pepper; stir well. Serve immediately, or cover and chill. Serve with corn chips or assorted crackers. Yield: 2 cups.

The Pasquotank Plate
Christ Episcopal Churchwomen
Elizabeth City, North Carolina

Red and Yellow Pepper Salsa with Croûtes

Croûte is the French word for "crust." You can also serve this colorful salsa with an assortment of crackers or breadsticks.

2 medium-size sweet red peppers, cut into very thin strips
1 medium-size sweet yellow pepper, cut into very thin strips
¼ cup olive oil, divided
8 small fresh basil leaves, torn into small pieces or 1½ teaspoons dried basil
1 tablespoon minced fresh oregano or 1 teaspoon dried oregano
1 teaspoon minced fresh thyme or ¼ teaspoon dried thyme
2 to 4 anchovy fillets, minced
3 cloves garlic, minced
1 tablespoon capers
½ teaspoon salt
¼ teaspoon pepper
Croûtes

Sauté sweet pepper strips in 2 tablespoons oil in a skillet over medium heat, stirring constantly, until tender. Set aside.

Combine remaining 2 tablespoons oil, basil, and next 5 ingredients in a bowl. Stir in reserved sweet pepper strips, salt, and pepper. Cover and let stand at room temperature 2 hours, or cover and chill at least 8 hours. Serve with Croûtes. Yield: 1¾ cups.

Croûtes

½ cup butter, melted
½ cup olive oil
2 cloves garlic, minced
2 (8-ounce) French baguettes, cut into ½-inch-thick slices
Paprika
Dried basil
Grated Parmesan cheese

Combine first 3 ingredients; brush on both sides of bread. Place on baking sheets. Bake at 300° for 20 minutes or until golden. Sprinkle with paprika, basil, or cheese. Yield: 3½ dozen.

Heart & Soul
The Junior League of Memphis, Tennessee

Sun-Dried Tomato and Roasted Red Pepper Dip

To add interest to this dip and hint at its flavor, serve it in a sweet red pepper cup. Just cut off the top of the pepper, and remove the seeds and membranes.

8 sun-dried tomatoes (without oil or salt)
2 (7-ounce) jars roasted red peppers, drained
1 clove garlic, crushed
2 tablespoons chopped fresh parsley
1 tablespoon lemon juice
⅛ teaspoon pepper
Dash of salt
½ (8-ounce) package cream cheese, cubed and softened
½ cup sour cream
Garnish: chopped fresh parsley

Place tomatoes in a bowl; add boiling water to cover, and let stand 10 minutes. Drain. Pat tomatoes and red peppers between paper towels to remove excess moisture. Position knife blade in food processor bowl. Add tomatoes, red peppers, and next 5 ingredients; cover and process until smooth, stopping once to scrape down sides. Add cream cheese and sour cream; cover and process until smooth, stopping once to scrape down sides. Serve dip immediately, or cover and chill. Garnish, if desired. Serve with pita bread chips. Yield: 2½ cups.

Jill Couhlin

Carol & Friends, A Taste of North County
Carol & Friends Steering Committee of the Carol Cox Re-Entry
Women's Scholarship Fund at CSU-San Marcos
San Marcos, California

Hot Macadamia Dip

11 ounces cream cheese, softened
2 tablespoons milk
1 (2¼-ounce) jar sliced dried beef, chopped
⅓ cup finely chopped onion
⅓ cup finely chopped green pepper
1 clove garlic, minced
½ teaspoon freshly ground pepper
¼ teaspoon ground ginger
¾ cup sour cream
½ cup chopped macadamia nuts
1 tablespoon butter or margarine, melted

Beat cream cheese and milk in a medium mixing bowl at medium speed of an electric mixer until creamy. Add dried beef and next 5 ingredients; stir well. Fold in sour cream. Pour into an ungreased 8-inch square baking dish. Set aside.

Sauté macadamia nuts in butter in a small skillet over medium heat, stirring constantly, until lightly browned. Sprinkle over dip mixture in baking dish. Bake, uncovered, at 350° for 20 to 25 minutes or until thoroughly heated. Serve dip with assorted crackers. Yield: about 4 cups.   Betty J. Hensley

A Cook's Tour of the Bayou Country
Churchwomen of the Southwest Deanery of the Episcopal
Diocese of Louisiana
Franklin, Louisiana

Cheese-Olive Dip

If you love olives, this warm dip is a "must try"—it contains both pimiento-stuffed and ripe olives.

1½ cups pimiento-stuffed
 olives, finely chopped
1 cup (4 ounces) shredded
 mozzarella cheese
1 cup (4 ounces) shredded
 Cheddar cheese

1 cup mayonnaise
¾ cup pitted ripe olives, finely
 chopped
2 small green onions, finely
 chopped

Combine all ingredients in a medium bowl; stir well. Spoon into an ungreased shallow 1-quart baking dish. Bake, uncovered, at 350° for 25 minutes or until thoroughly heated. Serve with corn chips or assorted crackers. Yield: 3½ cups.   Vicky Bussey

Under the Crabapple Tree
Northwestern Elementary School PTA
Alpharetta, Georgia

Amber Glow

1 (8-ounce) package cream
  cheese, softened
1 (10-ounce) jar apricot
  preserves
1½ teaspoons dry mustard
1 teaspoon prepared
  horseradish
⅛ teaspoon dried crushed red
  pepper
¼ cup chopped salted roasted
  peanuts

Line a 1-cup mold with plastic wrap, leaving a 1-inch overhang around edges. Firmly press cream cheese into mold. Cover and chill 2 hours or until firm. Unmold onto a serving platter; peel off plastic wrap. Combine apricot preserves, mustard, horseradish, and red pepper in a small bowl; stir well. To serve, spoon preserve mixture over cream cheese; sprinkle with peanuts. Serve with assorted crackers. Yield: 1 cup.   June Wierbicky

Feeding Our Flock
Cross of Christ Lutheran Church
Crown Point, Indiana

Layered Christmas Cheese Loaf

2 (8-ounce) packages cream
  cheese, softened
¼ cup butter or margarine,
  softened
3 tablespoons milk
2 (10-ounce) packages frozen
  chopped spinach, thawed
2 cups fresh parsley sprigs
½ cup chopped walnuts
2 cloves garlic, minced
1 teaspoon dried basil
1 teaspoon dried oregano
1½ cups grated Parmesan
  cheese
½ cup vegetable oil
1 tablespoon fresh lemon juice

Line an 8½- x 4½- x 3-inch loafpan with plastic wrap, leaving a 1-inch overhang around edges. Set aside.

Beat cream cheese, butter, and milk in a medium mixing bowl at medium speed of an electric mixer until creamy. Set aside.

Press spinach between paper towels to remove moisture. Position knife blade in food processor bowl; add spinach and next 5 ingredients. Cover and process until finely chopped, stopping once to scrape down sides. Add Parmesan cheese; cover and process until blended, stopping once to scrape down sides. With processor running, pour oil and lemon juice through food chute in a slow, steady stream, processing until combined. Set aside.

Spoon one-third of reserved cream cheese mixture into prepared pan, spreading evenly. Spread half of spinach mixture over cream cheese layer. Repeat layers once. Top with remaining cream cheese mixture. Cover and chill at least 8 hours.

Unmold onto a serving platter; peel off plastic wrap. Serve with assorted crackers. Yield: 5½ cups.   Jeff Mensch

Mifflinburg Bicentennial Cookbook
Mifflinburg Heritage and Revitalization Association
Mifflinburg, Pennsylvania

Gorgonzola-Pistachio Loaf

Gorgonzola is an Italian blue cheese with a slightly pungent flavor.

2 (8-ounce) packages cream
   cheese, softened
8 ounces Gorgonzola cheese,
   crumbled
½ cup unsalted butter or
   margarine, softened

1 cup pistachios
½ cup fresh basil leaves
½ cup fresh parsley sprigs
Garnish: fresh parsley sprigs

Line a 5-cup mold with plastic wrap, leaving a 1-inch overhang around edges. Set aside.

Combine first 3 ingredients in a large mixing bowl; beat at medium speed of an electric mixer until creamy. Set aside.

Position knife blade in food processor bowl; add pistachios, basil, and ½ cup parsley sprigs. Cover and process until finely chopped, stopping once to scrape down sides.

Spoon one-third of reserved cheese mixture into prepared mold, spreading evenly. Spread half of pistachio mixture over cheese layer. Repeat layers once. Top with remaining cheese mixture, spreading evenly. Cover and chill at least 8 hours. Unmold onto a serving platter; peel off plastic wrap. Garnish, if desired. Serve with assorted crackers. Yield: 5 cups.

Celebrate!
The Junior League of Sacramento, California

Tomato-Cheese Wreath

2 cups (8 ounces) shredded
  sharp Cheddar cheese
1 (8-ounce) package cream
  cheese, softened
½ cup butter, softened
½ to 1 teaspoon salt
⅛ teaspoon garlic powder

⅛ teaspoon ground red
  pepper
1 cup peeled, seeded, and
  diced tomato
⅓ cup chopped green onions
1½ cups chopped pecans,
  toasted

Combine first 6 ingredients in a mixing bowl; beat at medium speed of an electric mixer until blended. Stir in tomato and green onions. Cover and chill at least 45 minutes. Shape mixture into a 14-inch log; cover and chill 30 minutes. Roll in pecans; form into a ring. Serve with assorted crackers. Yield: one 6-inch cheese ring.

Augusta Cooks for Company, Past and Present
The Augusta Council of the Georgia Association for Children
and Adults with Learning Disabilities
Augusta, Georgia

Fancy Chicken Log

2 (8-ounce) packages cream
  cheese, softened
1 tablespoon commercial steak
  sauce
½ teaspoon curry powder
1½ cups minced cooked
  chicken

⅓ cup minced celery
¼ cup chopped fresh parsley,
  divided
¼ cup chopped almonds,
  toasted

Combine first 3 ingredients in a mixing bowl; beat at medium speed of an electric mixer until smooth. Stir in chicken, celery, and 2 tablespoons parsley. Cover and chill 1 hour. Shape into a 9-inch log. Combine remaining 2 tablespoons parsley and almonds. Roll log in almond mixture. Cover and chill at least 4 hours. Serve with assorted crackers. Yield: one 9-inch log.   Shelia Parker

Cookin' for the Kids
WalMart Distribution Center #6011
Brookhaven, Mississippi

Salsa Cheesecake

Cheesecake isn't just for dessert anymore. You'll love the Tex-Mex flavor of this unique appetizer cheesecake. You can serve it with corn chips as well as an assortment of crackers.

2 tablespoons butter or
   margarine, melted
½ cup fine, dry breadcrumbs,
   divided
12 ounces cream cheese,
   softened
4 ounces Roquefort cheese,
   crumbled
1 cup grated Parmesan cheese

1 (8-ounce) carton sour cream
½ cup commercial salsa
2 tablespoons all-purpose flour
4 large eggs
1 tablespoon chopped fresh
   cilantro
1 tablespoon minced fresh
   parsley
Garnish: fresh cilantro leaves

Brush bottom and sides of a 9-inch springform pan with butter; sprinkle with ¼ cup breadcrumbs.

Beat cream cheese and Roquefort in a large mixing bowl at high speed of an electric mixer until creamy. Add Parmesan cheese and next 3 ingredients, beating until blended. Add eggs, one at a time, beating just until yellow disappears.

Pour mixture into prepared pan; sprinkle with remaining ¼ cup breadcrumbs. Sprinkle with chopped cilantro and parsley. Bake at 300° for 1 hour and 5 minutes or until almost set. Turn oven off. Partially open oven door, and let cheesecake cool in oven 1 hour. Let cool completely in pan on a wire rack.

Carefully remove sides of springform pan. Serve at room temperature, or cover and chill thoroughly. Garnish, if desired. Serve with assorted crackers. Yield: 24 appetizer servings.

California Sizzles
The Junior League of Pasadena, California

Charley Brown's Beer-Cheese Croutons

4 cups (16 ounces) shredded
  Cheddar cheese
¾ cup grated Parmesan cheese
¾ cup beer
1 tablespoon Worcestershire
  sauce

½ teaspoon dry mustard
¼ teaspoon garlic powder
¼ teaspoon hot sauce
2 (8-ounce) French baguettes

Combine all ingredients except French baguettes in a large mixing bowl; beat at low speed of an electric mixer until blended. Cut baguettes into ¼-inch-thick slices; spread evenly with cheese mixture. Place on ungreased baking sheets. Bake at 400° for 8 to 10 minutes or until lightly browned. Serve croutons immediately. Yield: 7 dozen.   Marilyn Teghtmeyer

The Happy Cooker
Safeway, Inc.
Oakland, California

Cheese and Olive Balls

Imagine taking a cheese straw and wrapping it around an olive, and you'll get the picture for this tasty appetizer.

1 cup (4 ounces) shredded
  sharp Cheddar cheese
½ cup all-purpose flour
¼ cup butter or margarine,
  softened

Salt and ground red pepper to
  taste
24 pimiento-stuffed olives

Combine all ingredients except olives in a mixing bowl; beat at medium speed of an electric mixer until blended. Divide dough into 24 equal pieces. Place an olive in center of each piece of dough, shaping dough around olive to form a ball. Place balls on ungreased baking sheets. Bake at 400° for 10 to 12 minutes. Serve warm. Yield: 2 dozen.   GeDelle Young, Doris Farnbach

Overtures and Encores
Gainesville Chamber Orchestra
Gainesville, Florida

Fried Chick-Pea Patties with Sesame Seed Sauce

Kefalotiri is a hard goat cheese. If unavailable, substitute Parmesan cheese.

1 (19-ounce) can chick-peas (garbanzo beans), drained
½ cup minced onion
2 tablespoons butter or margarine, melted
1 large egg, lightly beaten
2 tablespoons grated kefalotiri cheese
2 tablespoons minced fresh parsley
¼ teaspoon salt
¼ teaspoon pepper
Dash of dried oregano
All-purpose flour
¼ cup vegetable oil, divided
Sesame Seed Sauce

Rinse chick-peas with cold water; drain well. Position knife blade in food processor bowl; add chick-peas. Cover and process until smooth, stopping once to scrape down sides. Set aside.

Sauté onion in butter in a saucepan over medium heat, stirring constantly, until tender. Remove from heat. Add chick-peas, egg, and next 5 ingredients; stir well. Drop mixture, 2 tablespoons at a time, into flour. Shape into 2-inch patties. Pour 2 tablespoons oil into a heavy skillet. Brown half of patties in oil over medium-high heat 2 to 3 minutes or until golden, turning once. Set aside; keep warm. Repeat procedure with remaining 2 tablespoons oil and patties. Serve immediately with sauce. Yield: 1½ dozen.

Sesame Seed Sauce

½ cup tahini (sesame seed paste)
1 tablespoon minced garlic
¼ cup plus 2 tablespoons fresh lemon juice
⅓ cup water
½ teaspoon ground cumin
¼ teaspoon salt

Combine tahini and garlic in a mixing bowl; beat at medium speed of an electric mixer until blended. Gradually add lemon juice and water; beat well. Stir in cumin and salt. Yield: 1 cup.

The Complete Book of Greek Cooking
Recipe Club of St. Paul's Greek Orthodox Cathedral
Hempstead, New York

French-Fried Dill Pickles

2 (22-ounce) jars sliced dill
  pickles, drained
½ cup milk
½ cup beer
1 large egg, beaten
1 tablespoon all-purpose flour
3 drops of hot sauce
3 cups all-purpose flour

2 teaspoons ground red
  pepper (optional)
1 teaspoon black pepper
½ teaspoon salt
¼ teaspoon garlic powder
Vegetable oil
Commercial Ranch-style
  dressing

Press pickle slices between paper towels to remove excess moisture. Set aside.

Combine milk and next 4 ingredients; stir well. Combine 3 cups flour, ground red pepper, if desired, and next 3 ingredients; stir well. Dip pickle slices in milk mixture; dredge in flour mixture.

Pour oil to depth of 4 inches into a Dutch oven; heat to 375°. Fry coated pickle slices, in batches, in hot oil 5 minutes or until golden, turning once. Drain on paper towels. Serve warm with dressing. Yield: 13 dozen. Susan McCarthy

Different, But Still Special!
The Service Association for the Retarded
Philadelphia, Pennsylvania

Pistachio-Stuffed Mushrooms

20 medium-size fresh
  mushrooms
3 tablespoons minced onion
¼ cup butter or margarine,
  melted
⅓ cup fine, dry breadcrumbs
¼ cup chopped pistachios

2 tablespoons chopped fresh
  parsley
¼ teaspoon salt
¼ teaspoon dried marjoram
3 tablespoons butter or
  margarine, melted

Clean mushrooms with damp paper towels; remove stems, and finely chop. Set mushroom caps aside.

Sauté stems and onion in ¼ cup butter in a skillet over medium-high heat, stirring constantly, until tender. Remove from heat; stir in breadcrumbs and next 4 ingredients. Spoon evenly into mushroom caps. Place in an ungreased 15- x 10- x 1-inch jellyroll pan;

drizzle with 3 tablespoons butter. Bake at 350° for 10 minutes. Serve immediately. Yield: 20 appetizers. Judith Peterson

Now We're Cookin'
Presbyterian Women of Northwood Presbyterian Church
Clearwater, Florida

Mushroom Palmiers

Puff pastry is a delicate, multilayered pastry made by repeatedly rolling butter between layers of dough. When baked, the steam created by moisture in the butter causes the dough to puff, forming hundreds of flaky layers.

18 ounces fresh mushrooms, finely chopped
2 cups finely chopped onion
¼ cup plus 1 tablespoon butter or margarine, melted
2 tablespoons all-purpose flour
1½ teaspoons dried thyme
1 teaspoon fresh lemon juice
½ teaspoon salt
¼ teaspoon pepper
1½ (17¼-ounce) packages frozen puff pastry, thawed
2 large eggs, lightly beaten
1 tablespoon plus 1 teaspoon water

Sauté mushrooms and onion in butter in a skillet over medium heat, stirring constantly, until liquid evaporates and vegetables are tender. Add flour, thyme, and lemon juice; cook, stirring constantly, 2 minutes. Stir in salt and pepper; let cool.

Place 1 pastry sheet on work surface; spread one-third of mushroom mixture evenly over pastry. Roll up pastry, jellyroll fashion, starting at short side, ending at middle of pastry. Roll up remaining pastry, starting at remaining short side until both rolls meet. Repeat procedure twice with remaining puff pastry and mushroom mixture. Cover and chill at least 1 hour or until firm.

Cut crosswise into ¼-inch-thick slices. (Slices will resemble a figure "8.") Place slices, cut side down, 1 inch apart on ungreased baking sheets. Combine eggs and water in a small bowl, stirring well. Brush slices with egg mixture. Bake at 400° for 20 minutes or until golden. Serve warm. Yield: 5 dozen. Debra Arthur

Five Star Sensations
Auxiliary of University Hospitals of Cleveland
Shaker Heights, Ohio

Herbed Spinach Tarts

Fresh chives and basil flavor these miniature spinach appetizer tarts.

2 cups all-purpose flour
¼ teaspoon salt
1 cup (4 ounces) shredded
  Cheddar cheese
⅔ cup butter or margarine
2 to 4 tablespoons cold water
1 (10-ounce) package frozen
  chopped spinach
1 cup small-curd cottage
  cheese

1 small onion, finely chopped
3 large eggs, lightly beaten
2 tablespoons grated Parmesan
  cheese
1 tablespoon chopped fresh
  chives
1 tablespoon chopped fresh
  basil or 1 teaspoon dried
  basil

Combine flour and salt; stir in shredded Cheddar cheese. Cut in butter with pastry blender until mixture is crumbly. Sprinkle cold water (1 tablespoon at a time) evenly over surface; stir with a fork until dry ingredients are moistened. Shape into a ball; chill 1 hour. Shape pastry into 36 balls. Place in greased miniature (1¾-inch) muffin pans, shaping each into a shell.

Cook spinach according to package directions; drain well. Press spinach between paper towels to remove excess moisture. Combine spinach, cottage cheese, and remaining ingredients in a medium bowl; stir well.

Spoon mixture evenly into prepared shells. Bake at 400° for 25 to 27 minutes or until golden. Cool in pans on wire racks 2 minutes. Loosen edges of tarts from pans with a sharp knife. Remove tarts from pans; serve warm. Yield: 3 dozen.   Jo Stecher

"City" Dining
City of Hope National Medical Center
and Beckman Research Institute
New York, New York

Spinach-Wrapped Chicken with Oriental Dip

2 whole chicken breasts
1¾ cups chicken broth
¼ cup soy sauce
1 tablespoon Worcestershire
  sauce

36 large fresh spinach leaves
  (about ¼ pound)
2 quarts boiling water
Lettuce leaves
Oriental Dip

Combine first 4 ingredients in a large saucepan. Bring to a boil; cover, reduce heat, and simmer 20 to 25 minutes or until chicken is done. Pour mixture through a wire-mesh strainer into a bowl, discarding broth. Skin and bone chicken; cut meat into 1-inch cubes. Set aside.

Remove and discard stems from spinach; wash leaves thoroughly, and pat dry. Place spinach in a colander; pour boiling water over spinach, and drain well. Rinse spinach with cold water until cool, and drain well. Press spinach between paper towels to remove excess moisture.

Place 1 reserved chicken cube at base of each spinach leaf. Fold bottom of spinach leaf over chicken. Fold sides over chicken, and roll up. Secure with wooden picks. Cover and chill at least 4 hours. Place on a lettuce-lined serving platter. Serve with Oriental Dip. Yield: 3 dozen.

Oriental Dip

1 (8-ounce) carton sour cream
2 teaspoons sesame seeds,
  toasted
½ teaspoon ground ginger

1 tablespoon plus 1 teaspoon
  soy sauce
2 teaspoons Worcestershire
  sauce

Combine all ingredients in a small bowl; stir well. Cover and chill at least 4 hours. Yield: 1 cup.

Hospitality: A Cookbook Celebrating Boston's North Shore
Salem Hospital Aid Association
Salem, Massachusetts

Coconut Chicken Bites

Tender bites of chicken breast are blanketed with a mixture of coconut, cumin, coriander, and ground red pepper before baking; afterwards they're dipped in Dijon mustard for a crowning touch of flavor.

3½ cups shredded coconut
2 teaspoons ground cumin
¾ teaspoon ground coriander
½ teaspoon salt
½ teaspoon ground red pepper
½ teaspoon freshly ground
  black pepper

2 pounds skinned and boned
  chicken breast halves, cut
  into 1-inch pieces
2 large eggs, beaten
Dijon mustard

Spread coconut on a large baking sheet. Bake at 325° for 15 to 20 minutes or until golden, stirring frequently. Let cool. Position knife blade in food processor bowl; add coconut. Cover and process until coarsely ground. Set aside.

Combine cumin and next 4 ingredients in a large bowl, and stir well. Add chicken pieces, stirring gently to coat. Add eggs, stirring gently to coat.

Dredge chicken in reserved shredded coconut, coating well. Place on lightly greased baking sheets. Cover and chill 1 hour. Bake, uncovered, at 400° for 8 minutes; turn chicken, and bake an additional 7 minutes or until golden and done. Serve warm with mustard. Yield: 16 appetizer servings.

Francie Fry

Kailua Cooks
Le Jardin Academy
Kailua, Hawaii

Rochester Wings

⅓ cup soy sauce
¼ cup honey
2 tablespoons vegetable oil
2 tablespoons chili sauce
1 teaspoon salt

½ teaspoon ground ginger
¼ teaspoon garlic powder
¼ teaspoon ground red
  pepper
3 pounds chicken wings

Combine all ingredients except chicken wings in a large heavy-duty, zip-top plastic bag. Add chicken wings; seal bag securely, and place in a large bowl. Marinate chicken wings in refrigerator 8 hours, turning occasionally.

Remove chicken wings, reserving marinade. Place chicken wings in an ungreased 15- x 10- x 1-inch jellyroll pan. Bake, uncovered, at 325° for 1 hour or until done, basting frequently with reserved marinade. Serve warm. Yield: 8 to 10 appetizer servings.

For Goodness Taste
The Junior League of Rochester, New York

Baked Crab Quesadillas

Unlike most quesadillas that are fried or broiled, these crabmeat- and cheese-filled appetizer quesadillas are baked.

⅓ cup unsalted butter or
  margarine, melted
¼ cup vegetable oil
½ cup chopped onion
2 jalapeño peppers, seeded
  and finely chopped
1 clove garlic, minced
1 pound lump crabmeat,
  drained

¼ cup mayonnaise
1 tablespoon chopped fresh
  cilantro
1 teaspoon salt
16 (8-inch) flour tortillas
⅓ cup (1.3 ounces) shredded
  Monterey Jack cheese with
  jalapeño peppers

Combine butter and oil; set aside. Sauté onion, peppers, and garlic in 2 tablespoons reserved butter mixture in a medium saucepan over medium heat, stirring constantly, until tender. Remove from heat. Gently stir in crabmeat and next 3 ingredients.

Place tortillas on baking sheets; brush 1 side of each tortilla with remaining butter mixture. Turn tortillas over; spread crabmeat mixture evenly over half of each tortilla, and sprinkle with cheese. Fold tortillas in half. Bake at 475° for 4 minutes or until golden. Cut each tortilla into thirds. Serve warm. Yield: 4 dozen.

Tampa Treasures
The Junior League of Tampa, Florida

Glazed Bacon

12 ounces sliced bacon
½ cup firmly packed light
  brown sugar

2 tablespoons Burgundy or
  other dry red wine
1 tablespoon Dijon mustard

Cut bacon slices in half crosswise. Place bacon in a single layer in an ungreased 15- x 10- x 1-inch jellyroll pan. Bake at 350° for 10 minutes or until almost crisp. Drain well. Return bacon to pan.

Combine sugar, wine, and mustard. Brush bacon with half of sugar mixture. Bake at 350° for 10 minutes. Turn bacon; brush with remaining sugar mixture. Bake 10 minutes or until golden. Serve warm or at room temperature. Yield: 8 appetizer servings.

Great Beginnings: The Art of Hors d'Oeuvres
Friends of the Arts of the Tampa Museum of Art
Tampa, Florida

Meatballs in Red Wine Sauce

2 pounds ground chuck
1 cup fine, dry breadcrumbs
1 cup finely chopped onion
¼ cup grated Parmesan cheese
3 large eggs, lightly beaten
¾ teaspoon curry powder
½ teaspoon salt
½ teaspoon pepper
½ teaspoon Worcestershire
  sauce

1 cup all-purpose flour
2 tablespoons vegetable oil
2 cups tomato sauce
1 cup Burgundy or other dry
  red wine
½ cup canned beef
  consommé, undiluted
⅛ teaspoon dried oregano

Combine first 9 ingredients in a bowl; stir well. Shape into 1-inch balls; dredge in flour. Brown meatballs, in batches, in oil in a skillet over medium heat. Remove from skillet; set aside.

Combine tomato sauce and remaining ingredients in a Dutch oven. Bring to a boil; add meatballs, reduce heat, and simmer, uncovered, 35 minutes. Yield: 9 dozen.   George Brox

Home at the Range with Wyoming B.I.L.'s
Chapter Y of P.E.O. Sisterhood
Casper, Wyoming

Lime-Tomato Sipper

1 teaspoon chicken-flavored
  bouillon granules
1 cup boiling water
3 cups tomato juice
2 tablespoons lime juice

1 teaspoon sugar
1 teaspoon Worcestershire sauce
¼ teaspoon celery salt
¼ teaspoon dried basil
Garnish: celery sticks

Combine bouillon granules and boiling water, stirring until granules dissolve. Add tomato juice and next 5 ingredients; stir well. Cover and chill thoroughly. To serve, pour into glasses. Garnish, if desired. Yield: 4 cups.   Terri Mattson

Golden Valley Women of Today Cookbook
Golden Valley Women of Today
Golden Valley, Minnesota

Bourbon Slush

The alcohol in this bourbon keeps this tea mixture from freezing solid.

2 cups boiling water
5 regular-size tea bags
1 cup sugar
7 cups water
2 cups bourbon
1 (16-ounce) can frozen orange
  juice concentrate, thawed
  and undiluted

1 (6-ounce) can frozen
  lemonade concentrate,
  thawed and undiluted
Garnishes: orange slices,
  maraschino cherries

Pour boiling water over tea bags; cover and let stand 1 hour. Remove tea bags, squeezing gently. Add sugar, stirring until sugar dissolves.

Combine tea mixture, 7 cups water, and next 3 ingredients. Pour into a 13- x 9- x 2-inch dish. Cover and freeze at least 48 hours (mixture will not freeze solid). To serve, scoop into glasses. Garnish, if desired. Yield: about 3½ quarts.   Alice Mary Hymel

A World of Good Taste
St. Bernadette's Home and School Guild
Springfield, Virginia

Hawaiian Mimosa

This popular brunch cocktail is best when served icy cold.

1 (12-ounce) can apricot nectar
1 (12-ounce) can unsweetened
  pineapple juice
1 (6-ounce) can frozen orange
  juice concentrate, thawed
  and undiluted

¾ cup water
1 (750-milliliter) bottle
  champagne, chilled

Combine all ingredients except champagne, stirring well. Cover and chill thoroughly. Gently stir in champagne just before serving. Yield: 2 quarts.

Barbara W. Deaton

Hopewell Heritage
Presbyterian Women of Hopewell Presbyterian Church
Huntersville, North Carolina

Strawberry Daiquiris

Here's a switch on the classic rum and lime cocktail. This version uses strawberries and pink lemonade.

3 cups water
2¼ cups light rum
1 (16-ounce) package frozen
  sliced strawberries in heavy
  syrup, thawed

1 (12-ounce) can frozen pink
  lemonade concentrate,
  thawed and undiluted
1 (2-liter) bottle lemon-lime
  carbonated beverage, chilled

Combine first 4 ingredients in freezer container of a 1-gallon hand-turned or electric freezer. Freeze according to manufacturer's instructions until mixture is slushy (mixture will not freeze solid). Gently stir in lemon-lime beverage just before serving. Yield: 4½ quarts.

Lyla L. Stuart

Reflections of the West
Telephone Pioneers of America, Skyline Chapter No. 67
Helena, Montana

Graduation Punch

4 quarts water
4 cups grapefruit juice
3 (6-ounce) cans frozen
  lemonade concentrate,
  thawed and undiluted
3 (6-ounce) cans frozen
  limeade concentrate, thawed
  and undiluted

1¾ cups sugar
2 (1-liter) bottles ginger ale,
  chilled
Garnishes: fresh strawberries,
  lime slices

Combine first 5 ingredients; stir well. Pour mixture into a large freezer container or into two 13- x 9- x 2-inch dishes; cover and freeze until firm. Partially thaw mixture; break into chunks, and transfer to a punch bowl. Gently stir in ginger ale just before serving. Garnish, if desired. Yield: 2¼ gallons.   Jessica Kleweno

Idalia Community Cookbook
Women's Fellowship of St. John United Church of Christ
Idalia, Colorado

Hot Fruited Tea Punch

3 (3-inch) sticks cinnamon
1 tablespoon whole cloves
5 quarts water, divided
2 family-size tea bags
1 (48-ounce) bottle cranberry-
  apple drink

1 (46-ounce) can pineapple
  juice
4 cups apple juice
4 cups orange juice
1½ to 2 cups sugar
1¼ cups lemon juice

Tie cinnamon sticks and cloves in a cheesecloth bag. Combine spice bag, 1 quart water, and tea bags in a stockpot. Bring to a boil over medium heat. Remove from heat; cover and let stand 30 minutes. Remove spice bag. Remove tea bags, squeezing gently. Add remaining 4 quarts water, cranberry-apple drink, and remaining ingredients. Cook over low heat until sugar dissolves; stir occasionally. Serve warm. Yield: 2½ gallons.   Staffie Webster

Rockingham County Cooks
Rockingham County Arts Council
Eden, North Carolina

Not-Your-Ordinary Nog

For a nonalcoholic nog, omit all three alcoholic beverages, and instead add 1 teaspoon brandy flavoring, 1 teaspoon rum flavoring, and 1 (6-ounce) can frozen apple juice concentrate, thawed and undiluted.

6 large eggs
½ cup sugar
4 cups milk, divided
1 cup bourbon
½ cup rum

½ cup Bourbon Apple or other
   apple-flavored brandy
½ gallon French vanilla ice
   cream, softened
Garnish: freshly grated nutmeg

Beat eggs at medium speed of an electric mixer until foamy; gradually add sugar, beating well.

Combine egg mixture and 2 cups milk in a medium saucepan; cook over medium-low heat, stirring constantly with a wire whisk, until mixture reaches 160°. Remove from heat, and let cool. Stir in remaining 2 cups milk. Cover and chill thoroughly. Gently stir in bourbon, rum, and Bourbon Apple. Stir in ice cream just before serving. Garnish, if desired. Yield: about 1 gallon.

Heavenly Hosts
Bryn Mawr Presbyterian Church
Bryn Mawr, Pennsylvania

Breads

*It's hard to top the tempting aroma of homemade bread
baking in the oven. You'll enjoy the satisfaction that comes from
making these quick breads and yeast breads.*

Scottish Scones, page 74

Blueberry Bread

⅔ cup shortening
1⅓ cups sugar
1 (15¼-ounce) can crushed
   pineapple, drained
4 large eggs
½ cup milk
1½ teaspoons lemon juice

3 cups all-purpose flour
2 teaspoons baking powder
1 teaspoon baking soda
½ teaspoon salt
2 cups fresh blueberries
1 cup chopped pecans
½ cup flaked coconut

Beat shortening at medium speed of an electric mixer until creamy; gradually add sugar, beating well. Add pineapple, eggs, milk, and lemon juice; beat well. Combine flour and next 3 ingredients; add to shortening mixture, beating until blended. Stir in blueberries, pecans, and coconut.

Spoon batter into 2 greased 9- x 5- x 3-inch loafpans. Bake at 350° for 40 to 45 minutes or until a wooden pick inserted in center comes out clean. Cool bread in pans on wire racks 10 minutes. Remove bread from pans, and let cool completely on wire racks. Yield: 2 loaves.   Barbara Reinecker

Cooking with the Congregation . . . Our Best to You
First Congregational Church
Billerica, Massachusetts

Cranberry-Banana Bread

2 cups fresh cranberries
1⅔ cups sugar, divided
1 cup water
⅓ cup shortening
2 large eggs
1¾ cups all-purpose flour

2 teaspoons baking powder
¼ teaspoon baking soda
½ teaspoon salt
1 cup mashed ripe banana
½ cup coarsely chopped
   walnuts

Line a greased 9- x 5- x 3-inch loafpan with wax paper; grease wax paper. Set aside. Combine cranberries, 1 cup sugar, and water in a saucepan. Cook over medium heat 5 minutes or until cranberry skins pop. Drain and set aside.

Beat shortening at medium speed of an electric mixer until creamy; gradually add remaining ⅔ cup sugar, beating well. Add eggs, one at a time, beating after each addition. Combine flour, baking powder, soda, and salt; add to shortening mixture alternately with banana, beginning and ending with flour mixture. Mix after each addition. Fold in reserved cranberries and walnuts.

Spoon batter into prepared pan. Bake at 350° for 1 hour to 1 hour and 5 minutes or until a wooden pick inserted in center comes out clean. Cool in pan on a wire rack 10 minutes. Remove from pan; remove wax paper, and let cool completely on wire rack. Yield: 1 loaf.   Audrey Dick

Hopewell Heritage
Presbyterian Women of Hopewell Presbyterian Church
Huntersville, North Carolina

Zucchini-Oatmeal Bread

2 cups all-purpose flour
1 cup quick-cooking oats,
  uncooked
1 teaspoon baking powder
1 teaspoon baking soda
½ teaspoon salt
½ cup sugar
½ cup firmly packed brown
  sugar
¾ teaspoon ground cinnamon
3 large eggs
¾ cup vegetable oil
1 teaspoon vanilla extract
3 cups shredded zucchini
1 cup chopped walnuts

Combine first 8 ingredients in a large mixing bowl; make a well in center of mixture. Set aside. Combine eggs, oil, and vanilla in a bowl; beat with a wire whisk until blended. Stir in zucchini and walnuts. Add to dry ingredients, stirring just until moistened.

Spoon batter into a greased 9- x 5- x 3-inch loafpan. Bake at 350° for 1 hour and 15 minutes or until a wooden pick inserted in center comes out clean. Cool in pan on a wire rack 10 minutes. Remove bread from pan, and let cool completely on wire rack. Yield: 1 loaf.   Verna J. Hennen

Country Church Favorites
St. John's United Church of Christ
Genoa, Ohio

Old-Fashioned Brown Bread

2 cups whole wheat flour
½ cup all-purpose flour
2 teaspoons baking soda
1 teaspoon salt

2 cups buttermilk
½ cup molasses
1 cup raisins

Combine first 4 ingredients in a large mixing bowl; stir well. Add buttermilk and molasses; beat at low speed of an electric mixer until blended. Stir in raisins.

Spoon batter into 2 greased and floured 1-pound coffee cans. Bake at 350° for 45 minutes or until a wooden pick inserted in center comes out clean. Cool in cans 10 minutes. Remove from cans; cool completely on wire racks. Yield: 2 loaves.   Carol Lee

Fellowship Family Favorites Cookbook
Word of Life Fellowship
Schroon Lake, New York

Cocoa-Apricot Swirl Coffee Cake

1½ cups dried apricots
¼ cup water
½ cup sugar
2 tablespoons butter or
  margarine
2 teaspoons grated lemon rind
⅓ cup cocoa
⅓ cup sugar
¾ cup butter or margarine,
  softened

1½ cups sugar
4 large eggs
1½ teaspoons vanilla extract
3 cups unbleached flour
1½ tablespoons baking powder
¾ teaspoon baking soda
¼ teaspoon salt
1 (8-ounce) carton sour cream
1 cup chopped walnuts
¼ cup sifted powdered sugar

Place apricots in a bowl; add boiling water to cover. Let stand 30 minutes; drain. Combine apricots and ¼ cup water in container of an electric blender or food processor; cover and process until smooth, stopping once to scrape down sides. Combine puree, ½ cup sugar, 2 tablespoons butter, and lemon rind in a saucepan. Cook over medium heat until sugar dissolves, stirring occasionally. Set aside. Combine cocoa and ⅓ cup sugar; set aside.

Beat ¾ cup butter at medium speed of an electric mixer until creamy; gradually add 1½ cups sugar, beating well. Add eggs, one at a time, beating well after each addition. Stir in vanilla. Combine flour and next 3 ingredients; add to butter mixture alternately with sour cream, beginning and ending with flour mixture (batter will be stiff).

Spoon one-third of batter into a greased and floured 12-cup Bundt pan. Spoon half of apricot mixture over batter; sprinkle with half of cocoa mixture and half of walnuts. Top with half of remaining batter. Spoon remaining apricot mixture over batter; sprinkle with remaining cocoa mixture and walnuts. Top with remaining batter. Bake at 350° for 55 to 60 minutes or until a wooden pick inserted in center comes out clean. Cool in pan on a wire rack 20 minutes; remove from pan, and let cool completely on wire rack. Sprinkle with powdered sugar. Yield: one 10-inch cake.

Taste the Magic!
The Junior Club of Twin Falls, Idaho

Applesauce Doughnuts

1 tablespoon shortening
¾ cup firmly packed brown
  sugar
½ cup applesauce
1 large egg
2 cups all-purpose flour
½ teaspoon baking soda

¼ teaspoon salt
¼ teaspoon ground nutmeg
¼ teaspoon ground cinnamon
Vegetable oil
½ cup sugar
2 teaspoons ground cinnamon

Beat shortening and brown sugar at medium speed of an electric mixer until blended. Add applesauce and egg; beat well. Combine flour and next 4 ingredients. Add to shortening mixture; beat well.

Roll dough to ½-inch thickness on a lightly floured surface. Cut dough with a floured 2½-inch doughnut cutter.

Pour oil to depth of 2 inches in a large Dutch oven; heat to 375°. Drop in 3 to 4 doughnuts at a time. Cook 1½ minutes on each side. Drain on paper towels. Combine ½ cup sugar and 2 teaspoons cinnamon. Roll doughnuts in cinnamon-sugar mixture. Cool on wire racks. Yield: 16 doughnuts. Marian Moscicki

Country Cookbook
Our Lady's Guild of St. Christopher's Parish
Red Hook, New York

Piña Colada Muffins

Muffin pans generally contain 12 muffin cups. When baking more than or less than 12 muffins, be sure to fill the empty cups with water so the muffins will bake evenly.

¼ cup butter or margarine, softened
½ cup sugar
1 large egg
1½ cups all-purpose flour
1 teaspoon baking powder
½ teaspoon baking soda
½ teaspoon salt

1 (8-ounce) carton sour cream
1 (8-ounce) can crushed pineapple, drained
½ cup flaked coconut
2 teaspoons rum extract
2 tablespoons sugar
½ teaspoon ground cinnamon

Beat butter at medium speed of an electric mixer until creamy; gradually add ½ cup sugar, beating well. Add egg; beat well. Combine flour and next 3 ingredients; add to butter mixture alternately with sour cream, beginning and ending with flour mixture. Mix after each addition. Stir in pineapple, coconut, and rum extract.

Spoon into greased muffin pans, filling three-fourths full. Combine 2 tablespoons sugar and cinnamon; stir well. Sprinkle evenly over batter. Bake at 350° for 20 minutes. Remove from pans immediately. Yield: 14 muffins.

Diane Gade

Concordia Seminary Cookbook 1992-1993
Concordia Seminary Women's Association
Clayton, Missouri

Pumpkin-Apple Strudel Muffins

1 (16-ounce) can pumpkin
1 cup honey
½ cup vegetable oil
1 tablespoon pumpkin pie spice
2 large eggs, beaten
2½ cups all-purpose flour
1 teaspoon baking soda
¼ teaspoon salt

1 cup sugar
2 cups peeled, diced cooking apples
¼ cup sugar
2 tablespoons all-purpose flour
½ teaspoon ground cinnamon
1 tablespoon plus 1 teaspoon butter or margarine

Combine first 4 ingredients. Add eggs; stir until blended. Combine 2½ cups flour, baking soda, salt, and 1 cup sugar in a bowl; make a well in center of mixture. Add pumpkin mixture to dry ingredients, stirring just until moistened. Stir in apple.

Spoon batter into greased muffin pans, filling two-thirds full. Combine ¼ cup sugar, 2 tablespoons flour, and cinnamon in a bowl; cut in butter with pastry blender until mixture is crumbly. Sprinkle evenly over batter. Bake at 375° for 20 minutes. Remove from pans immediately. Yield: 2½ dozen.   Helen Brown

From the Prince's Pantry
The Friends of Prince Memorial Library
Cumberland, Maine

Rhubarb-Walnut Muffins

These tender muffins are best served warm from the oven.

1¼ cups all-purpose flour
½ teaspoon baking powder
½ teaspoon baking soda
¼ teaspoon salt
½ cup plus 2 tablespoons
  firmly packed brown sugar
½ cup buttermilk
¼ cup butter or margarine,
  melted

1 large egg, beaten
1 teaspoon vanilla extract
¾ cup diced fresh rhubarb
½ cup chopped walnuts
¼ cup sugar
1 tablespoon butter or
  margarine, melted
¾ teaspoon ground cinnamon

Combine first 5 ingredients in a large bowl; make a well in center of mixture. Combine buttermilk, ¼ cup butter, egg, and vanilla; add to dry ingredients, stirring just until moistened. Stir in rhubarb and walnuts.

Spoon batter into a greased muffin pan, filling two-thirds full. Combine ¼ cup sugar, 1 tablespoon butter, and cinnamon in a small bowl, stirring well. Sprinkle sugar mixture evenly over batter. Bake at 400° for 18 to 20 minutes. Remove from pan immediately. Yield: 1 dozen.   Judi Jacobson Gilbertson

Feeding the Flock
Ellsborough Lutheran Church
Lake Wilson, Minnesota

Scottish Scones

Scones are a popular quick bread that come in a variety of shapes including rounds, squares, diamonds, and, as in this recipe, triangles.

2 cups all-purpose flour
2 teaspoons baking powder
½ teaspoon baking soda
¾ teaspoon salt
3 tablespoons sugar
¼ cup plus 1 tablespoon
  butter or margarine

½ cup currants
1 (8-ounce) carton sour cream
1 large egg, separated
1 teaspoon sugar
⅛ teaspoon ground cinnamon

Combine first 5 ingredients in a large bowl; stir well. Cut in butter with pastry blender until mixture is crumbly. Stir in currants. Combine sour cream and egg yolk, stirring well; add to flour mixture, stirring just until dry ingredients are moistened.

Turn dough out onto a lightly floured surface, and knead lightly 10 or 12 times. Shape dough into a 9-inch circle. Cut into 3 rounds, using a 4-inch cutter. Reroll remaining dough; cut into 2 rounds.

Place rounds on an ungreased baking sheet. Cut each round into 4 wedges, but do not separate. Lightly beat egg white, and brush over wedges.

Combine 1 teaspoon sugar and cinnamon; sprinkle evenly over wedges. Bake at 425° for 13 to 15 minutes or until lightly browned. Serve warm. Yield: 20 scones.   Ann A. Corscaden

M.D. Anderson Volunteers Cooking for Fun
University of Texas M.D. Anderson Cancer Center
Houston, Texas

Double-Orange Scones
with Orange Butter

For the flair of traditional English high tea, serve these scones on your best china and the Orange Butter in a small crystal bowl.

2 cups all-purpose flour
2½ teaspoons baking powder
3 tablespoons sugar
1 tablespoon grated orange
  rind
⅓ cup butter or margarine

1 (11-ounce) can mandarin
  oranges, drained
¼ cup milk
1 large egg, lightly beaten
1 tablespoon sugar
Orange Butter

Combine first 4 ingredients in a large bowl; stir well. Cut in butter with pastry blender until mixture is crumbly. Add oranges, milk, and egg, stirring just until dry ingredients are moistened.

Turn dough out onto a heavily floured surface, and knead lightly 4 or 5 times. Pat dough into a 6-inch circle on a greased baking sheet. Cut into 8 wedges; separate wedges slightly. Sprinkle with 1 tablespoon sugar. Bake at 400° for 15 to 20 minutes or until lightly browned. Serve warm with Orange Butter. Yield: 8 scones.

Orange Butter

¼ cup butter or margarine,
  softened

2 tablespoons orange
  marmalade

Combine butter and orange marmalade in a small bowl, stirring well. Yield: ⅓ cup.

California Sizzles
The Junior League of Pasadena, California

Buttermilk-Garlic Bread

5 cups bread flour, divided
⅓ cup grated Parmesan cheese
1 package rapid-rise yeast
1¾ cups buttermilk
¼ cup unsalted butter or
   margarine
1 tablespoon sugar
2 teaspoons salt

2 cloves garlic, crushed
3 egg yolks
1 large egg
2 tablespoons whipping cream
1 tablespoon caraway seeds
1 tablespoon poppy seeds
1 tablespoon sesame seeds

Combine 2 cups flour, cheese, and yeast in a large mixing bowl; stir well. Combine buttermilk and next 4 ingredients in a saucepan; heat until butter melts, stirring occasionally. Cool to 120° to 130°.

Gradually add liquid mixture to flour mixture, beating well at low speed of an electric mixer until blended. Beat an additional 2 minutes at medium speed. Add egg yolks, and beat 2 minutes. Gradually stir in enough remaining flour to make a soft dough.

Turn dough out onto a lightly floured surface, and knead until smooth and elastic (about 8 minutes). Place in a well-greased bowl, turning to grease top. Cover and let rise in a warm place (85°), free from drafts, 1 hour or until doubled in bulk.

Cut a piece of aluminum foil long enough to fit around a 2½-quart soufflé dish, allowing a 1-inch overlap; fold foil lengthwise into thirds. Butter 1 side of foil and soufflé dish. Wrap foil around outside of dish, buttered side against dish, allowing it to extend 3 inches above rim to form a collar; secure with string.

Punch dough down; divide into 3 equal portions. Shape each portion into a ball. Arrange in prepared dish, allowing balls to touch in center. Combine egg and whipping cream, beating until blended. Brush balls with egg mixture. Sprinkle 1 ball with caraway seeds, 1 ball with poppy seeds, and 1 ball with sesame seeds.

Cover and let rise in a warm place, free from drafts, 50 minutes or until doubled in bulk. Bake at 375° for 35 to 40 minutes or until bread sounds hollow when tapped. (Cover with aluminum foil the last 15 minutes of baking to prevent excessive browning, if necessary.) Remove from dish immediately; cool on a wire rack. Yield: 1 loaf.

Claire Furman

Cooking Up a Storm
L.Z. Aerobics Class
Lawrenceville, Georgia

Harvest Bread

The flavor of this hearty yeast bread comes from the wholesome ingredients it contains—honey, molasses, whole wheat flour, wheat germ, and crumbled whole wheat cereal biscuits.

1½ cups milk
⅓ cup butter or margarine
2 large shredded whole wheat
   cereal biscuits, crumbled
2 tablespoons honey
2 tablespoons molasses
2 teaspoons salt

2 packages active dry yeast
½ cup warm water (105° to
   115°)
2 cups whole wheat flour
¼ cup wheat germ
2 to 3 cups all-purpose flour

Combine first 6 ingredients in a saucepan; heat until butter melts, stirring occasionally. Cool to 105° to 115°. Combine yeast and warm water in a 1-cup liquid measuring cup; let stand 5 minutes.

Combine milk mixture, yeast mixture, and whole wheat flour in a large mixing bowl; beat at medium speed of an electric mixer until blended. Gradually stir in wheat germ and enough all-purpose flour to make a stiff dough.

Turn dough out onto a lightly floured surface, and knead until smooth and elastic (about 8 to 10 minutes). Place dough in a well-greased bowl, turning to grease top. Cover dough, and let rise in a warm place (85°), free from drafts, 1 hour or until dough is doubled in bulk.

Punch dough down, and divide in half. Roll 1 portion of dough into a 14- x 6-inch rectangle. Roll up dough, starting at short side, pressing firmly to eliminate air pockets; pinch seams to seal. Place dough, seam side down, in a greased 8½- x 4½- x 3-inch loafpan. Repeat procedure with remaining dough.

Cover and let rise in a warm place, free from drafts, 35 minutes or until doubled in bulk. Bake at 400° for 25 minutes or until loaves sound hollow when tapped. (Cover with aluminum foil the last 5 minutes of baking to prevent excessive browning, if necessary.) Remove from pans immediately; cool on wire racks. Yield: 2 loaves.   Norm Linde

Let Us Break Bread Together
St. Michael's Episcopal Churchwomen
Barrington, Illinois

Braided Potato Bread

Mashed potato added to the dough makes this bread moist and flavorful.

1 cup cooked mashed potato	1 package active dry yeast
⅔ cup milk	1½ teaspoons salt
¼ cup butter or margarine	2 large eggs
3½ cups all-purpose flour, divided	1 egg white, lightly beaten
¼ cup sugar	1 teaspoon water
	2 teaspoons poppy seeds

Combine potato, milk, and butter in a saucepan; heat until butter melts, stirring occasionally. Cool to 120° to 130°.

Combine 1½ cups flour, sugar, yeast, and salt in a large mixing bowl; stir well. Gradually add milk mixture and 2 eggs, beating at medium speed of an electric mixer 2 minutes. Stir in enough remaining flour to make a soft dough.

Turn dough out onto a lightly floured surface, and knead until smooth and elastic (about 10 minutes). Place dough in a well-greased bowl, turning to grease top. Cover and let rise in a warm place (85°), free from drafts, 1½ hours or until dough is doubled in bulk.

Punch dough down; divide into 3 equal portions. Shape each portion of dough into a 14-inch rope. Place ropes on a greased baking sheet (do not stretch); pinch ends together at one end to seal. Braid ropes; pinch loose ends together to seal. Cover and let rise in a warm place, free from drafts, 1 hour or until dough is doubled in bulk.

Combine egg white and water; stir well. Brush egg white mixture over top and sides of loaf. Sprinkle with poppy seeds. Bake at 350° for 30 to 35 minutes or until loaf sounds hollow when tapped. Remove bread from baking sheet immediately; let cool on a wire rack. Yield: 1 loaf.

Suzanne Towcimak

A World of Good Taste
St. Bernadette's Home and School Guild
Springfield, Virginia

Chocolate-Pecan Rolls

¾ cup milk
½ cup sugar
½ cup butter or margarine
1 (1-ounce) square
  unsweetened chocolate
2 teaspoons salt
1 package active dry yeast
¾ cup warm water (105° to 115°)
4 to 4½ cups all-purpose flour
1 large egg
1 teaspoon ground mace

2 cups firmly packed brown
  sugar
½ cup butter or margarine,
  melted
½ cup chopped pecans
1 tablespoon light corn syrup
2 teaspoons vanilla extract
½ cup butter or margarine,
  softened and divided
1 cup sugar
2 teaspoons ground cinnamon

Combine first 5 ingredients in a saucepan; heat until butter and chocolate melt, stirring occasionally. Cool to 105° to 115°. Combine yeast and warm water; let stand 5 minutes. Combine milk mixture, yeast mixture, 2 cups flour, egg, and mace in a mixing bowl; beat at medium speed of an electric mixer until blended. Gradually stir in enough remaining flour to make a soft dough. Cover and chill at least 2 hours or up to 3 days.

Combine brown sugar, ½ cup melted butter, pecans, corn syrup, and vanilla; stir well. Set aside.

Turn dough out onto a lightly floured surface, and knead lightly 4 or 5 times. Divide dough in half. Roll 1 portion of dough into an 18- x 9-inch rectangle. Spread ¼ cup softened butter over dough to within ½ inch of sides. Combine 1 cup sugar and cinnamon; sprinkle half of cinnamon-sugar mixture over dough. Roll up dough, starting at long side, pressing firmly to eliminate air pockets; pinch seam to seal (do not seal ends). Cut roll into 1-inch-thick slices. Sprinkle half of reserved pecan mixture evenly into the bottom of a buttered 13- x 9- x 2-inch pan. Place slices, cut side down, in prepared pan. Repeat procedure with remaining dough, cinnamon-sugar mixture, and pecan mixture.

Cover and let rise in a warm place (85°), free from drafts, 1 hour or until doubled in bulk. Bake at 350° for 25 minutes. Immediately invert pans onto serving platters. Let stand 1 minute. Remove pans from rolls. Yield: 3 dozen.   Rudela Watts

McMahan Fire Department and Ladies Auxiliary Cookbook
McMahan Fire Department Ladies Auxiliary
Dale, Texas

Cottage Cheese Rolls

2 packages active dry yeast
½ cup warm water (105° to 115°)
2 cups small-curd cottage
  cheese
¼ cup sugar
2 teaspoons salt

½ teaspoon baking soda
2 large eggs, lightly beaten
5 cups all-purpose flour
All-purpose flour
Melted butter or margarine
  (optional)

Combine yeast and warm water in a 1-cup liquid measuring cup; let stand 5 minutes. Combine yeast mixture, cottage cheese, and next 4 ingredients in a mixing bowl; beat at medium speed of an electric mixer until blended. Gradually stir in 5 cups flour until mixture forms a soft dough (dough will be sticky). Place in a well-greased bowl, turning to grease top. Cover and let rise in a warm place (85°), free from drafts, 1 hour or until doubled in bulk.

Punch dough down, and divide in half; shape each portion of dough into 12 balls. Roll each ball in flour, and place in a well-greased 13- x 9- x 2-inch pan. Cover and let rise in a warm place, free from drafts, 30 minutes or until doubled in bulk. Bake at 350° for 25 to 30 minutes or until golden. (Cover loosely with aluminum foil during the last 5 minutes of baking to prevent excessive browning, if necessary.) Immediately remove rolls from pan; brush with melted butter, if desired. Yield: 2 dozen.   Ruth Witcher

Treasured Recipes
Morton County Hospital Auxiliary
Elkhart, Kansas

Dilly Rolls

No kneading! Simply spoon the dough into muffin pans, let rise, and bake.

1½ cups milk
⅓ cup butter or margarine
3½ cups all-purpose flour,
  divided
¼ cup sugar

1 package active dry yeast
2 teaspoons dried dillweed
1 teaspoon salt
1 large egg

Combine milk and butter in a small saucepan; heat until butter melts, stirring mixture occasionally. Cool to 120° to 130°.

Combine 1½ cups flour, sugar, yeast, dillweed, and salt in a large mixing bowl, stirring well. Gradually add milk mixture to flour mixture, beating at low speed of an electric mixer until blended. Beat an additional 2 minutes at medium speed. Add egg, and beat well. Stir in enough remaining flour to make a soft dough.

Cover and let rise in a warm place (85°), free from drafts, 45 minutes or until doubled in bulk. Stir dough down to remove air bubbles. Spoon into greased muffin pans, filling two-thirds full. Let rise in a warm place, free from drafts, 30 minutes. Bake at 400° for 15 to 20 minutes or until golden. Remove from pans immediately. Serve warm. Yield: 1½ dozen.   Carol Edmondson

First United Methodist Church Centennial Cookbook, 1993
United Methodist Women of First United Methodist Church
Casper, Wyoming

Whole-Grain Pan Rolls

1 cup water
¼ cup honey
¼ cup butter or margarine
¾ cup whole wheat flour
½ cup regular oats, uncooked

2 packages active dry yeast
1 teaspoon salt
1 large egg
2½ to 2¾ cups all-purpose
  flour

Combine water, honey, and butter in a small saucepan; heat until butter melts, stirring occasionally. Cool to 120° to 130°. Combine wheat flour and next 3 ingredients in a large mixing bowl; stir well. Gradually add liquid mixture to flour mixture, beating at low speed of an electric mixer until blended. Beat an additional 2 minutes at medium speed. Add egg, and beat 2 minutes. Gradually stir in enough all-purpose flour to make a soft dough.

Turn dough out onto a lightly floured surface; knead until smooth and elastic (about 8 minutes). Divide into 24 equal portions; shape each portion into a ball. Place balls in a lightly greased 13- x 9- x 2-inch pan. Cover and let rise in a warm place (85°), free from drafts, 1 hour or until doubled in bulk. Bake at 375° for 18 to 20 minutes or until lightly browned. Yield: 2 dozen.

We're Really Cookin' Now!
Epsilon Sigma Alpha of Oklahoma
McAlester, Oklahoma

Whole-Grain Soft Pretzels

Serve these whole-grain pretzels with a spicy hot mustard for dipping.

1 package active dry yeast
1½ cups warm water (105° to
 115°)
1 tablespoon brown sugar
3¼ to 3½ cups whole wheat
 flour

1 teaspoon salt
½ cup toasted wheat germ
1 large egg, lightly beaten
1 tablespoon water
Kosher salt

Dissolve yeast in warm water in a 2-cup liquid measuring cup. Stir in brown sugar; let stand 5 minutes. Combine yeast mixture, 2 cups flour, and salt in a large mixing bowl; beat at medium speed of an electric mixer until blended. Gradually stir in wheat germ and enough remaining flour to make a soft dough.

Turn dough out onto a lightly floured surface, and knead until smooth and elastic (about 5 minutes). Place in a well-greased bowl, turning to grease top. Cover and let rise in a warm place (85°), free from drafts, 1 hour or until doubled in bulk.

Punch dough down; divide into 16 equal portions. Roll each portion into a 15-inch rope. Twist each rope into a pretzel shape. Place pretzels about 1½ inches apart on lightly greased baking sheets. Cover and let rise in a warm place, free from drafts, 20 minutes.

Combine egg and water; stir well. Brush pretzels with egg mixture; sprinkle with salt. Bake at 400° for 16 to 18 minutes or until lightly browned. Serve warm, or let cool on wire racks. Yield: 16 pretzels.

Stephanie Luke

Our Daily Bread
Women's Club of Our Lady of Mt. Carmel
Carmel, Indiana

Cakes

*Whether your celebration calls for a buttery pound cake,
a frosted sheet cake, or a creamy cheesecake, you're sure to find
some new favorites in this chapter.*

Lemon Cheesecake with Strawberries, page 101

Banana-Nutmeg Cream Cake

This cake will become more moist and flavorful the longer it chills.

1¾ cups all-purpose flour
1 teaspoon baking powder
1 teaspoon baking soda
¾ teaspoon salt
1 cup sugar
1 cup mashed ripe banana
⅔ cup buttermilk, divided
⅓ cup vegetable oil
1 teaspoon vanilla extract
2 large eggs, separated
⅓ cup sugar
½ cup finely chopped walnuts
Nutmeg Whipped Cream

Combine first 5 ingredients in a large mixing bowl; stir well. Add banana, ⅓ cup buttermilk, oil, and vanilla. Beat at low speed of an electric mixer until blended. Beat an additional minute at high speed. Add remaining ⅓ cup buttermilk and egg yolks, and beat at high speed 1 minute or until blended.

Beat egg whites at high speed until foamy. Gradually add ⅓ cup sugar, 1 tablespoon at a time, beating until stiff peaks form and sugar dissolves (2 to 4 minutes). Fold beaten egg white and walnuts into banana mixture.

Pour batter into 2 greased and floured 9-inch round cakepans. Bake at 350° for 30 to 35 minutes or until a wooden pick inserted in center comes out clean. Cool in pans on wire racks 10 minutes; remove from pans, and let cool completely on wire racks. Spread 3½ cups Nutmeg Whipped Cream between layers and on top and sides of cake. Spoon remaining Nutmeg Whipped Cream into a decorating bag fitted with a large star tip; decorate cake. Cover and chill. Yield: one 2-layer cake.

Nutmeg Whipped Cream

3 cups whipping cream
1 cup sifted powdered sugar
1½ teaspoons ground nutmeg

Beat whipping cream in a large mixing bowl until foamy; gradually add powdered sugar and nutmeg, beating until soft peaks form. Yield: 6 cups.

Fiddlers Canyon Ward Cookbook
Fiddlers Canyon Ward Relief Society
Cedar City, Utah

Cherry Nectar Cake

Maraschino cherry juice gives this cake a pretty light pink color.

1½ cups shortening, divided
2 cups sugar
4 large eggs
3 cups all-purpose flour
1 tablespoon baking powder
1 teaspoon salt
1¼ cups milk, divided
1 teaspoon almond extract
1 cup chopped maraschino
  cherries, divided

¼ cup maraschino cherry juice
¾ cup chopped pecans,
  divided
½ cup butter or margarine,
  softened
6 cups sifted powdered sugar
1 teaspoon almond extract

Grease four 8-inch round cakepans; line with wax paper. Grease and flour wax paper. Set aside.

Beat 1 cup shortening at medium speed of an electric mixer until creamy; gradually add 2 cups sugar, beating well. Add eggs, one at a time, beating after each addition.

Combine flour, baking powder, and salt; add to shortening mixture alternately with 1 cup milk, beginning and ending with flour mixture. Mix after each addition. Stir in 1 teaspoon almond extract, ½ cup cherries, cherry juice, and ½ cup pecans.

Pour batter into prepared pans. Bake at 350° for 20 to 25 minutes or until a wooden pick inserted in center comes out clean. Cool in pans on wire racks 10 minutes; remove from pans, and let cool completely on wire racks.

Beat butter and remaining ½ cup shortening at medium speed until creamy. Add powdered sugar to butter mixture alternately with remaining ¼ cup milk, beginning and ending with powdered sugar. Beat until blended after each addition. Stir in 1 teaspoon almond extract, remaining ½ cup cherries, and remaining ¼ cup chopped pecans. Spread frosting between layers and on top and sides of cake. Yield: one 4-layer cake.

Blooming Good
National Council of State Garden Clubs
St. Louis, Missouri

Old-Fashioned Caramel Cake

Be sure to spread the Caramel Frosting immediately after it reaches spreading consistency because it will harden quickly.

1 cup butter, softened
2 cups sugar
3 large eggs
3 cups all-purpose flour
1 teaspoon baking soda
3 tablespoons cocoa

1 cup buttermilk
½ cup warm water
1 teaspoon vanilla extract
Caramel Frosting
Garnishes: pecan halves,
   grated chocolate

Beat butter at medium speed of an electric mixer until creamy; gradually add sugar, beating well. Add eggs, one at a time, beating after each addition.

Combine flour, baking soda, and cocoa; add to butter mixture alternately with buttermilk and water, beginning and ending with flour mixture. Mix after each addition. Stir in vanilla.

Pour batter into 2 greased and floured 9-inch round cakepans. Bake at 350° for 35 minutes or until a wooden pick inserted in center comes out clean. Cool in pans on wire racks 10 minutes; remove from pans, and let cool completely on wire racks. Quickly spread Caramel Frosting between layers and on top and sides of cake. Garnish, if desired. Yield: one 2-layer cake.

Caramel Frosting

2 cups sugar
1 cup butter

1 cup evaporated milk
1 teaspoon vanilla extract

Combine sugar, butter, and milk in a large saucepan; bring to a boil over medium heat. Cover and cook 2 to 3 minutes to wash down sugar crystals from sides of pan. Uncover and cook, stirring constantly, until mixture reaches soft ball stage or candy thermometer registers 234°. Remove from heat, and add vanilla (do not stir). Let cool 10 minutes. Beat at medium speed of an electric mixer 8 to 10 minutes or until mixture is spreading consistency. Yield: 2½ cups.

Dining Al Fresco
Wolf Trap Associates
Vienna, Virginia

White Chocolate-Coconut Cake

4 ounces white chocolate,
  coarsely chopped
½ cup hot water
1 cup butter or margarine,
  softened
1¾ cups sugar, divided
4 large eggs, separated
2½ cups sifted cake flour,
  divided
1 teaspoon baking soda

1 cup buttermilk
¾ cup chopped blanched
  almonds, toasted
2 cups flaked coconut, divided
2 cups whipping cream
1 cup seedless raspberry jam
2 tablespoons powdered sugar
1½ ounces white chocolate,
  grated

Grease three 9-inch round cakepans; line with wax paper. Grease and flour wax paper; set aside.

Combine chopped chocolate and hot water in top of a double boiler; bring water in bottom of double boiler to a boil. Reduce heat to low; cook until chocolate melts, stirring occasionally. Cool.

Beat butter at medium speed of an electric mixer until creamy; gradually add 1½ cups sugar, beating well. Add egg yolks, one at a time, beating after each addition. Add white chocolate mixture, beating well. Combine 2¼ cups flour and soda; add to butter mixture alternately with buttermilk, beginning and ending with flour mixture. Mix after each addition. Combine remaining ¼ cup flour, almonds, and 1 cup coconut; toss to coat. Stir into batter.

Beat egg whites at high speed until foamy. Gradually add remaining ¼ cup sugar, 1 tablespoon at a time, beating until stiff peaks form and sugar dissolves (2 to 4 minutes); fold into batter.

Pour batter into prepared pans. Bake at 350° for 20 to 25 minutes or until a wooden pick inserted in center comes out clean. Cool in pans on wire racks 10 minutes; remove from pans, and let cool completely on wire racks.

Beat whipping cream until foamy. Gradually add 2 tablespoons powdered sugar, beating until soft peaks form. Spread ½ cup jam between each cake layer; spread whipped cream mixture on top and sides of cake. Press remaining 1 cup coconut onto sides of cake; sprinkle grated white chocolate on top. Cover and chill. Yield: one 3-layer cake.   Mary Ann Hawkins Pennel

Fairfax Heritage Cookbook
Fairfax Community Betterment
Fairfax, Missouri

Super Peanutty Layer Cake

¾ cup creamy peanut butter
½ cup shortening
2¼ cups firmly packed brown sugar
3 large eggs
3 cups all-purpose flour
1 tablespoon baking powder
½ teaspoon salt
1¼ cups milk
1 cup flaked coconut, toasted
1 cup chopped unsalted dry roasted peanuts
1½ teaspoons vanilla extract
Peanut Butter Frosting

Beat peanut butter and shortening at medium speed of an electric mixer until creamy; gradually add brown sugar, beating well. Add eggs, one at a time, beating after each addition.

Combine flour, baking powder, and salt; add to peanut butter mixture alternately with milk, beginning and ending with flour mixture. Mix after each addition. Stir in coconut, peanuts, and vanilla.

Pour batter into 3 greased and floured 9-inch round cakepans. Bake at 350° for 25 minutes or until a wooden pick inserted in center comes out clean. Cool in pans on wire racks 10 minutes; remove from pans, and let cool completely on wire racks. Spread Peanut Butter Frosting between layers and on top and sides of cake. Yield: one 3-layer cake.

Peanut Butter Frosting

½ cup butter or margarine, softened
3 tablespoons creamy peanut butter
6 cups sifted powdered sugar
⅓ cup plus 1 tablespoon half-and-half
1 teaspoon vanilla extract

Beat butter and peanut butter at medium speed of an electric mixer until creamy. Add sugar to butter mixture alternately with half-and-half, beginning and ending with sugar. Beat well after each addition. Stir in vanilla. Yield: 3½ cups.   Jane Taylor

Our Daily Bread
Women's Club of Our Lady of Mt. Carmel
Carmel, Indiana

Mango Cake with Lemon Icing

Pureed fresh mango gives this cake its delectable flavor and moist, tender texture. Carefully carve the fragrant fruit away from the large, flat seed, using a sharp knife.

1½ cups raisins
½ cup shortening
1½ cups firmly packed brown
  sugar
2 large eggs
3 cups sifted cake flour
1½ teaspoons baking soda

¾ teaspoon salt
1½ teaspoons ground
  cinnamon
¾ teaspoon ground nutmeg
¾ teaspoon ground cloves
1½ cups pureed fresh mango
Lemon Icing

Place raisins in a small bowl; add boiling water to cover. Let stand 15 minutes. Drain well, and set aside.

Beat shortening at medium speed of an electric mixer until creamy; gradually add brown sugar, beating well. Add eggs, one at a time, beating after each addition. Combine flour and next 5 ingredients; add to shortening mixture alternately with mango, beginning and ending with flour mixture. Mix after each addition. Stir in reserved raisins.

Pour batter into a greased and floured 13- x 9- x 2-inch pan. Bake at 325° for 50 minutes or until a wooden pick inserted in center comes out clean. Cool completely in pan on a wire rack. Spread Lemon Icing on top of cake. Yield: 15 servings.

Lemon Icing

⅓ cup butter or margarine,
  softened
3 cups sifted powdered sugar

2 to 3 tablespoons water
1 tablespoon plus 1 teaspoon
  grated lemon rind

Beat butter at medium speed of an electric mixer until creamy. Gradually add sugar, beating until blended. Add water and lemon rind, beating until spreading consistency. Yield: 1½ cups.

Tropical Seasons, A Taste of Life in South Florida
Beaux Arts of the Lowe Art Museum of the University of Miami
Coral Gables, Florida

Rhubarb Cake

The peak season for rhubarb is from April to June, although it's available in some areas of the country almost year-round. Fresh rhubarb will keep up to three days if wrapped in a plastic bag and refrigerated.

½ cup shortening
1½ cups firmly packed brown
  sugar
1 large egg
2 cups all-purpose flour
1 teaspoon baking soda
½ teaspoon salt

1 cup milk
2 cups chopped fresh rhubarb
2 teaspoons vanilla extract
2 cups flaked coconut
½ cup sugar
1 tablespoon ground cinnamon

Beat shortening at medium speed of an electric mixer until creamy; gradually add brown sugar, beating well. Add egg, beating just until yellow disappears.

Combine flour, baking soda, and salt; add to shortening mixture alternately with milk, beginning and ending with flour mixture. Mix after each addition. Stir in rhubarb and vanilla.

Pour batter into a greased and floured 13- x 9- x 2-inch pan. Combine coconut, ½ cup sugar, and cinnamon; sprinkle evenly over batter. Bake at 350° for 45 minutes or until a wooden pick inserted in center comes out clean. (Cover with aluminum foil to prevent excessive browning, if necessary.) Cool in pan on a wire rack. Yield: 15 servings.

Dorothy Rudolph

Family Cookbook: A Collection of Favorite Recipes
Women's Ministries of Trinity Assembly of God
Derry, New Hampshire

Absolutely Heavenly Amaretto Cake

1 cup butter or margarine
2½ cups sugar
6 large eggs
3 cups sifted cake flour
¼ teaspoon baking soda
½ teaspoon salt
1 (8-ounce) carton sour cream
2 teaspoons almond extract
1 teaspoon lemon extract

1 teaspoon orange extract
1 teaspoon vanilla extract
¾ cup amaretto, divided
¾ cup orange marmalade
¼ cup plus 2 tablespoons
  apricot preserves
½ to 1 cup chopped blanched
  almonds, toasted

Beat butter at medium speed of an electric mixer about 2 minutes or until soft and creamy. Gradually add sugar, beating at medium speed 5 to 7 minutes. Add eggs, one at a time, beating just until yellow disappears.

Combine flour, baking soda, and salt; add to butter mixture alternately with sour cream, beginning and ending with flour mixture. Mix at low speed just until blended after each addition. Stir in flavorings and ½ cup amaretto.

Pour batter into a greased and floured 12-cup Bundt pan. Bake at 325° for 1 hour and 15 minutes or until a wooden pick inserted in center comes out clean. Cool in pan on a wire rack 10 to 15 minutes; remove from pan, and let cool completely on wire rack.

Combine remaining ¼ cup amaretto, marmalade, and preserves in a small saucepan. Cook over medium heat until marmalade and preserves melt, stirring frequently. Drizzle over cake; sprinkle with almonds. Yield: one 10-inch cake.   Lee Caffery

A Cook's Tour of the Bayou Country
Churchwomen of the Southwest Deanery of the Episcopal
Diocese of Louisiana
Franklin, Louisiana

Chocolate-Walnut Upside-Down Cake

⅔ cup light corn syrup
½ cup plus 2 tablespoons
  butter or margarine,
  softened and divided
¼ cup firmly packed light
  brown sugar
¼ cup whipping cream
1 cup chopped walnuts
3 (1-ounce) squares
  unsweetened chocolate

1½ cups sugar
2 large eggs, separated
1 teaspoon vanilla extract
1¾ cups sifted cake flour
2 teaspoons baking powder
¼ teaspoon salt
1 cup milk
Whipped cream or sour cream

Combine corn syrup, ¼ cup butter, brown sugar, and whipping cream in a small saucepan. Cook over low heat, stirring constantly, just until mixture comes to a simmer (do not boil). Remove from heat; stir in walnuts (mixture will be thin). Pour into a heavily buttered 12-cup Bundt pan. Set aside.

Place chocolate in top of a double boiler; bring water to a boil. Reduce heat to low; cook until chocolate melts, stirring occasionally. Set aside.

Beat remaining ¼ cup plus 2 tablespoons butter at medium speed of an electric mixer about 2 minutes or until soft and creamy. Gradually add 1½ cups sugar, beating at medium speed 5 to 7 minutes. Add reserved melted chocolate, egg yolks, and vanilla, beating well.

Combine flour, baking powder, and salt; add to butter mixture alternately with milk, beginning and ending with flour mixture. Mix at low speed just until blended after each addition.

Beat egg whites in a small bowl at high speed until stiff peaks form. Gently fold beaten egg white into batter. Spoon batter over walnut mixture in pan. Bake at 350° for 45 minutes or until a wooden pick inserted in center comes out clean. Loosen cake from sides of pan, using a narrow metal spatula. Immediately invert cake onto a serving plate. Serve warm with whipped cream or sour cream. Yield: one 10-inch cake.   Rena Badessa

From Your Neighbor's Kitchen
Friends of Riverton Park
Riverton, New Jersey

Cranberry Christmas Cake

This cake is similar to a traditional fruitcake, but instead of candied fruit, it's full of cranberries and dates.

2½ cups all-purpose flour
1 teaspoon baking powder
1 teaspoon baking soda
1 teaspoon salt
1 cup sugar
1 cup chopped walnuts
1 cup fresh cranberries
1 cup chopped dates
2½ tablespoons grated orange
  rind

2 large eggs, beaten
¾ cup vegetable oil
⅓ cup buttermilk
1 cup sugar
1 cup orange juice
¼ cup brandy
Whipped cream

Combine first 5 ingredients in a large bowl; stir in walnuts, cranberries, dates, and orange rind. Combine eggs, oil, and buttermilk; add to flour mixture, stirring until blended.

Spoon batter into a heavily greased 10-inch tube pan. Bake at 350° for 1 hour or until a wooden pick inserted in center comes out clean. Cool in pan on a wire rack 10 minutes; remove from pan, and place on wire rack. Place rack in a large shallow pan.

Combine 1 cup sugar, orange juice, and brandy in a small bowl; stir well. Slowly drizzle orange juice mixture over cake. Let cool completely on wire rack.

Wrap cake in heavy-duty aluminum foil. Chill cake at least 24 hours or up to 8 weeks. Serve cake with whipped cream. Yield: one 10-inch cake.

Ann Ellis

Thymely Treasures
Hubbard Historical Society
Hubbard, Ohio

Tropical Dream Cake

The tropical flavors of pineapple and banana are spiced with cinnamon and orange in this dreamy glazed Bundt cake.

2 cups sugar
1 cup vegetable oil
3 large eggs
1 (8-ounce) can crushed
  pineapple, undrained
1½ teaspoons vanilla extract
3 cups all-purpose flour

1 teaspoon baking powder
1 teaspoon baking soda
1 teaspoon salt
1 teaspoon ground cinnamon
2 cups mashed ripe banana
1¾ cups sifted powdered sugar
2 to 3 tablespoons orange juice

Beat 2 cups sugar and oil at medium speed of an electric mixer 2 minutes. Add eggs, one at a time, beating just until yellow disappears. Add crushed pineapple and vanilla, beating just until blended.

Combine flour and next 4 ingredients; add to oil mixture alternately with banana, beginning and ending with flour mixture. Mix at low speed just until blended after each addition.

Pour batter into a greased and floured 12-cup Bundt pan. Bake at 350° for 1 hour or until a wooden pick inserted in center comes out clean. Cool in pan on a wire rack 10 minutes; remove from pan, and let cool completely on wire rack.

Combine powdered sugar and orange juice; stir well. Drizzle glaze over cake. Yield: one 10-inch cake.   Florence Johnson

A Collection of Excellent Recipes
Olathe Medical Center
Olathe, Kansas

Coffee Cloud Cake

If the frosting seems too thick, add an additional tablespoon of milk.

2 tablespoons instant coffee
 granules, divided
1 cup boiling water
2 cups all-purpose flour
1 tablespoon baking powder
½ teaspoon salt
6 large eggs, separated
2 cups sugar, divided
1 teaspoon vanilla extract

2½ cups chopped walnuts,
 divided
½ teaspoon cream of tartar
¼ cup milk
1 (16-ounce) package
 powdered sugar, sifted
¼ cup plus 2 tablespoons
 butter or margarine,
 softened

Dissolve 1 tablespoon granules in boiling water; set aside. Combine flour, baking powder, and salt; set aside.

Beat egg yolks in a large mixing bowl until thick and pale. Gradually add 1½ cups sugar; beat until blended. Beat an additional 5 minutes at high speed. Add reserved flour mixture to egg yolk mixture alternately with reserved coffee mixture, beginning and ending with flour mixture. Mix after each addition. Stir in vanilla and 1 cup walnuts. Beat egg whites and cream of tartar at high speed of an electric mixer until foamy. Gradually add remaining ½ cup sugar, 1 tablespoon at a time, beating until stiff peaks form and sugar dissolves (2 to 4 minutes). Fold one-fourth of egg white mixture into egg yolk mixture; carefully fold in remaining egg white mixture.

Pour batter into an ungreased 10-inch tube pan. Bake at 350° for 60 to 70 minutes or until cake springs back when lightly touched. Invert pan. Let cake cool in pan 40 minutes. Loosen from sides of pan, using a narrow metal spatula; remove from pan. Place on a serving plate.

Combine remaining 1 tablespoon granules and ¼ cup milk in a mixing bowl; stir until granules dissolve. Add powdered sugar and butter; beat at low speed until blended. Beat at medium speed until spreading consistency. Stir in remaining 1½ cups walnuts. Spread on top and sides of cake. Yield: one 10-inch cake.

Simply Heavenly
Woman's Synodical Union of the Associate Reformed
Presbyterian Church
Greenville, South Carolina

Chocolate-Buttermilk Pound Cake

4 (1.55-ounce) milk chocolate
  candy bars
½ cup chocolate syrup
1 cup butter, softened
2 cups sugar

4 large eggs
2½ cups all-purpose flour
½ teaspoon baking soda
1 cup buttermilk
2 teaspoons vanilla extract

Combine candy bars and syrup in top of a double boiler; bring water to a boil. Reduce heat to low; cook until chocolate melts, stirring occasionally. Set aside, and let cool.

Beat butter at medium speed of an electric mixer about 2 minutes or until soft and creamy. Gradually add sugar, beating at medium speed 5 to 7 minutes. Add eggs, one at a time, beating just until yellow disappears. Combine flour and baking soda; add to butter mixture alternately with buttermilk, beginning and ending with flour mixture. Mix at low speed just until blended after each addition. Stir in reserved candy bar mixture and vanilla.

Pour batter into a greased and floured 10-inch tube pan. Bake at 350° for 1 hour and 15 minutes or until a wooden pick inserted in center comes out clean. Cool in pan on a wire rack 10 to 15 minutes; remove from pan, and let cool completely on wire rack. Yield: one 10-inch cake. •

Tampa Treasures
The Junior League of Tampa, Florida

Pecan-Cranberry Pound Cake

1 cup unsalted butter or
  margarine, softened
2 cups sugar
5 large eggs
1¼ cups all-purpose flour
1 cup sifted cake flour
1 teaspoon grated orange rind
½ teaspoon salt

¼ cup sour cream
¼ cup Triple Sec or other
  orange-flavored liqueur
2 teaspoons vanilla extract
1½ cups chopped fresh
  cranberries
1 cup chopped pecans, toasted
Powdered sugar

Beat butter in a large mixing bowl at medium speed of an electric mixer about 2 minutes or until soft and creamy. Gradually add 2 cups sugar, beating at medium speed 5 to 7 minutes. Add eggs, one at a time, beating just until yellow disappears. Combine flours, orange rind, and salt; add to butter mixture alternately with sour cream and liqueur, beginning and ending with flour mixture. Mix at low speed just until blended after each addition. Stir in vanilla. Fold in cranberries and pecans.

Pour batter into 2 greased and floured 8½- x 4½- x 3-inch loaf-pans. Bake at 350° for 1 hour and 10 minutes or until a wooden pick inserted in center comes out clean. Cool in pans on wire racks 10 minutes; remove from pans. Cool on wire racks. Sprinkle with powdered sugar. Yield: 2 loaves.   Mrs. George P. Brown

Angels & Friends Favorite Recipes II
Angels of Easter Seal
Youngstown, Ohio

Montauk High-Bush Blueberry Shortcake

2 cups all-purpose flour
1 tablespoon baking powder
¾ teaspoon salt
3 tablespoons sugar
½ cup butter or margarine
½ cup milk
1 large egg, lightly beaten
6 cups fresh blueberries
1 cup water
½ cup sugar
Butter or margarine
Vanilla ice cream

Combine first 4 ingredients in a bowl. Cut in butter with pastry blender until mixture is crumbly. Combine milk and egg; add to flour mixture, stirring just until moistened. Drop batter by heaping ¼ cupfuls onto a lightly greased baking sheet. Bake at 400° for 14 minutes or until lightly browned. Let cool slightly on a wire rack.

Combine blueberries, water, and ½ cup sugar in a saucepan. Cook over medium heat 10 minutes, stirring gently. Split short-cakes in half horizontally. Spread butter over bottom; place in shallow soup bowls. Top with blueberry mixture. Place tops of shortcakes over blueberry mixture. Top each with ice cream. Serve immediately. Yield: 8 servings.   Mary Pospisil

The Montauk Lighthouse Cookbook
The Montauk Lighthouse Committee
Montauk, New York

Boston Cream Pie

⅓ cup shortening
1 cup sugar
2 large eggs
1¼ cups all-purpose flour
1½ teaspoons baking powder
½ teaspoon salt
¾ cup milk
1 teaspoon vanilla extract

3 tablespoons water
2 tablespoons butter or
 margarine
1 cup sifted powdered sugar
3 tablespoons cocoa
½ teaspoon vanilla extract
Custard Filling

Beat shortening at medium speed of an electric mixer until creamy; gradually add 1 cup sugar, beating well. Add eggs, one at a time, beating after each addition. Combine flour, baking powder, and salt; add to shortening mixture alternately with milk, beginning and ending with flour mixture. Mix after each addition. Stir in 1 teaspoon vanilla.

Pour batter into a greased and floured 9-inch round cakepan. Bake at 350° for 25 to 30 minutes or until a wooden pick inserted in center comes out clean. Cool in pan on a wire rack 10 minutes; remove from pan, and let cool completely on wire rack.

Combine water and butter in a saucepan; bring to a boil over medium heat. Remove from heat; add powdered sugar, cocoa, and ½ teaspoon vanilla, stirring until smooth. Set glaze aside

Split cake layer in half horizontally. Spread filling between layers; pour glaze over top of cake. Cover and chill. Yield: 8 to 10 servings.

Custard Filling

⅓ cup sugar
2 tablespoons cornstarch
1½ cups milk
2 egg yolks, lightly beaten

1 tablespoon butter or
 margarine
1 teaspoon vanilla extract

Combine sugar and cornstarch in a saucepan; gradually stir in milk and egg yolks. Cook over medium heat, stirring constantly, until thickened and bubbly. Remove from heat. Add butter and vanilla; stir until butter melts. Cool. Yield: 1¾ cups. Allyce North

Georgia Land
Medical Association of Georgia Alliance
Atlanta, Georgia

Marzipan Cake with Raspberry Sauce

Here's a luscious cake with the flavor of marzipan—a sweetened almond paste confection. Serve wedges of this rich cake in a pool of Raspberry Sauce.

½ cup butter or margarine, softened
⅔ cup sugar
1 (8-ounce) can almond paste, crumbled
4 large eggs, separated

2 tablespoons kirsch or orange juice
3 tablespoons all-purpose flour
¼ teaspoon baking powder
¼ teaspoon salt
Raspberry Sauce

Grease a 9-inch round cakepan; line with wax paper, and grease wax paper. Set aside.

Beat butter at medium speed of an electric mixer until creamy; gradually add sugar, beating well. Add almond paste; beat at low speed 2 to 3 minutes or until smooth. Add egg yolks, one at a time, beating after each addition. Stir in kirsch.

Combine flour, baking powder, and salt; add to butter mixture, beating until blended.

Beat egg whites at high speed until stiff peaks form; gently fold into batter.

Pour batter into prepared pan. Bake at 300° for 45 minutes or until a wooden pick inserted in center comes out clean. Cool in pan on a wire rack 10 minutes; remove from pan, and let cool completely on wire rack. Cut into wedges. Serve with Raspberry Sauce. Yield: 12 servings.

Raspberry Sauce

¼ cup sugar
½ cup seedless raspberry jam
½ cup water

1 teaspoon kirsch or
   ¼ teaspoon almond extract
⅔ cup fresh raspberries

Combine first 3 ingredients in a small saucepan; stir well. Bring to a boil; reduce heat, and cook, stirring constantly, until sugar dissolves and jam melts. Remove from heat, and stir in kirsch. Let sauce cool completely. Fold in raspberries. Cover and chill thoroughly. Yield: 1¼ cups.

Desert Treasures
The Junior League of Phoenix, Arizona

Chocolate-Irish Cream Cheesecake

You'll need to crush about 24 chocolate wafers in order to get 1¼ cups of the chocolate wafer crumbs.

1¼ cups chocolate wafer crumbs
¼ cup butter or margarine, melted
½ teaspoon ground cinnamon
8 (1-ounce) squares semisweet chocolate
3 (8-ounce) packages cream cheese, softened
1 (8-ounce) carton sour cream
1 cup sugar
3 large eggs
½ cup Irish Cream liqueur
2 tablespoons whipping cream
2 teaspoons vanilla extract
⅓ cup semisweet chocolate morsels
Garnish: fresh raspberries

Combine first 3 ingredients in a medium bowl, stirring well. Firmly press crumb mixture on bottom of a 10-inch springform pan, and set aside.

Place chocolate squares in top of a double boiler; bring water to a boil. Reduce heat to low; cook until chocolate melts, stirring occasionally. Set aside.

Beat cream cheese and sour cream at medium speed of an electric mixer until smooth. Add reserved melted chocolate and sugar, beating well. Add eggs, beating just until blended. Stir in liqueur, whipping cream, and vanilla.

Pour batter into prepared pan. Bake at 325° for 1 hour or until center is almost set. Let cool to room temperature in pan on a wire rack; cover and chill at least 8 hours. Carefully remove sides of springform pan.

Place chocolate morsels in top of double boiler; bring water to a boil. Reduce heat to low; cook until chocolate melts, stirring occasionally. Drizzle melted chocolate on top of cheesecake. Garnish, if desired. Yield: 12 servings.   Melissa Boden

Idalia Community Cookbook
Women's Fellowship of St. John United Church of Christ
Idalia, Colorado

Lemon Cheesecake with Strawberries

Beat the cheesecake filling just until creamy to avoid incorporating too much air. Overbeating can create a crack in the filling as it cools.

2 cups all-purpose flour
½ cup sugar
2 tablespoons grated lemon rind
1 cup unsalted butter or margarine
2 egg yolks, lightly beaten
½ teaspoon vanilla extract
3 (8-ounce) packages cream cheese, softened

1¾ cups sugar
1 teaspoon grated lemon rind
½ teaspoon vanilla extract
4 large eggs, lightly beaten
3 tablespoons all-purpose flour
1 teaspoon salt
2 egg yolks
¼ cup whipping cream
2 cups fresh strawberries, halved

Combine first 3 ingredients; cut in butter with pastry blender until mixture is crumbly. Add 2 egg yolks and ½ teaspoon vanilla; stir with a fork until dry ingredients are moistened. Firmly press one-third of flour mixture on bottom of a 10-inch springform pan. Bake at 400° for 8 minutes; cool in pan on a wire rack. Firmly press remaining flour mixture 2 inches up sides of pan. Set aside.

Beat cream cheese at medium speed of an electric mixer until creamy; gradually add 1¾ cups sugar, beating well. Add 1 teaspoon lemon rind and ½ teaspoon vanilla, beating well. Add eggs, 3 tablespoons flour, and salt, and beat well. Add 2 egg yolks, one at a time, beating after each addition. Add whipping cream, and beat until smooth.

Pour batter into prepared pan. Bake at 425° for 12 minutes. Reduce oven temperature to 300°, and bake 1 hour or until center is almost set. Let cool to room temperature in pan on wire rack; cover and chill at least 8 hours. Carefully remove sides of springform pan. Top with strawberry halves just before serving. Yield: 12 servings.

Celebrate!
The Junior League of Sacramento, California

Gingered Pumpkin Cheesecake

Gingersnap crumbs give this crust its spiciness, while crystallized ginger flavors the pumpkin-cream cheese filling. Crystallized ginger is gingerroot that's been cooked in a sugar syrup and coated with sugar.

1½ cups gingersnap crumbs
¼ cup sugar
¼ cup plus 2 tablespoons
  butter or margarine, melted
3 (8-ounce) packages cream
  cheese, softened
¾ cup sugar
¾ cup firmly packed light
  brown sugar

1 (16-ounce) can pumpkin
¼ cup whipping cream
¼ cup minced crystallized
  ginger
1½ teaspoons pumpkin pie
  spice
5 large eggs

Combine first 3 ingredients in a small bowl; stir well. Firmly press crumb mixture on bottom and 1½ inches up sides of a 9-inch springform pan. Chill.

Beat cream cheese at medium speed of an electric mixer until creamy; gradually add ¾ cup sugar and brown sugar, beating well. Add pumpkin and next 3 ingredients; beat until blended. Add eggs, one at a time, beating after each addition.

Pour batter into prepared pan. Bake at 325° for 1 hour and 35 minutes or until center is almost set. Remove from oven; let cheesecake cool to room temperature in pan on a wire rack. Cover and chill at least 8 hours. Carefully remove sides of springform pan. Yield: 12 servings.

Jeanne Jatkowski

Exclusively Pumpkin Cookbook
Coventry Historical Society
Coventry, Connecticut

Cookies & Candies

Will it be chewy, chocolate brownies or creamy divinity?
Whatever your pleasure, you can bet the cookie jar or candy dish
won't stay full very long!

Monte Carlos, page 107

Amaretto Apricot Chews

For even chewier cookies, bake them at 350° for 10 minutes.

1 cup butter or margarine,
  softened
¾ cup firmly packed brown
  sugar
½ cup sugar
1 large egg
1 tablespoon amaretto
1 cup all-purpose flour
1 teaspoon baking soda

2½ cups regular oats,
  uncooked
1 cup finely chopped dried
  apricots
½ cup finely chopped
  blanched almonds
2 cups sifted powdered sugar
3 to 4 tablespoons amaretto

Beat butter at medium speed of an electric mixer until creamy. Gradually add brown sugar and ½ cup sugar, beating well. Add egg and 1 tablespoon amaretto, beating well.

Combine flour and baking soda; add to butter mixture, beating well. Stir in oats, apricots, and almonds. Drop by rounded teaspoonfuls onto ungreased cookie sheets. Bake at 375° for 7 to 8 minutes or until lightly browned. Cool 1 minute on cookie sheets; remove to wire racks, and let cool completely. Combine powdered sugar and 3 to 4 tablespoons amaretto, stirring until smooth. Drizzle glaze over cookies. Yield: about 7 dozen.   Brenda Bragg

Country Church Favorites
St. John's United Church of Christ
Genoa, Ohio

Blueberry Cookies

¾ cup shortening
1½ cups sugar
2 large eggs
3 cups all-purpose flour
1 tablespoon baking powder
¾ teaspoon salt

⅓ cup milk
1¼ cups fresh blueberries
2½ tablespoons chopped
  pecans
2 teaspoons grated lemon rind

Beat shortening at medium speed of an electric mixer until creamy; gradually add sugar, beating well. Add eggs, one at a time, beating well after each addition.

Combine flour, baking powder, and salt in a medium bowl; add to shortening mixture alternately with milk, beginning and ending with flour mixture. Mix after each addition. Gently stir in blueberries, pecans, and lemon rind.

Drop by heaping tablespoonfuls onto lightly greased cookie sheets. Bake at 375° for 12 to 14 minutes or until lightly browned. Cool on wire racks. Yield: about 3½ dozen.   Marsha Strong

Palmetto Palate Cookbook
American Cancer Society, South Carolina Division
Columbia, South Carolina

Lemon Bonbons

These delicate lemon cookies are coated with finely chopped pecans and topped with a tangy lemon glaze.

1 cup butter or margarine, softened
⅓ cup sifted powdered sugar
1¼ cups all-purpose flour
¾ teaspoon cornstarch
½ cup finely chopped pecans or walnuts

1½ cups sifted powdered sugar
1½ teaspoons butter or margarine, melted
1½ tablespoons lemon juice

Beat 1 cup butter at medium speed of an electric mixer until creamy; gradually add ⅓ cup powdered sugar, beating well. Add flour and cornstarch, beating well. Cover and chill 1 hour.

Shape dough into 1-inch balls; roll in pecans. Place on ungreased cookie sheets. Flatten cookies with bottom of a glass dipped in flour. Bake at 350° for 14 to 16 minutes. Cool on wire racks.

Combine 1½ cups powdered sugar, 1½ teaspoons butter, and lemon juice in a small bowl, stirring until smooth. Drizzle glaze over cookies. Yield: 2 dozen.   Mary Atwood

Cooking Up a Storm
L.Z. Aerobics Class
Lawrenceville, Georgia

Chocolate Mint Snaps

Melting chocolate in the top of a double boiler ensures slow, even melting of the chocolate and prevents scorching.

4 (1-ounce) squares
  unsweetened chocolate
1¼ cups shortening
2¼ cups plus 2 tablespoons
  sugar, divided
2 large eggs
⅓ cup light corn syrup

2½ tablespoons water
2 teaspoons peppermint
  extract
1 teaspoon vanilla extract
4 cups all-purpose flour
2 teaspoons baking soda
½ teaspoon salt

Place chocolate squares in top of a double boiler; bring water to a boil. Reduce heat to low; cook until chocolate melts, stirring occasionally. Remove from heat; set aside, and let cool.

Beat shortening at medium speed of an electric mixer until creamy; gradually add 2 cups sugar, beating well. Add reserved chocolate, eggs, and next 4 ingredients; beat well.

Combine flour, baking soda, and salt; add to shortening mixture, beating well. Shape dough into 1-inch balls; roll in remaining ¼ cup plus 2 tablespoons sugar. Place 2 inches apart on ungreased cookie sheets. Bake at 350° for 9 to 11 minutes. Cool 5 minutes on cookie sheets; remove to wire racks, and let cool completely. Yield: 6 dozen.

Robin Lee

Pride of Gaithersburg
Gaithersburg Lioness Club
Gaithersburg, Maryland

Monte Carlos

These pretty coconut sandwich cookies contain a double filling of raspberry preserves and white frosting. Make a decorative crisscross pattern on top of the cookies with a fork dipped in flour.

¾ cup butter or margarine, softened
½ cup sugar
1 large egg
1½ teaspoons vanilla extract, divided
2 cups all-purpose flour
1½ teaspoons baking powder
½ teaspoon salt
½ cup flaked coconut
¼ cup butter or margarine, softened
¾ cup sifted powdered sugar
1 to 2 teaspoons milk
½ cup seedless raspberry preserves

Beat ¾ cup butter at medium speed of an electric mixer until creamy; gradually add ½ cup sugar, beating well. Add egg and 1 teaspoon vanilla, beating well.

Combine flour, baking powder, and salt; add to butter mixture, beating well. Stir in coconut.

Shape dough into 1-inch balls; place on lightly greased cookie sheets. Flatten cookies in a crisscross pattern with a fork dipped in flour. Bake at 350° for 12 to 14 minutes. Cool on wire racks.

Beat ¼ cup butter at medium speed of an electric mixer until creamy; gradually add powdered sugar, beating well. Add remaining ½ teaspoon vanilla and milk; beat well.

Spread 1 teaspoon powdered sugar mixture on flat side of half of cookies. Spread 1 teaspoon raspberry preserves on flat side of remaining cookies. Place preserve-topped cookies on top of powdered sugar mixture-topped cookies to form sandwiches. Yield: 22 cookies.

Rose Ciao

George Westinghouse Museum Cookbook
The George Westinghouse Museum Foundation
Wilmerding, Pennsylvania

Holoku Garden Party Cookies

Whether or not you're having a party, you'll love these fresh coconut cookies!

1 cup butter, softened
1 cup sugar
2 cups all-purpose flour

1 teaspoon salt
1½ cups freshly grated
   coconut

Beat butter at medium speed of an electric mixer until creamy; gradually add sugar, beating well. Combine flour and salt; add to mixture, beating well. Stir in coconut. Cover and chill 2 hours.

Shape dough into two 6-inch rolls. Wrap rolls in wax paper, and chill at least 8 hours. Slice dough into ¼-inch-thick slices; place on ungreased cookie sheets. Bake at 350° for 12 to 14 minutes or until lightly browned. Cool on wire racks. Yield: 4 dozen.

Kailua Cooks
Le Jardin Academy
Kailua, Hawaii

Stove-Top Cookies

1 cup sugar
2 large eggs, lightly beaten
1 cup chopped dates
1 tablespoon butter or
   margarine

2 cups crisp rice cereal
1 cup chopped pecans
1 teaspoon vanilla extract
Powdered sugar or flaked
   coconut

Combine 1 cup sugar and eggs in a large saucepan; stir well. Add dates and butter; cook over low heat, stirring constantly, 8 minutes or until mixture is thickened and bubbly. Remove from heat; stir in cereal, pecans, and vanilla.

Sprinkle powdered sugar or coconut onto a sheet of wax paper. Pour cereal mixture onto prepared wax paper; spread into a 15- x 10-inch rectangle. Let stand 15 minutes. Roll into a 15-inch log, beginning at long side. Let cool completely. Slice into ½-inch-thick slices. Yield: 2½ dozen.   Joe Ann Vann

Roll'n the Dough
Meals on Wheels of Central Arkansas
North Little Rock, Arkansas

Twice-Baked Walnut Cookies

These twiced-baked cookies are first baked in a loaf, and then sliced and baked again. They can be stored in an airtight container up to a month and still remain crunchy.

4 large eggs
1½ cups sugar
¾ cup butter or margarine, melted
2 teaspoons vanilla extract
1 teaspoon anise extract
1 teaspoon black walnut flavoring
½ teaspoon almond extract
5 cups all-purpose flour
1 tablespoon plus 1½ teaspoons baking powder
1 cup chopped walnuts

Beat eggs and sugar at medium speed of an electric mixer until blended. Add butter and flavorings, beating until blended. Combine flour and baking powder; gradually add to butter mixture, beating well. Stir in walnuts.

Divide dough into 8 equal portions. Roll each portion of dough into a 14-inch rope on a lightly floured surface. Place ropes 2 inches apart on greased cookie sheets. Bake at 325° for 25 minutes or until golden. Cool 2 minutes on cookie sheets.

Slice ropes into ½- to ¾-inch-thick slices. Place slices on cookie sheets, cut side down. Bake at 375° for 10 to 12 minutes or until crisp and lightly browned. Cool on wire racks. Yield: 12 dozen.

Steamboat Entertains
Steamboat Springs Winter Sports Club
Steamboat Springs, Colorado

Chocolate-Dipped Brandy Snaps

If the cookies become too crisp to roll around the handle of a wooden spoon, simply reheat them in the oven for 30 seconds to soften.

½ cup sugar
½ cup butter
⅓ cup dark corn syrup
½ teaspoon ground cinnamon
¼ teaspoon ground ginger
1 cup all-purpose flour

2 teaspoons brandy
1 (6-ounce) package semisweet
  chocolate morsels
1 tablespoon shortening
⅓ cup finely chopped pecans
  or walnuts

Combine first 5 ingredients in a medium saucepan. Cook over medium heat, stirring constantly, until sugar and butter melt. Remove from heat; stir in flour and brandy.

Spoon batter by rounded teaspoonfuls 3 inches apart onto an ungreased cookie sheet (do not bake more than six at a time). Bake at 300° for 10 to 12 minutes or until edges are lightly browned (cookies will spread during baking). Remove from oven, and cool 1 minute on cookie sheet.

When cookies are cool enough to hold their shape, quickly lift them with a metal spatula, and roll each around the handle of a wooden spoon or other cylindrical object. Cool on wire racks. When cookies have cooled, carefully remove wooden spoons. Repeat procedure with remaining batter.

Combine chocolate morsels and shortening in top of a double boiler; bring water to a boil. Reduce heat to low; cook until chocolate and shortening melt, stirring occasionally. Dip 1 end of each cookie in melted chocolate mixture, coating half of cookie. Sprinkle with pecans, and let cool on wax paper until chocolate is set. Yield: 3 dozen.   Marianne Schrader

A Dessert A-Fare
Anderson Area Chamber of Commerce
Cincinnati, Ohio

Almond Madeleines

¼ cup plus 2 tablespoons
  unsalted butter, softened
2 tablespoons almond oil
2 large eggs, separated
⅔ cup sugar

1 cup all-purpose flour
1 teaspoon baking powder
¼ cup ground blanched
  almonds, toasted

Beat butter and oil at medium speed of an electric mixer until creamy. Beat egg yolks and sugar until thick and pale; fold into butter mixture. Combine flour and baking powder; stir into butter mixture. Beat egg whites at high speed until stiff peaks form; gently fold into batter. Gently fold ground almonds into batter.

Spoon batter evenly into buttered and floured 3-inch madeleine molds. (If using 1 mold, let cool between batches.) Bake at 400° for 9 to 11 minutes or until lightly browned. Remove from molds, and cool on wire racks, flat side down. Yield: 2 dozen.

Blooming Good
National Council of State Garden Clubs
St. Louis, Missouri

Peek-a-Boo Bars

1 cup butter, softened
1½ cups sugar
4 large eggs
2 cups all-purpose flour

1 tablespoon lemon juice
1 (21-ounce) can cherry pie
  filling
Powdered sugar

Beat butter at medium speed of an electric mixer until creamy. Gradually add 1½ cups sugar; beat well. Add eggs, one at a time, beating after each addition. Add flour and lemon juice; beat well.

Pour batter into a greased and floured 15- x 10- x 1-inch jellyroll pan. Score batter into 20 bars; drop 1 heaping tablespoon pie filling into center of each bar. Bake at 350° for 40 to 45 minutes. Sprinkle powdered sugar over warm bars. Cool in pan on a wire rack. Cut into bars. Yield: 20 bars. Pauline Brtovich

American Heritage Cookbook
Brownsville General Hospital Auxiliary
Brownsville, Pennsylvania

Chocolate-Raspberry Bars

2 cups all-purpose flour
1 cup sugar
1 cup butter or margarine
1 large egg, lightly beaten
1 teaspoon almond extract
¾ cup seedless raspberry jam
1 (6-ounce) package semisweet
    chocolate morsels
1 cup chopped blanched
    almonds
1 cup sifted powdered sugar
1 to 2 tablespoons milk

Combine flour and 1 cup sugar in a large bowl; cut in butter with pastry blender until mixture is crumbly. Add egg and almond extract; stir well. Set aside 1 cup of flour mixture for topping. Press remaining flour mixture into a lightly greased 13- x 9- x 2-inch pan. Spread raspberry jam evenly over dough.

Combine reserved flour mixture, chocolate morsels, and almonds; stir well. Sprinkle topping over raspberry jam; gently press topping into jam with a fork. Bake at 350° for 35 to 40 minutes or until lightly browned. Cool in pan on a wire rack.

Combine powdered sugar and milk in a small bowl, stirring until mixture is smooth. Drizzle glaze over topping. Cut into bars. Yield: 2½ dozen.

Taste the Magic!
The Junior Club of Twin Falls, Idaho

Chocolate-Peanut Bars

A crispy meringue sweetened with brown sugar and studded with chocolate morsels and peanuts crowns these delicious bar cookies.

½ cup butter or margarine,
    softened
1½ cups firmly packed brown
    sugar, divided
½ cup sugar
2 large eggs, separated
1 teaspoon vanilla extract
2 cups all-purpose flour
1 teaspoon baking soda
½ teaspoon salt
1 (6-ounce) package semisweet
    chocolate morsels
¾ cup chopped salted roasted
    peanuts, divided

Beat butter at medium speed of an electric mixer until creamy; gradually add ½ cup brown sugar and sugar, beating well. Add egg yolks and vanilla, beating well.

Combine flour, baking soda, and salt; add to butter mixture, mixing well (dough will be crumbly). Press dough evenly into a greased 13- x 9- x 2-inch pan. Sprinkle with chocolate morsels and ½ cup peanuts; press lightly into dough.

Beat egg whites at high speed of an electric mixer until foamy. Gradually add remaining 1 cup brown sugar, 1 tablespoon at a time, beating until stiff peaks form and sugar dissolves (2 to 4 minutes). Spread over chocolate morsels and peanuts. Sprinkle with remaining ¼ cup peanuts; press lightly into egg white mixture. Bake at 325° for 40 minutes. Cut into bars while warm. Cool in pan on a wire rack. Yield: 2 dozen.   Mary Ann Edman

Family Cookbook: A Collection of Favorite Recipes
Women's Ministries of Trinity Assembly of God
Derry, New Hampshire

Katie's Peanut Bars

Whole wheat flake cereal and crisp rice cereal give these no-bake bar cookies their chewy texture.

1 cup sugar	4 cups whole wheat flake
1 cup light corn syrup	cereal
1 cup chunky peanut butter	2 cups crisp rice cereal
¼ cup butter or margarine	1 cup salted roasted peanuts

Combine sugar and corn syrup in a large saucepan; cook over medium heat, stirring constantly, until sugar dissolves. Add peanut butter and butter; cook, stirring constantly, until smooth. Remove from heat, and stir in cereals and peanuts.

Spoon mixture into a buttered 13- x 9- x 2-inch pan. Firmly press mixture into pan. Cool completely in pan on a wire rack. Cut into bars. Yield: 2 dozen.   Katie Pruitt

Favorite Recipes by the Students and Staff of St. John's School
St. John's Home and School Association
Beloit, Kansas

Chocolate-Cherry Brownies

1 (16-ounce) jar maraschino
  cherries, drained
⅔ cup butter or margarine
½ cup semisweet chocolate
  morsels
1½ cups all-purpose flour
1 teaspoon baking powder
¼ teaspoon salt
¾ cup quick-cooking oats,
  uncooked

1 cup sugar
2 large eggs, beaten
1 teaspoon vanilla extract
½ cup chopped pecans or
  walnuts (optional)
½ cup semisweet chocolate
  morsels
2 teaspoons shortening

Cut 12 cherries in half, and set aside. Chop remaining cherries, and set aside.

Combine butter and ½ cup chocolate morsels in top of a double boiler; bring water to a boil. Reduce heat to low; cook until butter and chocolate melt, stirring occasionally. Remove from heat, and let cool slightly.

Combine flour and next 3 ingredients in a large mixing bowl; stir well, and set aside.

Add sugar, eggs, and vanilla to reserved chocolate mixture, stirring with a wire whisk until blended. Add to reserved flour mixture, beating at low speed of an electric mixer until blended. Stir in reserved chopped cherries and pecans, if desired.

Spread mixture in a greased 13- x 9- x 2-inch pan. Bake at 350° for 25 to 28 minutes or until a wooden pick inserted in center comes out clean. Cool in pan on a wire rack. Cut into squares. Top each square with a reserved cherry half.

Combine ½ cup chocolate morsels and shortening in top of double boiler; bring water to a boil. Reduce heat to low; cook until chocolate and shortening melt, stirring occasionally. Drizzle over brownies. Yield: 2 dozen.   Bruce Everhart

Favorite Recipes from Our Best Cooks
Daniel Electric Generating Plant
Escatawpa, Mississippi

Cinnamon-Chocolate Brownies

A layer of brown sugar, pecans, and cinnamon in the middle of this brownie creates an unexpected burst of flavor.

½ cup plus 2 tablespoons
  butter or margarine,
  softened
1 cup sugar
2 large eggs
¾ cup all-purpose flour
½ teaspoon baking powder
¼ teaspoon salt

¼ cup plus 2 tablespoons
  cocoa
1½ teaspoons vanilla extract
½ cup firmly packed light
  brown sugar
½ cup chopped pecans
1 tablespoon ground cinnamon

Beat butter at medium speed of an electric mixer until creamy; gradually add 1 cup sugar, beating well. Add eggs, one at a time, beating after each addition.

Combine flour, baking powder, salt, and cocoa in a medium mixing bowl; stir well. Add flour mixture to butter mixture, beating well. Stir in vanilla. Spoon half of batter into a greased 8-inch square pan, spreading evenly.

Combine brown sugar, pecans, and cinnamon in a small bowl; stir well. Sprinkle brown sugar mixture evenly over batter in pan. Spoon remaining batter over brown sugar mixture, spreading evenly. Bake at 350° for 45 to 50 minutes or until a wooden pick inserted in center comes out clean. Cool in pan on a wire rack. Cut into squares. Yield: 1 dozen.   LuAnn Warner-Prokos

Celebration: Saint Andrew's School 30th Anniversary
of Celebrated Recipes
Saint Andrew's School Parents' Association
Boca Raton, Florida

Cappuccino Caramels

Coffee afficionados will delight in these rich espresso- and steamed milk-flavored confections.

2¼ cups firmly packed brown sugar
1 (14-ounce) can sweetened condensed milk
1 cup butter or margarine, melted
1 cup light corn syrup

3 tablespoons instant coffee granules
½ to 1 teaspoon grated orange rind
1 cup chopped walnuts or pecans
1 teaspoon vanilla extract

Line an 8-inch square pan with aluminum foil; butter foil, and set pan aside.

Combine first 6 ingredients in a large heavy saucepan; stir well. Cook over medium heat until mixture reaches firm ball stage or candy thermometer registers 248° (about 15 to 17 minutes), stirring frequently. Remove from heat; stir in walnuts and vanilla.

Pour mixture into prepared pan. Cool in pan on a wire rack at least 5 hours. Cut into squares, using a buttered knife. Wrap each caramel piece in plastic wrap. Yield: 3 pounds.

Some Like It Hot
The Junior League of McAllen, Texas

Mother's Perfect Cherry Divinity

Be sure you make divinity on a relatively dry day. If the humidity level is high (above 60%), the sugar in the candy will absorb moisture from the air, and the divinity will not hold its shape.

2½ cups sugar
½ cup water
½ cup light corn syrup
¼ teaspoon salt

2 egg whites
½ cup chopped candied cherries
1 teaspoon vanilla extract

Combine first 4 ingredients in a heavy 3-quart saucepan; stir well. Cook over low heat, stirring constantly, until sugar dissolves. Cover and cook over medium heat 2 to 3 minutes to wash down sugar crystals from sides of pan. Uncover and cook, without stirring, until mixture reaches hard ball stage or until candy thermometer registers 260°. Remove from heat.

Beat egg whites in a large mixing bowl at high speed of an electric mixer until stiff peaks form. Pour hot sugar mixture in a very thin stream over beaten egg white while beating constantly at high speed until mixture holds it shape (5 to 8 minutes). Quickly fold in candied cherries and vanilla. Drop mixture by rounded teaspoonfuls onto a sheet of wax paper. Cool completely. Yield: 1¼ pounds.

Betsy Bennett

Under the Mulberry Tree
United Methodist Women of Mulberry Street
United Methodist Church
Macon, Georgia

Butterscotch Fudge

Sour cream makes this butterscotch-flavored fudge extra rich and creamy. Be sure to let the fudge cool completely before cutting it into squares so it will cut cleanly and evenly.

1 cup sugar	¼ cup butter
1 cup firmly packed brown sugar	1 teaspoon vanilla extract
¾ cup sour cream	1 cup chopped pecans or walnuts

Combine sugar, brown sugar, sour cream, and butter in a large heavy saucepan. Cook over medium heat, stirring constantly, until sugars dissolve and mixture comes to a boil. Cover and cook 2 to 3 minutes to wash down sugar crystals from sides of pan. Uncover and cook until mixture reaches soft ball stage or candy thermometer registers 240°, stirring occasionally. Remove from heat, and let cool 30 minutes.

Add vanilla, and beat with a wooden spoon until mixture thickens and begins to lose its gloss. Stir in pecans. Pour into a lightly buttered 8-inch square pan. Cool completely. Cut into squares. Yield: 1¼ pounds.

Mary Moore

A Centennial Sampler
The American Association of University Women, Elkins Branch
Elkins, West Virginia

Fruitcake Fudge

This fancy fudge is studded with nuts, dried fruit, and candied fruit.

1½ cups flaked coconut
18 ounces milk chocolate, finely chopped
12 ounces semisweet chocolate, finely chopped
2 (1-ounce) squares unsweetened chocolate, finely chopped
2 teaspoons vanilla extract
1 (7-ounce) jar marshmallow cream
½ cup chopped pecans
½ cup chopped blanched almonds, toasted
½ cup hazelnuts, toasted, skinned, and chopped

½ cup chopped dates
½ cup raisins
½ cup dried figs, chopped
½ cup candied pineapple, diced
½ cup red and green candied cherries, chopped
4½ cups sugar
1 (12-ounce) can evaporated milk
¼ cup butter or margarine, melted
½ teaspoon salt

Sprinkle coconut into a heavily buttered 18- x 12- x 1-inch jellyroll pan; press coconut lightly into butter. Chill.

Combine milk chocolate and next 3 ingredients in a large bowl. Add marshmallow cream, and stir well. Add nuts, dried fruit, and candied fruit; stir well. (Mixture will be very thick.) Set aside.

Combine sugar, evaporated milk, butter, and salt in a large saucepan; stir well. Cook over medium heat until mixture reaches soft ball stage or candy thermometer registers 238°, stirring occasionally. Remove from heat, and pour over reserved chocolate mixture, stirring until chocolate and marshmallow cream melt.

Pour into prepared pan; spread evenly. Cool completely. Cut into small squares. Yield: about 7 pounds.   Ella Gobetz

Big Brutus: Treasured Recipes from Coal Mining Families
Big Brutus, Inc.
West Mineral, Kansas

Desserts

*Give your next meal a grand finale with an
elegant chocolate mousse or a luscious fruit sorbet. And get ready
for rave reviews!*

Mocha Brûlée, page 125

Melon Balls with Rum and Lime Sauce

⅔ cup sugar
½ cup water
1 teaspoon grated lime rind
¼ cup plus 2 tablespoons lime juice

½ cup light rum
8 cups melon balls (cantaloupe, honeydew, and watermelon)
Garnish: fresh mint sprigs

Combine sugar and water in a saucepan. Bring to a boil over medium heat, stirring until sugar dissolves. Reduce heat; simmer, uncovered, 5 minutes. Stir in lime rind. Let cool. Stir in lime juice and rum. Combine melon balls and rum mixture in a large bowl; toss gently. Cover and chill 3 to 5 hours. Garnish, if desired. Yield: 8 cups.   Alice Burke

Cooking in Cade
The Episcopal School of Acadiana
Cade, Louisiana

Spiced Pears in Port Wine

Originally made in Portugal, port is a sweet fortified wine made by adding brandy to the wine partway through the fermentation process.

4 medium-size firm ripe pears
2 cups water
1 cup port wine
½ cup sugar

2 (3-inch) sticks cinnamon
6 to 8 whole cloves
1 teaspoon ground cinnamon
½ teaspoon ground cloves

Peel and core pears. Cut pears in half lengthwise, and set aside.
Combine water and remaining ingredients in a saucepan. Bring to a boil; cook, stirring constantly, until sugar dissolves. Add pear halves; cover, reduce heat, and simmer 20 to 25 minutes or until tender. Spoon pear halves and liquid into individual serving dishes. Serve warm. Yield: 4 servings.   DeDe Munn

M.D. Anderson Volunteers Cooking for Fun
University of Texas M.D. Anderson Cancer Center
Houston, Texas

Chocolate-Banana Meringue Torte

3 egg whites
1 cup superfine sugar
6 (1-ounce) squares semisweet
   chocolate
3 tablespoons water

3 cups whipping cream
¼ cup sugar
3 medium bananas, thinly
   sliced

Line 3 large baking sheets with parchment paper. Trace a 9½-inch circle on each piece of parchment paper. Turn paper circles over, and set aside.

Beat egg whites at high speed of an electric mixer until soft peaks form. Gradually add 1 cup sugar, 2 tablespoons at a time, beating until stiff peaks form and sugar dissolves (2 to 4 minutes). Spoon meringue mixture evenly inside circles on prepared baking sheets. Form mixture on each sheet into a smooth circle, spreading with back of a large spoon. Place in a 400° oven; turn oven off. Let meringues dry in oven 8 hours (do not open oven door). Remove meringues from oven; peel off paper. Set meringues aside.

Combine chocolate squares and water in top of a double boiler; bring water in bottom to a boil. Reduce heat to low; cook, stirring constantly, until chocolate melts. Remove from heat; keep top of double boiler over warm water. Set aside.

Beat whipping cream in a large mixing bowl at high speed until soft peaks form; gradually add ¼ cup sugar, beating until stiff peaks form.

To assemble torte, place 1 meringue circle on a serving plate. Arrange half of banana slices on top of meringue; drizzle one-third of reserved melted chocolate mixture over banana slices. Top with one-fourth of whipped cream mixture. Repeat layers once. Top with remaining meringue circle. Spread top and sides of torte with remaining whipped cream mixture; drizzle with remaining melted chocolate mixture.

Place torte in an airtight cake storage container, and chill at least 2 hours or up to 8 hours before serving. Yield: 10 servings.

The Virginia Hostess
The Junior Woman's Club of Manassas, Virginia

Blueberry Cream Dessert

1¼ cups graham cracker
  crumbs
¼ cup sugar
¼ cup plus 2 tablespoons
  butter or margarine, melted
1 envelope unflavored gelatin
¾ cup cold water
½ cup sugar

1 (8-ounce) carton sour cream
1 (8-ounce) carton blueberry
  yogurt
½ teaspoon vanilla extract
⅔ cup whipping cream
1 cup fresh or frozen
  blueberries, thawed

Combine first 3 ingredients; stir well. Reserve ¼ cup crumb mixture for topping. Firmly press remaining crumb mixture into an ungreased 11- x 7- x 1½-inch dish. Set aside.

Sprinkle gelatin over cold water in a small saucepan; let stand 1 minute. Add ½ cup sugar; cook over low heat, stirring constantly, until gelatin and sugar dissolve. Remove from heat. Combine sour cream and yogurt; gradually add to gelatin mixture, stirring until blended. Stir in vanilla. Cover and chill 1 hour or until mixture is consistency of unbeaten egg white.

Beat whipping cream at high speed until soft peaks form. Gently fold whipped cream into gelatin mixture. Stir in blueberries. Spoon blueberry mixture into prepared dish. Sprinkle with reserved crumb mixture. Cover and chill 8 hours. Cut into squares. Yield: 8 servings.

Plain & Elegant: A Georgia Heritage
West Georgia Medical Center Auxiliary
LaGrange, Georgia

Blueberry Buckle

½ cup shortening
¾ cup sugar
1 large egg
2 cups all-purpose flour
2½ teaspoons baking powder
¼ teaspoon salt

½ cup milk
2 cups fresh blueberries
½ cup sugar
½ cup all-purpose flour
½ teaspoon ground cinnamon
¼ cup butter or margarine

Beat shortening and ¾ cup sugar at medium speed of an electric mixer until blended. Add egg, and beat until fluffy. Combine 2 cups flour, baking powder, and salt; add flour mixture to shortening mixture alternately with milk, beginning and ending with flour mixture. Spread batter in a greased 11- x 7- x 1½-inch pan. Sprinkle blueberries on top of batter.

Combine ½ cup sugar, ½ cup flour, and cinnamon; cut in butter with pastry blender until mixture is crumbly. Sprinkle topping over blueberries. Bake at 350° for 45 minutes. Cut into squares; serve warm. Yield: 6 to 8 servings.   Denise Vetter

I'm at the Ballpark, No Time to Cook
Jupiter-Tequesta Athletic Association
Jupiter, Florida

Rhubarb-Raspberry Crunch

1½ cups all-purpose flour
1 cup quick-cooking oats, uncooked
1 cup firmly packed brown sugar
1 teaspoon ground cinnamon
½ cup butter or margarine

1 (12-ounce) package frozen raspberries in syrup, thawed and undrained
½ cup sugar
3 tablespoons cornstarch
2 cups chopped fresh rhubarb
Whipped cream (optional)

Combine first 4 ingredients in a large bowl; cut in butter with pastry blender until mixture is crumbly. Reserve ¼ cup oat mixture for topping. Press remaining oat mixture into bottom of an ungreased 9-inch square pan.

Drain raspberries, reserving syrup. Set raspberries aside. Add enough water to syrup to measure 1 cup; place mixture in a small saucepan. Add sugar and cornstarch; cook over medium heat, stirring constantly, until mixture is thickened and bubbly. Remove from heat, and set aside.

Top oat mixture in pan with reserved raspberries and chopped rhubarb. Pour cornstarch mixture over fruit; sprinkle with reserved oat mixture. Bake at 325° for 1 hour. Cool in pan on a wire rack. Cut into squares. Serve with whipped cream, if desired. Yield: 9 servings.   Rose Anne Millette

Ritzy Rhubarb Secrets Cookbook
Litchville Committee 2,000
Litchville, North Dakota

Baked Fudge Dessert with Kahlúa Topping

Enjoy two treats in one—a crusty yet tender chocolate cake tops a creamy chocolate-fudge pudding.

2 cups sugar
¾ cup cocoa
½ cup all-purpose flour
5 large eggs
1 cup plus 2 tablespoons
    butter or margarine, melted

2 teaspoons vanilla extract
1½ cups chopped pecans
Kahlúa Topping

Combine first 3 ingredients in a medium mixing bowl, stirring well. Add eggs; beat at medium speed of an electric mixer until smooth. Add butter and vanilla, beating well. Stir in pecans.

Spoon mixture into eight 6-ounce custard cups. Place in a 13- x 9- x 2-inch pan; add hot water to pan to depth of 1 inch. Bake, uncovered, at 300° for 1 hour. Remove custard cups from water. Let stand 10 minutes before serving. Serve warm with Kahlúa Topping. Yield: 8 servings.

Kahlúa Topping

1 cup whipping cream
½ cup sifted powdered sugar

3 tablespoons Kahlúa or other
    coffee-flavored liqueur

Beat whipping cream in a large mixing bowl until foamy; gradually add powdered sugar and Kahlúa, beating until soft peaks form. Yield: 2⅓ cups.

Abe and Charlene Gutmore

From the Kitchens of . . . Columbia Employees
Columbia Gas Distribution Companies
Columbus, Ohio

Mocha Brûlée

⅔ cup sugar
3 tablespoons water
2 cups half-and-half
4 ounces imported milk
  chocolate, chopped
¼ cup sugar
2½ teaspoons instant coffee
  granules
3 egg yolks

1 large egg
1 teaspoon almond extract
4 ounces imported milk
  chocolate, chopped
¼ cup whipping cream
1½ teaspoons instant coffee
  granules
Garnish: fresh strawberries

Combine ⅔ cup sugar and water in a heavy saucepan. Cook over medium heat, stirring constantly with a wooden spoon, until sugar crystallizes into lumps. Continue cooking, stirring constantly, until sugar melts and turns a light golden brown (about 10 minutes). Quickly pour hot caramel mixture into six 4-ounce ramekins or six 6-ounce custard cups, tilting to coat bottom evenly; set aside (mixture will harden).

Combine half-and-half and next 3 ingredients in a large saucepan. Cook over medium heat until chocolate melts, stirring occasionally. Combine egg yolks, egg, and almond extract in a small bowl. Gradually stir about one-fourth of hot half-and-half mixture into yolk mixture; add to remaining hot half-and-half mixture, stirring constantly.

Pour custard mixture evenly into ramekins. Place ramekins in a 13- x 9- x 2-inch pan; add hot water to pan to depth of 1 inch. Cover and bake at 350° for 45 minutes. Remove ramekins from water; cool. Cover and chill at least 4 hours.

Combine 4 ounces chocolate, whipping cream, and 1½ teaspoons coffee granules in top of a double boiler; bring water to a boil. Reduce heat to low; cook until chocolate melts, stirring occasionally. Spread evenly over chilled custard. Cover and chill at least 30 minutes. To serve, loosen edge of each custard with a spatula, and invert onto an individual dessert plate. Garnish, if desired. Serve immediately. Yield: 6 servings.   Kate Zoercer

Georgia Land
Medical Association of Georgia Alliance
Atlanta, Georgia

Caramelized Coffee Flan

¾ cup sugar
2 large eggs
2 egg yolks
1 (14-ounce) can sweetened
  condensed milk

1 cup milk
1 teaspoon instant coffee
  granules

Place sugar in a small heavy saucepan. Cook over medium heat, stirring constantly with a wooden spoon, until sugar crystallizes into lumps (about 15 minutes). Continue cooking, stirring constantly, until sugar melts and turns a light golden brown (about 15 minutes). Quickly pour hot caramel mixture into an ungreased 8-inch round cakepan, tilting to coat bottom evenly. Set aside (mixture will harden).

Combine eggs and remaining ingredients in a large bowl; beat with a wire whisk until coffee granules dissolve. Pour egg mixture over caramelized sugar in cakepan.

Place cakepan in a large shallow baking dish. Pour hot water into baking dish to depth of 1 inch. Cover with aluminum foil, and bake at 350° for 55 minutes or until a knife inserted near center of flan comes out clean. Remove pan from water, and let cool. Cover and chill at least 8 hours.

To serve, loosen edge of custard with a spatula, and invert onto a serving plate. Yield: 6 servings.

Southwest Cooks! The Tradition of Native American Cuisines
Southwest Museum
Los Angeles, California

Chocolate Mousse

A mold with smooth sides rather than an intricate pattern works best for this rich mousse. If you would rather not mold this classic dessert, serve it instead in elegant individual dessert dishes.

2 (1-ounce) squares
  unsweetened chocolate
1 cup milk
½ cup sifted powdered sugar
1 envelope unflavored gelatin

3 tablespoons cold water
¾ cup sugar
1 teaspoon vanilla extract
¼ teaspoon salt
2 cups whipping cream

Place chocolate squares in top of a double boiler; bring water to a boil. Reduce heat to low; cook until chocolate melts, stirring occasionally. Remove from heat; keep top of double boiler over warm water. Set aside.

Heat milk in a small saucepan over low heat until hot (do not boil). Add hot milk and powdered sugar to reserved chocolate in double boiler; cook over medium heat, stirring constantly, just until mixture comes to a simmer (do not boil). Remove from heat. Set aside.

Sprinkle gelatin over cold water; let stand 1 minute. Add gelatin mixture, ¾ cup sugar, vanilla, and salt to reserved chocolate mixture, stirring well. Chill 30 minutes or until consistency of unbeaten egg white, stirring occasionally.

Beat chocolate mixture at high speed of an electric mixer 3 minutes. Beat whipping cream until soft peaks form. Gently fold whipped cream into chocolate mixture. Spoon chocolate mixture into a lightly greased, smooth 6-cup mold. Cover and chill at least 8 hours. To serve, unmold onto a serving plate. Serve immediately. Yield: 8 servings.   Mary Portivent Redwine

Windows: Reflections of Taste
Brenau University Alumnae Association
Gainesville, Georgia

Frozen Kahlúa Crème

1 pint vanilla ice cream,
 softened
¼ cup Kahlúa or other
 coffee-flavored liqueur

1 cup whipping cream
⅓ cup finely chopped
 almonds, toasted

Combine ice cream and Kahlúa in a large bowl, stirring until blended. Beat whipping cream in a large mixing bowl until soft peaks form; gently fold whipped cream into ice cream mixture. Spoon mixture evenly into paper-lined muffin cups. Sprinkle evenly with toasted almonds. Cover and freeze at least 8 hours. Yield: 12 servings.   Deborah Van Keuren

A Taste of Reno
The Food Bank of Northern Nevada
Sparks, Nevada

Double-Chocolate Cookies and Cream Ice Cream

The double chocolate in this ice cream is semisweet chocolate mini-morsels and cream-filled chocolate sandwich cookies. If you count the cocoa, the dessert could be called a triple chocolate delight!

2 cups half-and-half
1½ cups sugar
½ cup cocoa
2 cups whipping cream
1 teaspoon vanilla extract

⅔ cup semisweet chocolate
  mini-morsels
11 cream-filled chocolate
  sandwich cookies, crushed

Combine first 3 ingredients in container of an electric blender; cover and process until sugar dissolves, stopping once to scrape down sides.

Pour half-and-half mixture into freezer container of a 2-quart hand-turned or electric freezer. Gently stir in whipping cream and vanilla. Freeze ice cream mixture according to manufacturer's instructions.

Remove ice cream mixture from freezer container, and gently stir in chocolate mini-morsels and crushed sandwich cookies. Pour ice cream mixture into a 13- x 9- x 2-inch dish; cover and freeze until firm. Yield: 7½ cups.

The Wild Wild West
The Junior League of Odessa, Texas

Mint Ice Cream

Serve this fresh mint ice cream with a delicate chocolate cookie for a refreshing finish to your next dinner party. The green crème de menthe gives the ice cream a pretty color and the fresh pineapple lends an unexpected flavor.

2 cups firmly packed fresh
  mint leaves
1½ cups sugar
1½ cups water
1 cup cubed fresh pineapple
1 cup light corn syrup

1 cup unsweetened pineapple
  juice
2 cups milk
2 cups whipping cream
½ cup green crème de menthe
Garnish: fresh mint sprigs

Combine first 6 ingredients in a large bowl; stir well. Pour half of mint mixture into container of an electric blender; cover and process until smooth, stopping once to scrape down sides. Repeat procedure with remaining mint mixture.

Pour mixture into freezer container of a 1-gallon hand-turned or electric freezer. Add milk, whipping cream, and crème de menthe; stir well. Freeze according to manufacturer's instructions. Pack freezer with additional ice and rock salt, and let stand 1 hour before serving.

To serve, spoon into individual dessert dishes. Garnish, if desired. Yield: 12 cups.

Heart & Soul
The Junior League of Memphis, Tennessee

Nestletoe Ice Cream

This ice cream title was inspired by Nesselrode—a creamy custard mixed with chestnut puree, candied fruits, currants, raisins, and maraschino-flavored liqueur.

1 (10-ounce) jar maraschino cherries, undrained
½ cup chopped pecans
18 almond macaroons
¼ cup bourbon
½ gallon vanilla ice cream, softened

Drain cherries, reserving juice. Coarsely chop cherries. Combine cherries, cherry juice, and pecans; stir well, and set aside.

Break macaroons into fourths; place in a medium bowl. Drizzle with bourbon. Fold reserved cherry mixture and macaroon mixture into ice cream. Spoon into a 13- x 9- x 2-inch pan. Cover and freeze until firm. Yield: 10 cups.   Lula Barnett

Southern Savoir Faire
The Altamont School
Birmingham, Alabama

Strawberry Ice Cream Cheesecake

Don't let the name of this dessert fool you—it's actually a luscious ice cream that tastes like strawberry cheesecake.

4 cups milk, divided
2 cups sugar
¼ teaspoon salt
4 large eggs, beaten
1 quart fresh strawberries,
  hulled and quartered
⅓ cup firmly packed brown
  sugar

1 (8-ounce) package cream
  cheese, softened
¾ cup half-and-half
1 tablespoon vanilla extract
1 tablespoon lemon juice
¾ cup finely chopped pecans

Combine 2 cups milk, 2 cups sugar, and salt in container of an electric blender; cover and process until sugar and salt dissolve, stopping once to scrape down sides. Add eggs, and process until blended, stopping once to scrape down sides. Pour milk mixture into a medium saucepan; cook over medium heat, stirring constantly, 8 minutes or until mixture begins to thicken. Remove from heat; cover and chill at least 4 hours.

Combine strawberries and brown sugar, stirring well. Set aside.

Combine half of chilled milk mixture and cream cheese in container of electric blender; cover and process until smooth, stopping once to scrape down sides. Pour cream cheese mixture into freezer container of a 1-gallon hand-turned or electric freezer.

Combine half of reserved strawberry mixture, remaining chilled milk mixture, half-and-half, vanilla, and lemon juice in container of electric blender; cover and process until smooth, stopping once to scrape down sides. Add to cream cheese mixture in freezer container. Add remaining 2 cups milk, remaining strawberry mixture, and pecans; stir well. Freeze according to manufacturer's instructions. Pack freezer with additional ice and rock salt, and let stand 1 hour before serving. Yield: 12 cups.   Rebecca Riley

A Fanfare of Flavors
Stanton Buffalo Bands
Stanton, Texas

Pink Grapefruit Sorbet

1 cup water
1 cup superfine sugar
1¾ cups fresh pink grapefruit
  juice

¼ cup Grand Marnier or other
  orange-flavored liqueur
Garnish: orange peel

Combine water and sugar in a saucepan; bring to a boil. Reduce heat, and simmer 10 minutes or until sugar dissolves; cool.

Combine sugar syrup, grapefruit juice, and liqueur. Pour into freezer container of a 2-quart hand-turned or electric freezer. Freeze according to manufacturer's instructions until thickened (mixture will not freeze firm). Spoon into an 11- x 7- x 1½-inch dish; cover and freeze until firm. To serve, spoon into dessert dishes. Garnish, if desired. Yield: 4 cups.   Mariana M. Grove

Cooking with Diplomacy
Association of American Foreign Service Women
Washington, DC

Three-Five Ice

Three fruits and a total of five ingredients inspire this catchy recipe title.

3 cups sugar
3 cups water
1 cup fresh orange juice

⅓ cup fresh lemon juice
3 ripe bananas, mashed

Combine sugar and water in a saucepan. Bring to a boil; boil 5 minutes or until sugar dissolves, stirring occasionally. Cool.

Combine sugar syrup, juices, and banana in a mixing bowl; beat at medium speed of an electric mixer until blended. Pour mixture into a 13- x 9- x 2-inch dish. Cover and freeze until almost firm (about 4 hours), stirring occasionally. Spoon into a chilled mixing bowl; beat just until smooth. Return mixture to dish; cover and freeze until firm. Let stand at room temperature 10 minutes before serving. Yield: 9 cups.   Mrs. Ross Culpepper

A Centennial Sampler
The American Association of University Women, Elkins Branch
Elkins, West Virginia

Café Cream Toffee Torte

Substitute Kahlúa or other coffee-flavored liqueur for the light rum, if desired.

6 (1.4-ounce) English toffee-flavored candy bars, coarsely chopped
1 quart coffee ice cream, softened
2 tablespoons light rum
1 (10¾-ounce) pound cake, cut into ½-inch-thick slices

4 ounces bittersweet chocolate
⅓ cup slivered almonds, toasted
1 quart chocolate ice cream, softened
2 tablespoons crème de cacao or Irish Cream liqueur

Reserve half of chopped candy bars for topping. Sprinkle remaining chopped candy bars in bottom of an ungreased 10-inch springform pan; set aside.

Combine coffee ice cream and rum; spread ice cream mixture over candy bar layer. Cover and freeze until firm. Arrange pound cake slices over frozen ice cream layer; cover and freeze until firm.

Place chocolate in top of a double boiler; bring water to a boil. Reduce heat to low; cook until chocolate melts, stirring occasionally. Remove from heat, and stir in almonds. Spread mixture over frozen pound cake layer; cover and freeze until firm.

Combine chocolate ice cream and crème de cacao; spread over frozen chocolate layer. Sprinkle with half of reserved chopped candy bars; cover and freeze until firm.

Let stand at room temperature 5 minutes before serving. Carefully remove sides of springform pan. Gently pat remaining chopped candy bars onto sides of torte. Serve immediately. Yield: 10 to 12 servings.

Cranbrook Reflections: A Culinary Collection
Cranbrook House and Gardens Auxiliary
Bloomfield Hills, Michigan

Eggs & Cheese

*Whether you choose a hearty omelet to start the day
or a satisfying meatless meal to end it, you'll appreciate the
versatility of these egg and cheese creations.*

Eggs in a Nest, page 134

Eggs in a Nest

To serve more than one, multiply the ingredients by the number of people. If you prefer a very firm egg yolk, bake up to 2 minutes longer.

1 slice white bread
1 teaspoon butter or
   margarine, softened

1 large egg, separated
½ teaspoon salt
¼ teaspoon pepper

Place bread on an ungreased baking sheet. Spread butter on 1 side of bread slice. Beat egg white at high speed of an electric mixer until stiff peaks form. Spoon beaten egg white onto bread. Make a well in center of beaten egg white with back of a spoon. Place egg yolk in well. Bake at 350° for 15 minutes or until meringue is golden and egg yolk is set. Sprinkle with salt and pepper. Serve immediately. Yield: 1 serving.   Helen C. Felton

Cooking with Grace
Grace Church School Parents' Association
New York, New York

Fancy Egg Scramble

4 ounces Canadian bacon,
   diced
¼ cup chopped green onions
3 tablespoons butter or
   margarine, melted
12 large eggs, beaten
2 tablespoons butter or
   margarine
2 tablespoons all-purpose flour
2 cups milk

1 cup (4 ounces) shredded
   process American cheese
½ teaspoon salt
⅛ teaspoon pepper
2¼ cups soft breadcrumbs
¼ cup butter or margarine,
   melted
⅛ teaspoon paprika
1 (3-ounce) can mushroom
   stems and pieces, drained

Sauté Canadian bacon and green onions in 3 tablespoons melted butter in a large skillet over medium heat, stirring constantly, until bacon is lightly browned and green onions are tender. Reduce heat to medium-low; add beaten eggs, and cook, without stirring, until egg mixture begins to set on bottom. Draw a spatula across bottom of pan to form large curds. Continue cooking until eggs are firm but still moist (do not stir constantly). Set eggs aside.

Melt 2 tablespoons butter in a heavy saucepan over low heat; add flour, stirring until smooth. Cook 1 minute, stirring constantly. Gradually add milk, and cook over medium heat, stirring constantly, until mixture is thickened and bubbly. Stir in cheese, salt, and pepper. Set aside.

Combine breadcrumbs, ¼ cup melted butter, and paprika; set aside. Add reserved cheese sauce and mushrooms to reserved egg mixture. Pour into an ungreased 11- x 7- x 1½-inch baking dish. Sprinkle with reserved breadcrumb mixture. Bake, uncovered, at 350° for 30 minutes or until lightly browned. Serve immediately. Yield: 8 to 10 servings.   Patricia Ashley

The Nineteenth Century Woman's Club Historical Centennial Cookbook
Nineteenth Century Woman's Club
Oak Park, Illinois

Garden Scramble

1 cup diced zucchini
½ cup asparagus tips
½ cup shredded carrot
¼ cup diced sweet red pepper
2 green onions, thinly sliced
2 tablespoons butter or
  margarine, melted
4 large eggs

¼ cup milk
½ teaspoon dried basil
½ teaspoon dried savory
1 tablespoon butter or
  margarine
¼ cup (1 ounce) shredded
  Swiss or Gruyère cheese

Sauté first 5 ingredients in 2 tablespoons butter in a skillet over medium heat, stirring constantly, until tender. Set aside; keep warm.

Combine eggs, milk, basil, and savory; beat with a wire whisk until blended. Melt 1 tablespoon butter in a large skillet over low heat. Add egg mixture, and cook over medium-low heat, without stirring, until mixture begins to set on bottom. Draw a spatula across bottom of pan to form large curds. Continue cooking until eggs are firm but still moist (do not stir constantly). Gently stir reserved sautéed vegetables into egg mixture; sprinkle with cheese. Serve immediately. Yield: 2 to 3 servings.

Cooking with Herb Scents
Western Reserve Herb Society
Bay Village, Ohio

Creamy Corn Omelet

4 ears fresh corn (about 2
  pounds)
½ cup half-and-half
½ teaspoon salt

Dash of pepper
4 large eggs, separated
2 tablespoons butter or
  margarine

Cut corn from cobs, scraping cobs well to remove milk. Combine corn and next 3 ingredients in a large bowl. Beat egg yolks at medium speed of an electric mixer until thick and pale; add to corn mixture, stirring well.

Beat egg whites at high speed until stiff peaks form; gently fold into corn mixture.

Melt butter in a 10-inch ovenproof skillet over medium-low heat. Pour corn mixture into skillet; cook, uncovered, 15 minutes. Transfer skillet to oven, and bake, uncovered, at 350° for 15 to 18 minutes or until golden. Cut into wedges. Serve immediately. Yield: 4 servings.

Tampa Treasures
The Junior League of Tampa, Florida

Crabmeat Egg Foo Yong

Egg foo yong is a Chinese-American dish made with eggs, bean sprouts, and green onions. Other vegetables and meats are often added, and the mixture is then cooked in small portions on a griddle, much like pancakes.

½ cup soy sauce
½ cup water
2 tablespoons sugar
2 tablespoons white vinegar
½ teaspoon minced garlic
1 tablespoon all-purpose flour
2 tablespoons water
1 (16-ounce) can bean sprouts,
  drained

1 (6-ounce) can crabmeat,
  drained
1 (4-ounce) can sliced
  mushrooms, drained
1 small onion, chopped
3 green onions, chopped
4 large eggs, beaten

Combine first 5 ingredients in a small saucepan. Bring to a boil; reduce heat, and simmer, uncovered, 2 minutes. Combine flour and 2 tablespoons water, stirring with a wire whisk until smooth.

Stir flour mixture into soy sauce mixture; cook, stirring constantly, until mixture is thickened and bubbly. Set sauce aside; keep warm.

Combine bean sprouts, crabmeat, mushrooms, onion, and green onions in a medium bowl; stir in beaten eggs.

Preheat griddle to 350°; lightly grease griddle. For each patty, pour about ¼ cup batter onto hot griddle. Cook patties until edges look cooked and lightly browned; turn and cook other side. Serve patties with reserved sauce. Yield: 4 servings.   Libby Lane

The Montauk Lighthouse Cookbook
The Montauk Lighthouse Committee
Montauk, New York

Cheesy Eggs Baked with Tarragon and Leeks

2 large leeks, coarsely chopped
¼ cup unsalted butter or
  margarine, melted
1½ cups (6 ounces) shredded
  Gruyère cheese
½ cup freshly grated Parmesan
  cheese
8 large eggs

2 cups whipping cream
2 tablespoons plus 2 teaspoons
  chopped fresh tarragon
½ teaspoon salt
¼ teaspoon freshly ground
  pepper
Garnish: fresh tarragon sprigs

Sauté chopped leeks in butter in a medium skillet over medium heat, stirring constantly, until tender. Spoon into a lightly greased 13- x 9- x 2-inch baking dish. Combine cheeses, reserving ½ cup cheese mixture for topping. Sprinkle remaining cheese mixture over leeks.

Combine eggs and next 4 ingredients in a bowl, stirring with a wire whisk until blended. Pour egg mixture over leek mixture. Bake, uncovered, at 375° for 30 minutes or until set and lightly browned. Sprinkle with reserved cheese mixture; bake an additional 5 minutes or until cheeses melt. Garnish, if desired. Serve immediately. Yield: 8 to 10 servings.

Tropical Seasons, A Taste of Life in South Florida
Beaux Arts of the Lowe Art Museum of the University of Miami
Coral Gables, Florida

Spinach-Mushroom Brunch Bake

1 pound fresh spinach
¼ cup water
¼ cup chopped sun-dried
  tomatoes (without oil and
  salt)
1 pound fresh mushrooms,
  sliced
½ cup unsalted butter or
  margarine, melted and
  divided
2 tablespoons chopped fresh
  basil
½ teaspoon dried thyme
½ cup chopped onion

1 cup ricotta cheese
⅔ cup grated Parmesan
  cheese, divided
3 slices bacon, cooked and
  crumbled
12 croissants
1 cup (4 ounces) shredded
  mozzarella cheese
6 large eggs, beaten
2 cups milk
1 teaspoon salt
½ teaspoon pepper
¼ teaspoon ground nutmeg

Remove stems from spinach; wash leaves thoroughly, and pat dry. Tear spinach into bite-size pieces. Bring ¼ cup water to a boil in a large Dutch oven; add spinach. Cover and cook over medium-high heat 2 minutes or until spinach wilts. Drain and set aside.

Place tomatoes in a small bowl; add boiling water to cover, and let stand 10 minutes. Drain and set aside.

Sauté mushrooms in 3 tablespoons butter in a skillet over medium heat, stirring constantly, until tender. Stir in reserved tomatoes, basil, and thyme; remove mixture from skillet, and set aside. In same skillet, sauté onion in 2 tablespoons butter over medium heat, stirring constantly, until tender. Stir in reserved spinach, ricotta cheese, ⅓ cup Parmesan cheese, and bacon; set aside.

Slice croissants horizontally into thirds. Place bottom third of croissants, crust side down, in a lightly greased 13- x 9- x 2-inch baking dish. Spread reserved spinach mixture evenly over croissant layer. Top with middle slices of croissants; spread with reserved mushroom mixture, and sprinkle with mozzarella cheese. Place remaining slices of croissants over cheese, cut side down.

Combine eggs and next 4 ingredients; pour over croissants. Cover and chill 8 hours. Sprinkle with remaining ⅓ cup Parmesan cheese. Drizzle with remaining 3 tablespoons butter. Bake, uncovered, at 350° for 1 hour. Serve immediately. Yield: 12 servings.

Desert Treasures
The Junior League of Phoenix, Arizona

Zucchini-Tomato Strata

A strata is a layered casserole typically composed of bread, cheese, and vegetables. It's moistened with an egg-milk mixture that's poured over the layers before baking. But this strata uses saltine crackers instead of bread.

½ cup chopped onion
1 clove garlic, crushed
1 tablespoon butter or
  margarine, melted
1 large zucchini
40 saltine crackers, divided
1 cup (4 ounces) shredded
  Cheddar cheese, divided
1 cup (4 ounces) shredded
  mozzarella cheese, divided

¼ cup grated Parmesan
  cheese, divided
3 small tomatoes, sliced
4 large eggs, beaten
1½ cups milk
1 teaspoon dried basil
½ teaspoon dried oregano

Sauté onion and garlic in butter in a small skillet over medium-high heat, stirring constantly, until tender. Set aside.

Slice zucchini lengthwise into ¼-inch-thick slices; set aside. Arrange 18 crackers overlapping in 3 rows in a greased 11- x 7- x 1½-inch baking dish. Sprinkle with ½ cup Cheddar cheese, ½ cup mozzarella cheese, and half of reserved onion mixture. Top with half of zucchini slices, and sprinkle with 1 tablespoon Parmesan cheese. Repeat layers once.

Arrange tomato slices around edge of baking dish. Arrange remaining 4 crackers overlapping down center. Combine eggs, milk, basil, and oregano; pour egg mixture over mixture in baking dish. Sprinkle with remaining 2 tablespoons Parmesan cheese. Bake, uncovered, at 350° for 50 to 55 minutes or until set and lightly browned. Let stand 10 minutes before serving. Yield: 6 servings.

Judy Keesler

"Show-me" Fine Dining
United Guardsman Foundation
St. Joseph, Missouri

Cheese Pie

You can substitute fresh mushrooms for canned, if you'd like. Just sauté the chopped mushrooms in butter, and drain them before adding to this pie.

Pastry for 9-inch pie
1½ cups (6 ounces) shredded
  Monterey Jack cheese
1 cup (4 ounces) shredded
  Cheddar cheese, divided
1 (4-ounce) can whole green
  chiles, drained, seeded, and
  finely chopped
⅓ cup finely chopped onion

⅓ cup drained, chopped
  canned mushrooms
⅓ cup drained, chopped
  canned tomatoes
3 large eggs
1 cup half-and-half
¼ teaspoon salt
⅛ teaspoon ground cumin
Dash of Worcestershire sauce

Roll pastry to ⅛-inch thickness on a floured surface. Place in a 9-inch deep-dish pieplate; trim off excess along edges. Fold edges under; crimp. Prick bottom and sides with a fork. Bake at 400° for 10 minutes or until lightly browned. Cool on a wire rack.

Sprinkle Monterey Jack cheese and ½ cup Cheddar cheese over bottom of pastry shell. Layer chiles and next 3 ingredients over cheese. Combine eggs and remaining ingredients; beat with a wire whisk until blended. Pour egg mixture into pastry shell. Sprinkle with remaining ½ cup Cheddar cheese. Bake, uncovered, at 350° for 45 minutes or until set and lightly browned. Let stand 15 minutes before serving. Yield: one 9-inch pie.　　Joan McClendon

Home Cooking with SMRMC
Southwest Mississippi Regional Medical Center Auxiliary
McComb, Mississippi

Crustless Crab Quiche

½ pound fresh mushrooms,
  sliced
4 green onions, chopped
2 tablespoons butter or
  margarine, melted
4 large eggs
1 cup small-curd cottage cheese
1 (8-ounce) carton sour cream

½ cup grated Parmesan cheese
¼ cup all-purpose flour
¼ teaspoon salt
4 drops of hot sauce
2 cups (8 ounces) shredded
  Monterey Jack cheese
6 ounces fresh crabmeat,
  drained and flaked

Sauté mushrooms and green onions in butter in skillet over medium-high heat, stirring constantly, until tender. Drain; set aside.

Combine eggs and next 6 ingredients in container of an electric blender or food processor; cover and process until blended, stopping once to scrape down sides. Pour mixture into a bowl. Stir in reserved mushroom mixture, Monterey Jack cheese, and crabmeat. Pour into a greased 10-inch pieplate or shallow 1½-quart casserole. Bake, uncovered, at 350° for 45 minutes or until set and lightly browned. Let stand 15 minutes before serving. Yield: 6 to 8 servings.

Family & Company
The Junior League of Binghamton, New York

San José Quiche

1 pound ground beef
1 medium onion, chopped
1 medium-size green pepper, chopped
1 clove garlic, minced
1 teaspoon dried oregano
1 teaspoon ground cumin
1 teaspoon chili powder
1 cup green chile salsa

6 (6-inch) corn tortillas, cut into 1-inch pieces
2 (4-ounce) cans whole green chiles, drained and cut lengthwise into 1-inch strips
2 cups (8 ounces) shredded Cheddar cheese
6 large eggs, beaten
1½ cups milk

Combine first 7 ingredients in a skillet; cook until meat is browned, stirring until it crumbles. Drain; stir in salsa. Set aside.

Place half of tortillas in bottom of an ungreased 11- x 7- x 1½-inch baking dish. Spread half of reserved meat mixture over tortillas. Place half of green chile strips over meat mixture; sprinkle with 1 cup Cheddar cheese. Repeat layers once.

Combine eggs and milk; pour egg mixture over mixture in baking dish. Bake, uncovered, at 350° for 40 to 45 minutes or until set and lightly browned. Let stand 5 minutes before serving. Yield: 6 to 8 servings. Candy Trout

Carol & Friends, A Taste of North County
Carol & Friends Steering Committee of the Carol Cox Re-Entry Women's Scholarship Fund at CSU-San Marcos
San Marcos, California

Zucchini, Leek, and Chèvre Tart in Wild Rice Crust

Chèvre is a white goat's milk cheese with a distinctive tart flavor. Some of the most popular chèvres include banon, Bûcheron, and Montrachet.

⅓ cup grated Parmesan cheese
1 large egg
3 tablespoons butter or margarine, melted
2 tablespoons lemon juice
2½ cups cooked wild rice
¼ teaspoon salt
¼ teaspoon freshly ground pepper
2 cups thinly sliced leeks
½ cup butter or margarine, melted

2 cups coarsely shredded zucchini
1½ cups whipping cream
4 large eggs
1 cup crumbled chèvre cheese
1 tablespoon chopped fresh marjoram or 1 teaspoon dried marjoram
1 teaspoon Dijon mustard
¼ teaspoon salt
¼ teaspoon freshly ground pepper

Combine first 4 ingredients in a large bowl; beat with a wire whisk until blended. Stir in rice, ¼ teaspoon salt, and ¼ teaspoon pepper. Spoon into a lightly greased 10-inch pieplate; press mixture in bottom and up sides of pieplate with back of a spoon. Bake at 350° for 15 minutes. Let cool on a wire rack.

Sauté leeks in ½ cup butter in a large skillet over medium heat, stirring constantly, 3 minutes or until crisp-tender. Add zucchini; sauté, stirring constantly, an additional 2 minutes or until vegetables are tender. Set aside.

Combine whipping cream and remaining ingredients in a large bowl; beat with a wire whisk until blended. Stir in reserved vegetable mixture. Pour into pastry shell. Bake, uncovered, at 350° for 45 minutes or until set and golden. Let stand 15 minutes before serving. Yield: one 10-inch tart.   Camille Tareshawty

Angels & Friends Favorite Recipes II
Angels of Easter Seal
Youngstown, Ohio

Baked French Toast with Berries

1 (8-ounce) day-old French
  baguette
3 large eggs, beaten
2¼ cups milk
3 tablespoons sugar
1 teaspoon vanilla extract
1 cup fresh or frozen
  blueberries, thawed

½ cup all-purpose flour
¼ cup plus 2 tablespoons
  firmly packed dark brown
  sugar
½ teaspoon ground cinnamon
¼ cup butter or margarine
1 cup fresh or frozen
  strawberries, thawed

Cut bread diagonally into 10 slices. Arrange bread slices in a greased 13- x 9- x 2-inch baking dish.

Combine eggs and next 3 ingredients; stir well. Pour egg mixture over bread slices. Cover and chill 8 hours.

Sprinkle blueberries over bread mixture. Combine flour, brown sugar, and cinnamon. Cut in butter with pastry blender until mixture is crumbly; sprinkle over blueberries. Bake, uncovered, at 375° for 40 to 45 minutes or until set and golden. Serve immediately with strawberries. Yield: 10 servings.

California Sizzles
The Junior League of Pasadena, California

French Toast Casserole

8 slices white bread
2 (8-ounce) packages cream
  cheese, cubed

12 large eggs, beaten
2 cups milk
⅓ cup maple syrup

Remove crusts from bread; cut bread into 1-inch cubes. Place bread cubes in a greased 13- x 9- x 2-inch baking dish; top with cream cheese cubes.

Combine eggs, milk, and syrup in a large bowl, stirring with a wire whisk until blended; pour over mixture in baking dish. Bake, uncovered, at 350° for 45 to 50 minutes or until set and golden. Serve immediately. Yield: 8 servings.   Mala Reich

A Jewish Family Cookbook
Valley Beth Shalom Nursery School
Encino, California

Goat Cheese Fritters

½ cup milk
1 tablespoon butter or
  margarine
1 cup quick-cooking grits,
  uncooked
⅛ teaspoon salt
2 egg yolks
2 ounces chèvre cheese,
  crumbled

1 tablespoon dry mustard
2 tablespoons honey
⅛ teaspoon salt
⅓ cup all-purpose flour
1 to 2 large eggs, beaten
⅔ cup fine, dry breadcrumbs
¼ cup butter or margarine,
  melted

Combine milk and 1 tablespoon butter in a medium saucepan; bring to a boil. Stir in grits and ⅛ teaspoon salt. Remove from heat; let cool. Stir in egg yolks and next 4 ingredients. Shape mixture into a 9-inch roll; wrap in parchment paper, and chill 2 hours.

Unwrap roll, and cut into ¼-inch-thick slices. Dredge slices in flour; dip in beaten eggs, and coat with breadcrumbs. Cook fritters in ¼ cup butter in a large skillet over medium-high heat 2 minutes on each side or until lightly browned. Serve fritters immediately. Yield: 3 dozen. The Tutwiler

Recipes from Historic Hotels
National Trust for Historic Preservation
Washington, DC

Eggplant and Mozzarella Sandwich

1 medium eggplant
3 tablespoons olive oil,
  divided
2 medium-size purple onions,
  cut into very thin strips
3 cloves garlic, minced
¼ teaspoon freshly ground
  pepper
Dash of dried thyme

2 plum tomatoes, seeded and
  cut into very thin strips
2 tablespoons chopped fresh
  parsley
1 teaspoon white wine vinegar
1 (16-ounce) loaf Italian bread
  or French baguette
6 ounces mozzarella cheese,
  thinly sliced

Line a baking sheet with aluminum foil; lightly oil foil. Cut eggplant lengthwise into ½-inch-thick slices. Place on prepared baking sheet; brush with 1 tablespoon olive oil. Broil 5½ inches from heat (with electric oven door partially opened) 6 to 7 minutes or until tender and golden. Coarsely chop eggplant, and set aside.

Sauté onion and next 3 ingredients in remaining 2 tablespoons olive oil in a large skillet over medium-high heat, stirring constantly, until tender. Stir in reserved eggplant, tomato, parsley, and vinegar. Remove from heat, and set aside.

Cut bread in half lengthwise; place on an ungreased baking sheet. Broil until lightly browned. Place reserved eggplant mixture on bottom half of toasted bread; top with mozzarella cheese slices. Broil 5½ inches from heat 1 to 2 minutes or until cheese melts. Cover with top half of bread. Cut into 4 portions, and serve immediately. Yield: 4 servings. Sherri Frost

A Feast for All Seasons
The Junior Women's Club of Mt. Lebanon
Pittsburgh, Pennsylvania

Mexican Egg Salad Sandwich

Green chiles and taco sauce add a south-of-the-border flavor to this egg-salad sandwich filling.

⅓ cup sour cream
3 tablespoons canned chopped green chiles, drained
1 tablespoon lemon juice
1 teaspoon salt
2 teaspoons commercial taco sauce

9 hard-cooked eggs, chopped
6 slices tomato
6 slices whole wheat bread, toasted
1 cup (4 ounces) shredded Cheddar cheese

Combine first 5 ingredients in a medium bowl; stir well. Gently stir in chopped eggs. Place 1 tomato slice on each slice of toasted bread. Spread about ½ cup egg mixture over each tomato slice. Sprinkle evenly with cheese. Place on an ungreased baking sheet. Broil 5½ inches from heat (with electric oven door partially opened) 3 minutes or until cheese melts. Serve sandwiches immediately. Yield: 6 servings. Kathy Green

First United Methodist Church Centennial Cookbook, 1993
United Methodist Women of First United Methodist Church
Casper, Wyoming

Ham Strudel

To most, a strudel is a rolled flaky pastry with a sweet fruit filling. This savory variation is filled with ham, rice, and cheese.

1 large onion, finely chopped
1 cup butter or margarine, melted and divided
1½ cups chicken broth
¾ cup long-grain rice, uncooked
1 to 2 tablespoons minced fresh parsley
10 sheets frozen phyllo pastry, thawed

4 ounces thinly sliced cooked ham, cut into very thin strips
1 cup (4 ounces) shredded Swiss cheese
1 cup (4 ounces) shredded Cheddar cheese
Paprika

Sauté onion in 1 tablespoon melted butter in a large saucepan over medium-high heat, stirring constantly, until tender. Add chicken broth; bring to a boil. Stir in rice; cover, reduce heat, and simmer 15 to 20 minutes or until rice is tender and liquid is absorbed. Set aside, and let cool. Stir in parsley.

Work with 1 sheet of phyllo at a time, keeping remaining sheets covered with slightly damp towel. Layer phyllo sheets on work surface, brushing each sheet with remaining ¾ cup plus 3 tablespoons melted butter. Spoon reserved rice mixture over phyllo, spreading to within 1 inch of sides. Sprinkle ham over rice mixture, and top with cheeses.

Starting at short side, fold phyllo over 1 inch; fold each long side over 1 inch. Roll up phyllo, starting with short side. Place phyllo, seam side down, on a lightly greased broiling rack in a broiler pan. Brush with any remaining melted butter. Make several diagonal slits, about ¼ inch deep, across top of pastry with a sharp knife. Sprinkle with paprika. Bake, uncovered, at 375° for 35 to 40 minutes or until golden. Let stand 5 minutes before serving. Yield: 6 to 8 servings.

For Goodness Taste
The Junior League of Rochester, New York

Fish & Shellfish

*From savory grilled tuna and succulent stuffed sole,
to juicy oysters on the half shell and delicate crabmeat, fish and
shellfish score high in flavor and nutrition.*

Baked Oysters Macadamia, page 162

Savory Sea Bass

For a subtle nutty flavor, replace the butter or margarine with sesame oil.

1 medium onion, chopped
1 tablespoon plus 1 teaspoon
   butter or margarine, melted
2 teaspoons curry powder
2 teaspoons peeled, minced
   gingerroot

2 teaspoons minced garlic
2 teaspoons soy sauce
4 sea bass fillets (about
   2 pounds)

Combine first 6 ingredients in a bowl; stir well, and set aside.

Cut 4 (12- x 9-inch) pieces of heavy-duty aluminum foil; fold in half lengthwise, creasing firmly. Trim each piece into a large heart shape. Place foil on an ungreased baking sheet.

Place 1 fillet on each piece of foil near the crease. Top evenly with reserved onion mixture. Fold over remaining halves of foil hearts. Starting with rounded edge of each heart, pleat and crimp edges together to seal. Twist end tightly to seal. Bake at 450° for 20 minutes or until fish flakes easily when tested with a fork. To serve, remove from foil. Yield: 4 servings.   Barbara Alba

Carol & Friends, A Taste of North County
Carol & Friends Steering Committee of the Carol Cox Re-Entry
Women's Scholarship Fund at CSU-San Marcos
San Marcos, California

Fish Plaki

Plaki is a Greek method of baking or braising fish with vegetables. As in this sea bass recipe, onions and tomatoes are commonly used.

2 large onions, thinly sliced
½ cup olive oil
3 tomatoes, thinly sliced
3 green onions, chopped
1 cup coarsely chopped celery
1 cup chopped fresh parsley
1 tablespoon minced garlic
1 bay leaf
2 to 3 pounds sea bass fillets

2 teaspoons dried oregano
½ teaspoon salt
¼ teaspoon pepper
2 medium lemons, thinly sliced
½ cup Chablis or other dry
   white wine
3 tablespoons fresh lemon
   juice
¼ cup soft breadcrumbs

Sauté sliced onion in olive oil in a large skillet over medium heat, stirring constantly, until tender. Add tomato and next 5 ingredients; cook, stirring constantly, until liquid evaporates. Remove from heat; set aside.

Place fillets in a lightly greased 13- x 9- x 2-inch baking dish; sprinkle with oregano, salt, and pepper. Spread reserved vegetable mixture over fish; top with lemon slices. Pour wine and lemon juice over vegetable mixture; sprinkle with breadcrumbs. Bake, uncovered, at 350° for 45 minutes or until fish flakes easily when tested with a fork. Remove and discard bay leaf. Yield: 6 servings.

The Complete Book of Greek Cooking
Recipe Club of St. Paul's Greek Orthodox Cathedral
Hempstead, New York

Catfish Amandine

Amandine is a French term that means "garnished with almonds."

¼ cup butter or margarine, melted
3 tablespoons lemon juice
6 farm-raised catfish fillets (about 2 pounds)

1½ teaspoons Creole seasoning
½ cup sliced natural almonds

Combine melted butter and lemon juice in a shallow dish. Dip fillets in butter mixture, and place in an ungreased 13- x 9- x 2-inch baking dish.

Sprinkle fillets evenly with Creole seasoning. Bake, uncovered, at 375° for 20 minutes. Sprinkle fillets evenly with almonds, and bake an additional 10 minutes or until fish flakes easily when tested with a fork. Transfer fillets to a serving platter. Serve immediately. Yield: 6 servings.

Jeanette Farmer

Attaché . . . A Decade of Delicacies
Attaché Booster Club of Clinton High School
Clinton, Mississippi

Catfish Capers

Capers spark the flavor of this grilled catfish entrée. Be sure to rinse the capers before using to remove excess salt.

2 tablespoons plus ½ teaspoon
olive oil, divided
6 farm-raised catfish fillets
(about 2 pounds)
1 teaspoon dried dillweed
¾ teaspoon lemon-pepper
seasoning
½ teaspoon salt
¼ cup chopped onion
1 cup mayonnaise
1 (2-ounce) jar diced pimiento,
drained

1 tablespoon plus 1 teaspoon
capers
1 tablespoon chopped fresh
parsley
1 tablespoon lemon juice
¼ teaspoon cracked pepper
2 lemons, thinly sliced
2 limes, thinly sliced
Garnish: fresh parsley sprigs

Brush a 13- x 9- x 2-inch disposable aluminum pan with ½ teaspoon olive oil. Place fillets in pan; brush fillets with 1 tablespoon olive oil. Sprinkle fillets evenly with dillweed, lemon-pepper seasoning, and salt.

Place pan on grill rack; grill, covered, over medium-hot coals (350° to 400°) about 25 minutes or until fish flakes easily when tested with a fork. Transfer fillets to a serving platter; set aside, and keep warm.

Sauté onion in remaining 1 tablespoon olive oil in a large skillet over medium-high heat, stirring constantly, until tender. Remove from heat; stir in mayonnaise and next 5 ingredients. Cook over low heat, stirring frequently, just until thoroughly heated.

Arrange lemon and lime slices around fillets. Garnish, if desired. Serve fillets with warm sauce. Yield: 6 servings.

Heart & Soul
The Junior League of Memphis, Tennessee

Baked Haddock

A mixture of beaten egg white, tartar sauce, and onion spread over these fish fillets creates an appealing puffy topping.

1 pound haddock fillets
¼ teaspoon salt
¼ teaspoon pepper

2 egg whites
⅓ cup commercial tartar sauce
¼ cup grated onion

Place fillets in a lightly greased 15- x 10- x 1-inch jellyroll pan; sprinkle with salt and pepper. Beat egg whites at high speed of an electric mixer until stiff peaks form. Gently fold tartar sauce and onion into beaten egg white. Spoon evenly over fillets. Bake, uncovered, at 300° for 35 minutes or until fish flakes easily when tested with a fork. Yield: 4 servings.   Dorothy Mollins

Fabulous Fare
Women's Fellowship of Center Harbor Congregational Church
Center Harbor, New Hampshire

Halibut and Sour Cream Bake

2 (8-ounce) halibut steaks,
  1 inch thick
¼ cup sour cream
¼ cup mayonnaise
¼ cup sliced green onions
1 teaspoon lemon juice

¼ teaspoon salt
⅛ teaspoon ground red
  pepper
¼ cup (1 ounce) shredded
  Cheddar cheese

Cut fish in half; arrange in a lightly greased 11- x 7- x 1½-inch baking dish. Bake, uncovered, at 450° for 12 to 15 minutes or until fish flakes easily when tested with a fork.

Combine sour cream and next 5 ingredients in a medium bowl; stir well. Spoon sour cream mixture evenly over fish. Sprinkle with shredded cheese. Bake, uncovered, an additional 3 to 4 minutes or until cheese melts and sauce is thoroughly heated. Serve immediately. Yield: 4 servings.   Georgene Baer

Reflections of the West
Telephone Pioneers of America, Skyline Chapter No. 67
Helena, Montana

Grilled Halibut in Lemon Mustard-Tarragon

6 (8-ounce) halibut steaks
1 tablespoon grated lemon
   rind
½ cup fresh lemon juice
¼ cup olive oil
¼ cup Dijon mustard
3 tablespoons finely chopped
   fresh tarragon
2 tablespoons finely chopped
   green onions
¼ teaspoon pepper
Garnishes: lemon slices, fresh
   tarragon sprigs

Place steaks in a large heavy-duty, zip-top plastic bag. Combine lemon rind and next 6 ingredients in a small bowl; stir well. Pour marinade mixture over steaks. Seal bag securely; place in a large bowl. Marinate in refrigerator 30 minutes.

Remove steaks from marinade, discarding marinade. Grill, covered, over medium-hot coals (350° to 400°) 5 to 7 minutes on each side or until fish flakes easily when tested with a fork. Garnish, if desired. Yield: 6 servings.   Nancy Vieburg

Golden Valley Women of Today Cookbook
Golden Valley Women of Today
Golden Valley, Minnesota

Grilled Mahimahi in Red Onion Butter

Mahimahi, also called dolphin fish and dorado, is a warm-water fish with a firm flesh and moderate fat content.

4 (8-ounce) mahimahi fillets
2 tablespoons extra virgin olive
   oil
2 medium-size purple onions,
   cut into ⅛-inch-thick slices,
   divided
⅛ teaspoon freshly ground
   white pepper
3 tablespoons extra virgin
   olive oil
½ cup Chablis or other dry
   white wine
½ teaspoon finely chopped
   fresh thyme
½ cup whipping cream
¼ cup unsalted butter or
   margarine
¼ teaspoon salt
⅛ teaspoon black pepper
Garnish: fresh thyme sprigs

Place fillets in a large shallow dish; drizzle with 2 tablespoons olive oil. Top each fillet with 1 onion slice, and sprinkle evenly with white pepper. Cover and marinate in refrigerator 2 hours.

Sauté remaining onion slices in 3 tablespoons olive oil in a large skillet over medium heat, stirring constantly, until almost tender. Add wine and chopped thyme; cook, stirring constantly, until wine is reduced by half. Stir in cream; cook, stirring constantly, until slightly reduced. Add butter, ¼ teaspoon salt, and ⅛ teaspoon pepper, stirring until butter melts. Set sauce aside, and keep warm.

Remove fillets from marinade, discarding marinade. Grill, covered, over medium-hot coals (350° to 400°) 5 minutes on each side or until fish flakes easily when tested with a fork.

Spoon reserved sauce onto a serving platter; top with grilled fillets. Garnish, if desired. Yield: 4 servings. Glenda Barrow

Texas Cookin' Lone Star Style
Telephone Pioneers of America, Lone Star Chapter 22
Dallas, Texas

Lime-Baked Orange Roughy

**2 tablespoons butter or
 margarine, melted**
**2 (6-ounce) orange roughy
 fillets**
2 tablespoons lime juice
1 teaspoon freeze-dried chives

¼ teaspoon salt
**¼ teaspoon dried tarragon
 (optional)**
⅛ teaspoon pepper
¼ teaspoon paprika
Garnish: lime wedges

Pour butter into an 8-inch square baking dish; arrange fillets over butter, turning to coat both sides. Drizzle lime juice over fillets. Combine chives, salt, tarragon, if desired, and pepper; sprinkle evenly over fillets. Bake, uncovered, at 450° for 15 minutes or until fish flakes easily when tested with a fork.

To serve, spoon pan juices over fillets; sprinkle with paprika. Garnish, if desired. Yield: 2 servings. Fern Branstad

Favorites from First
First Lutheran Churchwomen
St. James, Minnesota

Fourth of July Salmon with Egg Sauce

If you're curious about the connection between salmon and the Fourth of July, you're probably not from the East Coast. There, it's a tradition to serve salmon in celebration of this holiday.

1 lemon, thinly sliced
6 (6- to 8-ounce) salmon steaks
¼ cup butter or margarine
¼ cup all-purpose flour
2 cups milk
2 hard-cooked eggs, coarsely chopped

3 tablespoons chopped fresh parsley
1 tablespoon capers
¼ teaspoon salt
¼ teaspoon pepper

Place half of lemon slices on a large square of heavy-duty aluminum foil; top with steaks. Place remaining lemon slices on top of steaks. Top with another large square of heavy-duty aluminum foil; wrap securely, sealing edges well. Place foil packet in an ungreased 15- x 10- x 1-inch jellyroll pan. Bake at 425° for 35 minutes or until fish flakes easily when tested with a fork. Transfer steaks to a serving platter; set aside, and keep warm.

Melt butter in a small heavy saucepan over low heat; add flour, stirring until smooth. Cook 1 minute, stirring constantly. Gradually add milk; cook over medium heat, stirring constantly, until mixture is thickened and bubbly. Stir in eggs and remaining ingredients, and cook until thoroughly heated. Serve salmon with warm sauce. Yield: 6 servings.

Hospitality: A Cookbook Celebrating Boston's North Shore
Salem Hospital Aid Association
Salem, Massachusetts

Salmon Patties

2 green onions, chopped
1 stalk celery, chopped
1 tablespoon butter or
  margarine, melted
1 (14¾-ounce) can pink
  salmon, drained
1 large egg, lightly beaten
2 tablespoons mayonnaise
1 tablespoon lemon juice

Dash of salt
Dash of ground red pepper
Dash of lemon-pepper
  seasoning
½ cup all-purpose flour
¼ cup butter or margarine,
  melted
Mushroom Sauce

Sauté green onions and celery in 1 tablespoon butter in a skillet over medium-high heat, stirring constantly, until tender. Set aside.

Remove and discard skin and bones from salmon, if desired. Combine salmon, reserved green onions mixture, egg, and next 5 ingredients. Shape mixture into 4 patties (mixture will be sticky). Dredge in flour. Cook in ¼ cup butter in a skillet over medium heat 5 minutes on each side or until browned. Serve patties with warm sauce. Yield: 4 servings.

Mushroom Sauce

¾ pound whole fresh
  mushrooms
3 tablespoons butter or
  margarine, melted
1 tablespoon all-purpose flour
¾ cup half-and-half

¼ cup Chablis or other dry
  white wine
1 teaspoon soy sauce
¼ teaspoon lemon-pepper
  seasoning

Sauté mushrooms in butter in a large saucepan over medium-high heat, stirring constantly, until tender. Remove mushrooms from saucepan, reserving drippings in pan. Reduce heat to low.

Add flour to drippings, stirring until smooth. Cook 1 minute, stirring constantly. Gradually add half-and half, wine, soy sauce, and lemon-pepper seasoning; cook over medium heat, stirring constantly, until thickened and bubbly. Return mushrooms to pan; cook until heated. Yield: 2 cups.   Ruthie Grajczyk

Sisseton Centennial Cookbook
Sisseton Centennial Committee
Sisseton, South Dakota

Scrod Marsala

New England is a fresh seafood lover's delight! Among the region's readily available fresh fish is scrod, a popular name for young cod or haddock.

¾ pound fresh mushrooms, sliced
1 clove garlic, minced
1 tablespoon butter or margarine, melted
1 tablespoon olive oil
⅔ cup saltine cracker crumbs
¼ cup grated Parmesan cheese
½ teaspoon salt

½ teaspoon dried basil
½ teaspoon dried oregano
¼ teaspoon garlic powder
4 (4-ounce) scrod fillets
3 tablespoons butter or margarine, melted
Paprika
2 tablespoons Marsala

Sauté mushrooms and garlic in 1 tablespoon butter and olive oil in a large skillet over medium-high heat, stirring constantly, until tender. Set aside, and keep warm.

Combine cracker crumbs and next 5 ingredients in a medium bowl; dredge fillets in crumb mixture. Pour 3 tablespoons melted butter into an 11- x 7- x 1½-inch baking dish. Arrange fillets over butter, turning to coat both sides; sprinkle with paprika. Bake, uncovered, at 350° for 15 minutes.

Drizzle Marsala evenly over fillets, and bake 5 minutes or until fish flakes easily when tested with a fork. Spoon reserved mushroom mixture over fillets. Serve immediately. Yield: 4 servings.

A Taste of New England
The Junior League of Worcester, Massachusetts

Broiled Oriental Shark Steaks

Shark is a flavorful fish with a dense, meaty texture. It can be grilled, baked, poached, fried, or as in this recipe, broiled.

2 (4-ounce) shark steaks, 1¼ inches thick
2 tablespoons soy sauce
2 tablespoons fresh lemon juice
1 tablespoon olive oil

1 tablespoon peeled, minced gingerroot
1 clove garlic, minced
1 green onion, thinly sliced diagonally
1 lemon, cut in half

Place steaks in a large heavy-duty, zip-top plastic bag. Combine soy sauce and next 4 ingredients in a small bowl; pour marinade mixture over steaks. Seal bag securely; place in a large bowl. Marinate in refrigerator 1 hour, turning occasionally.

Remove steaks from marinade, reserving marinade. Place on a lightly greased rack in a broiler pan. Broil 5½ inches from heat (with electric oven door partially opened) 4 to 5 minutes on each side or until fish flakes easily when tested with a fork, basting occasionally with reserved marinade.

Remove steaks to a serving platter, and sprinkle with sliced green onion. Serve with lemon halves, squeezing lemon juice over steaks. Yield: 2 servings.

Culinary Arts, Volume II
Society of the Arts of Allentown Art Museum
Allentown, Pennsylvania

Sole Stuffed with Shrimp

1 pound frozen cooked salad shrimp
2 cups water
1½ cups finely chopped celery
½ cup finely chopped onion
1 cup mayonnaise
1 cup finely crushed potato chips
Dash of ground red pepper
16 (6-ounce) sole fillets

Combine first 4 ingredients in a large saucepan. Bring to a boil; boil 1 minute. Drain well, and place in a medium bowl. Add mayonnaise, potato chips, and red pepper; stir well.

Place 1 fillet in each of 8 lightly greased individual 2½-cup baking dishes; spread shrimp mixture evenly over fillets. Place remaining fillets over shrimp mixture. Bake, uncovered, at 350° for 20 to 25 minutes or until fish flakes easily when tested with a fork. Yield: 8 servings.   Marilyn Branham Caradonna

A Taste of Twin Pines
Twin Pines Alumni of Twin Pines Cooperative House
West Lafayette, Indiana

Grilled Swordfish
with Cantaloupe Relish

These steaks can also be broiled. Place on a lightly greased rack in a broiler pan; broil 5½ inches from heat (with electric oven door partially opened) 8 minutes on each side or until fish flakes easily when tested with a fork.

4 (8-ounce) swordfish steaks (1 inch thick)	2 tablespoons dark sesame oil
½ cup commercial teriyaki sauce	2 tablespoons honey
	Cantaloupe Relish

Place steaks in a large shallow dish. Combine teriyaki sauce, oil, and honey in a small bowl; stir well. Pour marinade mixture over steaks; cover and marinate in refrigerator 8 hours, turning steaks occasionally.

Remove steaks from marinade, discarding marinade. Grill steaks, covered, over medium-hot coals (350° to 400°) about 5 minutes on each side or until fish flakes easily when tested with a fork. Serve with Cantaloupe Relish. Yield: 4 servings.

Cantaloupe Relish

1 medium-size ripe cantaloupe, peeled, seeded, and diced (about 2 pounds)	1 tablespoon seeded, minced serrano pepper
½ cup diced green pepper	2 tablespoons fresh lemon juice
¼ cup diced purple onion	2 tablespoons vegetable oil
1 tablespoon minced fresh cilantro	1 tablespoon sugar
1 tablespoon minced fresh parsley	½ teaspoon salt

Combine first 6 ingredients in a medium bowl; stir well. Combine lemon juice and remaining ingredients, stirring well. Pour lemon juice mixture over cantaloupe mixture, and toss gently to coat. Cover and chill at least 1 hour. Yield: 3 cups.

Still Gathering: A Centennial Celebration
Auxiliary to the American Osteopathic Association
Chicago, Illinois

Shrimp and Crab Stuffed Trout

This shrimp and crabmeat stuffing should hold together loosely. If necessary, you can add up to ½ cup additional fine, dry breadcrumbs to the stuffing mixture to achieve the right consistency.

¾ cup finely chopped onion
½ cup finely chopped green pepper
1 clove garlic, crushed
2 tablespoons butter or margarine, melted
¼ pound fresh crabmeat, drained and flaked
¼ pound frozen cooked salad shrimp, thawed
¼ cup plus 2 tablespoons fine, dry breadcrumbs

1 tablespoon minced fresh parsley
1 tablespoon minced fresh chives
¼ teaspoon salt
⅛ teaspoon pepper
4 dressed freshwater trout (about 2¾ pounds)
2 tablespoons butter or margarine, melted

Sauté onion, green pepper, and garlic in 2 tablespoons butter in a large skillet over medium-high heat, stirring constantly, until tender. Remove from heat; stir in crabmeat and next 6 ingredients. Set aside.

Brush trout cavities with 2 tablespoons melted butter; spoon reserved crabmeat mixture evenly into cavities. Place trout in an ungreased shallow 3-quart baking dish; cover and bake at 350° for 15 minutes. Uncover and bake an additional 30 minutes or until fish flakes easily when tested with a fork. Serve immediately. Yield: 4 servings.

Steamboat Entertains
Steamboat Springs Winter Sports Club
Steamboat Springs, Colorado

Grilled Tuna Steaks with Herb Vinaigrette

If you prefer a milder vinaigrette with your grilled tuna steaks, just omit or reduce the amount of the fiery jalapeño pepper.

1 medium tomato, peeled, seeded, and diced
¼ cup finely chopped green onions
¼ cup chopped fresh basil
¼ cup olive oil
2 cloves garlic, minced
2 tablespoons red wine vinegar
1 teaspoon seeded, finely chopped jalapeño pepper
¼ teaspoon salt
⅛ teaspoon freshly ground pepper

4 (6- to 8-ounce) tuna steaks, ¾ inch thick
2 tablespoons olive oil
2 tablespoons soy sauce
1 tablespoon fresh lemon juice
1 tablespoon chopped fresh thyme
1 teaspoon peeled, grated gingerroot
¼ teaspoon salt
⅛ teaspoon freshly ground pepper
Vegetable cooking spray

Combine first 9 ingredients in a small bowl; stir well. Cover and let stand at room temperature at least 1 hour.

Place tuna steaks in a large heavy-duty, zip-top plastic bag. Combine 2 tablespoons olive oil and next 6 ingredients in a small bowl; stir well. Pour marinade mixture over steaks. Seal bag securely; place in a large bowl. Marinate in refrigerator 30 minutes.

Remove steaks from marinade, discarding marinade. Spray a grill basket with cooking spray, and place steaks in basket. Grill steaks, covered, over medium coals (300° to 350°) 5 minutes on each side or until fish flakes easily when tested with a fork. Remove steaks to a serving platter, and serve with reserved tomato mixture. Yield: 4 servings.

Beth Kotek

YUMMM . . . Delicious & Fun Recipes
The YWCA of Ridgewood Children's Educational Services
Ridgewood, New Jersey

Spicy Crab Cakes with Corn

If the crabmeat mixture seems too moist to shape into patties, you can add more cracker crumbs to help bind the mixture.

1 pound fresh lump crabmeat, drained
1 cup frozen whole kernel corn, cooked
½ cup minced onion
½ cup minced celery
½ cup minced green pepper
1 teaspoon seeded, minced jalapeño pepper
1 cup mayonnaise
½ teaspoon salt
½ teaspoon dry mustard
1 teaspoon Old Bay seasoning, divided
¼ teaspoon freshly ground black pepper
⅛ teaspoon ground red pepper
1 large egg, lightly beaten
1 cup crushed saltine crackers, divided
2 tablespoons butter or margarine, melted and divided
2 tablespoons vegetable oil, divided
Old Bay seasoning (optional)
Commercial tartar sauce
Lemon wedges

Combine first 6 ingredients in a large bowl, and toss gently.

Combine mayonnaise, salt, dry mustard, ½ teaspoon Old Bay seasoning, black pepper, and red pepper; add to crabmeat mixture, and stir well. Gently fold in egg and ¼ cup cracker crumbs. Shape crabmeat mixture into 8 patties. Dredge each patty in remaining ¾ cup cracker crumbs. Sprinkle both sides of each patty with remaining ½ teaspoon Old Bay seasoning. Cover and chill 30 minutes.

Heat 1 tablespoon butter and 1 tablespoon oil in a large skillet over medium-high heat until hot. Add 4 patties, and cook 4 to 5 minutes on each side or until golden. Sprinkle patties with additional Old Bay seasoning, if desired. Repeat procedure with remaining butter, oil, and patties. Serve immediately with tartar sauce and lemon wedges. Yield: 8 servings.

Sugar Snips & Asparagus Tips
Woman's Auxiliary of Infant Welfare Society of Chicago
Chicago, Illinois

Crab Imperial, Chesapeake

¾ cup mayonnaise or salad
  dressing, divided
⅔ cup diced green pepper
1 large egg, beaten
¼ cup diced pimiento,
  drained
2 teaspoons dry mustard

½ teaspoon salt
¼ teaspoon ground white
  pepper
2 pounds fresh lump
  crabmeat, drained
Paprika

Combine ½ cup plus 2 tablespoons mayonnaise and next 6 ingredients in a large bowl; stir well. Add crabmeat, and stir gently.

Spoon crabmeat mixture evenly into 8 ungreased (6-ounce) custard cups or individual baking dishes. Spread remaining 2 tablespoons mayonnaise evenly over crabmeat mixture; sprinkle with paprika. Bake, uncovered, at 350° for 15 to 20 minutes or until thoroughly heated. Yield: 8 servings.   Vera Butts

From Zion's Kitchen
The Semper Fidelis Sunday School Class of Zion Lutheran
Evangelical Church
Williamsport, Maryland

Baked Oysters Macadamia

Try nestling Baked Oysters Macadamia on a bed of rock salt to keep the uneven shells from tipping. Serve with lemon wedges and seafood sauce.

1 cup unsalted butter or
  margarine, softened
½ cup finely chopped
  macadamia nuts
2 tablespoons soft
  breadcrumbs
2 tablespoons minced garlic
2 tablespoons finely chopped
  shallots

1 tablespoon finely chopped
  fresh parsley
¼ teaspoon salt
⅛ teaspoon freshly ground
  pepper
3 dozen fresh oysters (in the
  shell)

Combine first 8 ingredients in a bowl; stir well, and set aside.

Scrub oyster shells, and open, discarding tops. Arrange shell bottoms (containing oysters) in a 15- x 10- x 1-inch jellyroll pan.

Top each oyster with 1 heaping teaspoon reserved butter mixture. Bake at 450° for 6 to 8 minutes or until butter melts and edges of oysters begin to curl. Serve immediately. Yield: 6 servings.

Tampa Treasures
The Junior League of Tampa, Florida

Scallops with Tomato and Basil Sauce

Two popular types of scallops are bay and sea scallops. Bay scallops are tiny and have a sweet flavor. Sea scallops are larger and slightly chewier.

1½ pounds sea scallops
¼ cup milk
½ teaspoon salt
¼ teaspoon pepper
1 (28-ounce) can whole
   tomatoes, drained and
   coarsely chopped
2 tablespoons olive oil
2 tablespoons chopped fresh
   basil

½ cup all-purpose flour
¼ cup plus 2 tablespoons
   vegetable oil
3 tablespoons butter or
   margarine
1 tablespoon minced garlic
2 tablespoons minced fresh
   parsley

Combine first 4 ingredients in a bowl; stir well, and set aside.

Sauté tomatoes in olive oil in a large skillet over medium-high heat, stirring constantly, 5 minutes. Stir in chopped basil; set aside, and keep warm.

Drain scallops; dredge in flour. Fry scallops in hot vegetable oil in a large heavy skillet over medium-high heat 5 minutes on each side or until golden. Drain, reserving drippings in skillet. Set scallops aside, and keep warm.

Add butter to drippings; cook over low heat until butter melts. Add garlic, and sauté over medium heat, stirring constantly, until garlic is tender.

Spoon reserved tomato mixture onto a serving platter; top with reserved scallops. Pour garlic mixture over scallops; sprinkle with parsley. Serve immediately. Yield: 4 to 6 servings.   Dana Max

From Your Neighbor's Kitchen
Friends of Riverton Park
Riverton, New Jersey

Dancing Shrimp

1 pound unpeeled large fresh
   shrimp
2 tablespoons egg white
1 teaspoon cornstarch
2 teaspoons dry sherry

¼ teaspoon sugar
¼ teaspoon salt
2 tablespoons vegetable oil
1 green onion, cut into 1-inch
   pieces

Peel and devein shrimp; pat dry with a paper towel. Combine egg white and cornstarch in a bowl, stirring with a wire whisk until blended. Add shrimp, tossing to coat. Cover and chill 45 minutes. Combine sherry, sugar, and salt in a bowl; stir well. Set aside.

Pour oil around top of preheated wok, coating sides. Heat at medium-high (375°) for 2 minutes. Add shrimp; stir-fry 1 to 2 minutes or until shrimp turn pink. Remove shrimp with a slotted spoon; set aside. Add green onion to wok; stir-fry 1 minute. Return shrimp to wok; add reserved sherry mixture, and stir-fry 30 seconds or until heated. Serve immediately. Yield: 4 servings.

Virginia Celebrates
The Council of the Virginia Museum of Fine Arts
Richmond, Virginia

Shrimp Rosemary

24 unpeeled large fresh shrimp
1 (16-ounce) package spinach
   angel hair pasta
⅓ cup minced onion
2 cloves garlic, minced
2 tablespoons butter or
   margarine, melted
1 tablespoon olive oil

½ teaspoon dried rosemary
½ teaspoon pepper
½ cup cream sherry
½ cup minced fresh tomato
2 tablespoons minced fresh
   parsley
¼ teaspoon garlic salt

Peel shrimp; devein and butterfly shrimp. Set shrimp aside.

Cook pasta according to package directions; drain well. Set aside, and keep warm.

Sauté onion and garlic in butter and olive oil in a large skillet over medium heat, stirring constantly, until tender. Add reserved shrimp, rosemary, and pepper; sauté over high heat, stirring constantly, 1 minute. Add sherry, tomato, parsley, and garlic salt; sauté, stirring constantly, 4 minutes or until shrimp turn pink. Serve immediately over reserved pasta. Yield: 4 to 6 servings.

Tropical Seasons, A Taste of Life in South Florida
Beaux Arts of the Lowe Art Museum of the University of Miami
Coral Gables, Florida

Corn-Shrimp Fritters

½ pound unpeeled medium-size fresh shrimp
1 (10-ounce) package frozen whole kernel corn, thawedand drained
4 green onions, chopped
2 stalks celery, finely chopped
2 large eggs, beaten
2 cloves garlic, crushed

½ cup all-purpose flour
2 tablespoons chopped fresh cilantro
1 teaspoon salt
1 teaspoon ground coriander
½ teaspoon ground cumin
Vegetable oil
Orange-Coriander Chili Dipping Sauce

Peel and devein shrimp; cut into ½-inch pieces. Combine shrimp, corn, and next 9 ingredients in a large bowl; stir well.

Pour oil to depth of 1 inch in a heavy saucepan; heat to 375°. Drop shrimp mixture by tablespoonfuls into hot oil; fry 2 minutes on each side or until golden. Drain on paper towels. Serve immediately with sauce. Yield: 4 to 6 servings.

Orange-Coriander Chili Dipping Sauce

¼ cup plus 2 tablespoons soy sauce
2 teaspoons grated orange rind
⅓ cup fresh orange juice
2 tablespoons sugar
2 tablespoons chopped fresh cilantro

1 tablespoon white vinegar
1 tablespoon light sesame oil
2 cloves garlic, minced
2 teaspoons peeled, minced gingerroot
2 teaspoons hot chili oil

Combine all ingredients; stir well. Yield: 1 cup.   Jo Rita Jordan

Rosie's Place Recipes
Rosie's Place
Boston, Massachusetts

Holiday Seafood Newburg

A rich sherry-cream sauce blankets this elegant combination of delicately flavored seafood and vegetables. If you prefer, you can substitute fresh crabmeat for frozen.

10 commercial frozen puff
  pastry patty shells
1 pound unpeeled medium-size
  fresh shrimp
¼ cup plus 3 tablespoons
  butter or margarine, divided
1 pound fresh mushrooms,
  sliced
⅓ cup all-purpose flour
4 cups half-and-half
1 teaspoon salt (optional)
⅛ teaspoon pepper

1 pound fresh bay scallops
1 (10-ounce) package frozen
  English peas, thawed
1 (6-ounce) package frozen
  crabmeat, thawed
¼ cup dry sherry
¾ cup (3 ounces) shredded
  sharp Cheddar cheese
1 (4-ounce) jar sliced pimiento,
  drained
Paprika

Bake patty shells according to package directions; set aside, and keep warm. Peel and devein shrimp; set aside.

Melt 3 tablespoons butter in a large Dutch oven over medium-high heat; add mushrooms, and sauté, stirring constantly, until tender. Remove mushrooms from Dutch oven with a slotted spoon; set mushrooms aside.

Melt remaining ¼ cup butter in Dutch oven over low heat. Add flour, stirring until smooth. Cook 1 minute, stirring constantly. Gradually add half-and-half; cook over medium heat, stirring constantly, until mixture is thickened and bubbly. Stir in salt, if desired, and pepper.

Add reserved shrimp, reserved mushrooms, scallops and next 3 ingredients; stir gently. Cook, uncovered, 10 minutes or until shrimp turn pink and scallops are opaque. Stir in cheese and pimiento. Cook just until cheese melts and mixture is thoroughly heated, stirring frequently.

Place reserved patty shells on a serving platter. Spoon seafood mixture evenly into shells, and sprinkle lightly with paprika. Serve immediately. Yield: 10 servings. Kathie Harper

From the Prince's Pantry
The Friends of Prince Memorial Library
Cumberland, Maine

Meats

You'll find just the right entrée in this chapter—
from simple to sensational! Try marinated kabobs for casual
entertaining and stuffed crown roast for the holidays.

Marinated Sirloin Kabobs, page 173

Peppered Rib-Eye Roast

To make a lump-free gravy, dissolve the cornstarch in cold water to form a thin, smooth paste before slowly stirring it into the hot mixture.

½ cup cracked pepper
1 (5- to 6-pound) boneless
  rib-eye roast, trimmed
1 cup soy sauce
¾ cup red wine vinegar

1 tablespoon tomato paste
1 teaspoon paprika
½ teaspoon garlic powder
1 tablespoon cornstarch
1 tablespoon cold water

Lightly press cracked pepper on top and sides of roast. Place roast in a large shallow dish. Combine soy sauce and next 4 ingredients; pour over roast. Cover and marinate in refrigerator 8 hours, turning occasionally.

Remove roast from marinade, discarding marinade. Place roast on rack in a shallow roasting pan; insert meat thermometer into thickest part of roast, making sure it does not touch fat. Bake at 325° for 2½ hours or until thermometer registers 140° (rare). (Bake roast until thermometer registers 150° for medium rare or 160° for medium.)

Remove roast to a serving platter, reserving drippings. Set roast aside, and keep warm. Add enough water to reserved drippings to make 1½ cups; return to pan. Combine cornstarch and 1 tablespoon water, stirring until smooth. Add cornstarch mixture to pan; cook, stirring constantly, until mixture is smooth and slightly thickened. Serve roast with gravy. Yield: 12 to 14 servings.

The Wild Wild West
The Junior League of Odessa, Texas

Tenderloin Stuffed with Lobster

Beef tenderloin and lobster tails—we don't know of a more elegant duo!

2 (8-ounce) lobster tails
1 (3- to 4-pound) beef
  tenderloin, trimmed
1 tablespoon butter or
  margarine, melted
1½ teaspoons lemon juice
6 slices bacon

½ cup sliced green onions
½ cup butter or margarine,
  melted
½ cup Chablis or other dry
  white wine
⅛ teaspoon garlic salt

Place lobster tails in boiling water to cover; return to a boil, reduce heat, and simmer 4 to 5 minutes. Drain well; carefully remove lobster meat from shells. Cut lobster meat in half lengthwise. Set aside.

Slice tenderloin lengthwise to, but not through, the center, leaving 1 long side connected. Place reserved lobster, end to end, inside tenderloin. Combine 1 tablespoon melted butter and lemon juice; drizzle over lobster. Fold top side of tenderloin over lobster, and tie securely with heavy string at 2-inch intervals. Place tenderloin, seam side down, on a rack in a roasting pan. Insert meat thermometer into thickest part of tenderloin. Bake, uncovered, at 425° for 45 minutes. Cut strings, and remove from tenderloin.

Partially cook bacon until almost crisp. Arrange bacon slices in a crisscross pattern over tenderloin; secure at ends with wooden picks. Bake an additional 5 minutes or until bacon is crisp and thermometer registers 140° (rare). (Bake tenderloin until thermometer registers 150° for medium rare or 160° for medium.) Remove wooden picks.

Sauté green onions in ½ cup butter in a small saucepan over low heat, stirring constantly, until tender. Add wine and garlic salt; cook until thoroughly heated. Serve tenderloin with sauce. Yield: 8 servings.

Still Gathering: A Centennial Celebration
Auxiliary to the American Osteopathic Association
Chicago, Illinois

Chinese Pot Roast

Chinese five-spice powder is a ground mixture of five spices—cinnamon, cloves, fennel seed, star anise, and Szechuan peppercorns.

1 clove garlic, minced
1½ teaspoons peeled, minced gingerroot
1 teaspoon salt
¼ teaspoon Chinese five-spice powder
1 (4- to 4½-pound) boneless chuck roast
¼ cup soy sauce
2 tablespoons brown sugar
1 tablespoon sherry
2 tablespoons vegetable oil

1½ cups water
3 medium potatoes, peeled and cubed (about 3 cups)
3 carrots, scraped and cut into 2-inch pieces
1 stalk celery, cut into 2-inch pieces
1 onion, cut into wedges
2 tablespoons cornstarch
¼ cup cold water
2 green onions, chopped

Combine first 4 ingredients; stir well. Rub garlic mixture over entire surface of roast. Place roast in an ungreased 13- x 9- x 2-inch dish. Combine soy sauce, brown sugar, and sherry; pour marinade mixture over roast. Cover and marinate in refrigerator 30 minutes, turning once.

Remove roast from marinade, reserving marinade. Brown roast in oil in a large Dutch oven over medium heat. Pour reserved marinade and 1½ cups water over roast. Bring to a boil; cover, reduce heat, and simmer 2 hours. Add potato, carrot, celery, and onion. Cook an additional 30 minutes or until vegetables are tender. Remove roast and vegetables to a serving platter, reserving pan juices. Set roast and vegetables aside, and keep warm.

Combine cornstarch and ¼ cup water, stirring until smooth. Add cornstarch mixture and green onions to pan juices; cook over medium heat, stirring constantly, until thickened and bubbly. Serve roast with warm sauce. Yield: 12 servings.   Terry Lock

A Collection of Favorite Recipes
Po'okela Church
Makawao, Hawaii

Italian Beef

1 (5-pound) chuck roast
1½ cups water
6 cloves garlic, crushed
2 bay leaves
2 tablespoons dried basil

1½ tablespoons salt
1½ tablespoons dried oregano
1 teaspoon dried crushed red
  pepper
½ teaspoon garlic powder

Place roast in a large Dutch oven. Combine water and remaining ingredients; stir well. Pour over roast; bring to a boil. Cover, reduce heat, and simmer 3 hours or until tender. Let cool. Cover and chill.

Remove roast from broth; cut into very thin slices. Return meat to broth; cook over medium heat until thoroughly heated. Remove bay leaves. Yield: 12 servings. Father Joseph W. Carlo

Cooking with Grace
Grace Episcopal Church
Kirkwood, Missouri

Bourbon Beef Broil

½ cup plus 2 tablespoons soy
  sauce
½ cup water
½ cup bourbon
3 tablespoons brown sugar
2 tablespoons fresh lemon juice

2 tablespoons Worcestershire
  sauce
1 to 2 cloves garlic, minced
1 (2-pound) flank steak
Pepper to taste

Combine first 7 ingredients in a small bowl; stir well. Place steak in a large shallow dish. Pour marinade mixture over steak; cover and marinate in refrigerator 8 hours.

Remove steak from marinade, reserving marinade. Place on a rack in a broiler pan. Broil 5½ inches from heat (with electric oven door partially opened) 5 minutes. Turn; brush with marinade. Broil an additional 4 to 6 minutes or to desired degree of doneness. Sprinkle with pepper to taste. To serve, slice steak diagonally across grain into thin slices. Yield: 6 servings. Alice Pahl

Quilted Quisine
Paoli Memorial Hospital Auxiliary
Paoli, Pennsylvania

Southwestern Flank Steak

Ask your butcher to butterfly the flank steak to save you time. If you prefer to do it yourself, use a sharp knife to cut the steak in half, cutting almost to, but not completely through, the opposite side, to form a butterfly shape.

¾ cup lemon juice
¾ cup vegetable oil
¼ cup Worcestershire sauce
1 clove garlic, minced
1 teaspoon liquid smoke
¼ teaspoon pepper
1 (1½- to 1¾-pound) flank
   steak, butterflied
1 (8-ounce) package frozen
   chopped spinach, thawed
   and well drained

1 (12-ounce) jar roasted red
   peppers in oil, drained and
   cut into very thin strips
1 cup finely chopped onion
2 (4-ounce) cans chopped
   green chiles, drained
1 clove garlic, minced
1 teaspoon ground cumin
1 teaspoon chili powder
¼ cup (1 ounce) shredded
   Monterey Jack cheese

Combine first 6 ingredients in a bowl; stir well. Place steak in a large heavy-duty, zip-top plastic bag. Pour marinade mixture over steak. Seal bag securely, and place in a large bowl. Marinate in refrigerator 8 hours, turning occasionally.

Remove steak from marinade, discarding marinade. Spread spinach over steak to within ½ inch of edges; top with red peppers and onion. Combine chiles, garlic, cumin, and chili powder; spread chile mixture over pepper and onion layer. Sprinkle with cheese. Roll steak, starting at short side. Secure with heavy string at 2-inch intervals. Place in a shallow roasting pan. Bake at 350° for 45 minutes. Let stand 5 minutes before serving. Yield: 6 to 8 servings.

A Cleveland Collection
The Junior League of Cleveland, Ohio

Barbecued Beef Strips

1½ pounds sirloin steak
¼ cup plus 2 tablespoons soy
   sauce
1 green onion, thinly sliced
2 cloves garlic, minced
2 tablespoons sugar

1 tablespoon sesame seeds,
   toasted
2 tablespoons dark sesame
   oil
1 teaspoon peeled, grated
   gingerroot

Trim excess fat from steak; slice steak diagonally across grain into ¼-inch-thick strips. Combine soy sauce and remaining ingredients in a glass bowl; add steak strips, and toss to coat. Cover and marinate in refrigerator 1½ to 2 hours.

Remove steak strips from marinade, reserving marinade. Thread steak strips onto skewers. Grill, uncovered, over medium-hot coals (350° to 400°) 9 minutes or to desired degree of doneness, turning and basting steak strips frequently with reserved marinade. Yield: 4 servings.

Gateways
Auxiliary-Twigs . . . Friends of St. Louis Children's Hospital
St. Louis, Missouri

Marinated Sirloin Kabobs

¼ cup lemon-lime carbonated
  beverage
¼ cup dry sherry
¼ cup soy sauce
3 tablespoons sugar
3 tablespoons white vinegar
½ teaspoon garlic powder
¼ teaspoon salt
¼ teaspoon pepper
2 pounds sirloin steak, cut into
  1-inch cubes

2 cups cherry tomatoes
2 medium onions, cut into
  eighths
½ pound fresh mushroom
  caps
2 medium-size green peppers,
  cut into 1-inch pieces
1 small pineapple, cut into
  1-inch pieces

Combine first 8 ingredients in a large shallow bowl. Add beef cubes; cover and marinate in refrigerator 2 hours, stirring occasionally. Remove beef cubes from marinade, reserving marinade.

Alternately thread beef cubes, tomatoes, onion, mushroom caps, green pepper, and pineapple onto skewers. Grill, covered, over medium-hot coals (350° to 400°) 10 to 12 minutes or to desired degree of doneness, turning and basting occasionally with marinade. Yield: 4 to 5 servings.   Janet Holland Johnson

The Heritage Collection
Western Kentucky University Home Economics
Alumni Association
Bowling Green, Kentucky

Mexican Beef Stir-Fry

This beef stir-fry goes Mexican with the addition of jalapeño peppers, cumin, and oregano. Serve it on a bed of shredded lettuce instead of rice.

1 pound top round steak
1 tablespoon vegetable oil
1 clove garlic, minced
1 teaspoon ground cumin
1 teaspoon dried oregano
1 medium onion, cut into thin
  wedges

1 sweet red pepper, cut into
  very thin strips
1 to 2 jalapeño peppers,
  seeded and cut into very thin
  strips
3 cups shredded iceberg
  lettuce

Trim excess fat from steak; slice steak diagonally across grain into ⅛-inch-thick strips. Set aside.

Combine oil and next 3 ingredients; stir well. Heat half of oil mixture in a large nonstick skillet over medium-high heat for 2 minutes. Add onion, red pepper, and jalapeño pepper, and stir-fry 2 minutes or until crisp-tender. Remove vegetables from skillet; set aside, and keep warm. Add remaining oil mixture to skillet. Add reserved beef strips, and stir-fry 2 minutes. Return vegetables to skillet, and stir-fry until thoroughly heated. Serve over lettuce. Yield: 4 servings.

Carol J. Boden

Idalia Community Cookbook
Women's Fellowship of St. John United Church of Christ
Idalia, Colorado

Horseradish Meat Loaf

Horseradish in both the meat mixture and the saucy topping creates a pleasantly pungent flavor throughout this meat loaf.

2 pounds ground beef
¾ cup regular oats, uncooked
1 large onion, chopped
½ cup catsup
¼ cup milk
2 large eggs, lightly beaten
1 tablespoon prepared
  horseradish

1½ teaspoons salt
½ teaspoon pepper
½ cup catsup
3 tablespoons brown sugar
1 tablespoon prepared
  horseradish
2 teaspoons spicy brown
  mustard

Combine first 9 ingredients in a large bowl; stir well. Form beef mixture into a loaf, and place in a 9- x 5- x 3-inch loafpan.

Combine ½ cup catsup, brown sugar, 1 tablespoon horseradish, and mustard in a small bowl, stirring well. Spoon half of catsup mixture over top of meat loaf. Bake, uncovered, at 375° for 45 minutes. Spoon remaining catsup mixture over meat loaf, and bake an additional 10 minutes. Remove to a serving platter. Yield: 8 servings.   Maxine Johnston Scholtz

Pride of Gaithersburg
Gaithersburg Lioness Club
Gaithersburg, Maryland

Dutch East Indies Meatballs

1 (20-ounce) can pineapple
  chunks in heavy syrup,
  undrained
1 pound ground round
½ cup fine, dry breadcrumbs
½ cup milk
1 large egg, lightly beaten
2 tablespoons chopped onion
1 teaspoon chopped fresh
  parsley

2 tablespoons butter or
  margarine, melted
2 tablespoons vegetable oil
⅛ teaspoon curry powder
⅓ cup white vinegar
¼ cup sugar
1 tablespoon cornstarch
1 tablespoon soy sauce

Drain pineapple chunks, reserving ½ cup syrup; set aside.

Combine ground round and next 5 ingredients. Shape mixture into 16 meatballs, inserting a pineapple chunk into center of each meatball. Set any remaining pineapple chunks aside.

Combine butter, oil, and curry powder in a large skillet. Brown meatballs in butter mixture over medium heat. Drain meatballs, discarding drippings. Set aside, and keep warm.

Combine reserved pineapple syrup, vinegar, sugar, cornstarch, and soy sauce in a saucepan; stir well. Add pineapple chunks; cook over medium heat, stirring constantly, until thickened and bubbly. Serve meatballs with sauce. Yield: 6 servings.   Carolyn Bale

Landon Legends: Memories and Recipes
Landon School
Potomac, Maryland

Sauerbraten Meatballs

These meatballs borrow their sweet-sour flavor from sauerbraten—a German specialty of marinated beef roast with a gingersnap-thickened sauce.

1 pound lean ground beef
⅓ cup fine, dry breadcrumbs
¼ cup finely chopped onion
1 large egg, lightly beaten
2 tablespoons peeled, grated
  Granny Smith apple
2 tablespoons Burgundy or
  other dry red wine
½ teaspoon salt

¼ teaspoon pepper
¼ teaspoon ground cloves
3 tablespoons vegetable oil
1¼ cups apple juice or apple
  cider
1 (8-ounce) can tomato sauce
3 tablespoons red wine vinegar
6 gingersnaps, crushed

Combine first 9 ingredients in a large bowl; stir well. Shape mixture into 1½-inch meatballs. Brown meatballs in oil in a large skillet over medium heat. Drain meatballs, discarding drippings. Set meatballs aside, and keep warm.

Add apple juice, tomato sauce, and vinegar to skillet; bring to a boil over medium heat, stirring frequently. Add reserved meatballs; cover, reduce heat, and simmer 10 minutes or until meatballs are done. Add gingersnaps, and cook until mixture is thickened, stirring frequently. Yield: 6 servings.   Phyllis Koob

German Heritage Recipes
American/Schleswig-Holstein Heritage Society
Davenport, Iowa

Unstuffed Cabbage

Looking for a quick and easy alternative to individually stuffing cabbage leaves with ground beef? Try this streamlined ground beef and cabbage dish.

1 small cabbage (about 2
  pounds)
1 (28-ounce) can whole
  tomatoes, undrained and
  coarsely chopped
1 pound ground beef
¼ cup diced onion

½ cup long-grain rice, uncooked
1 (8-ounce) can tomato sauce
⅓ cup firmly packed light
  brown sugar
¼ cup cider vinegar
¼ cup lemon juice
½ teaspoon salt

Discard any tough outer leaves from cabbage. Coarsely shred cabbage, and place in a large Dutch oven. Add tomatoes; cover and cook over medium heat 25 minutes.

Brown beef and onion in a skillet over medium heat, stirring until meat crumbles. Drain; add to cabbage mixture. Stir in rice. Combine tomato sauce and remaining ingredients; pour over cabbage mixture. Bring to a boil; cover, reduce heat, and simmer 35 to 40 minutes or until rice is tender. Yield: 6 servings.   Al Pimentel

Tiger Favorites
American School for the Deaf Alumni Association
West Hartford, Connecticut

Moroccan Peppers

8 large green peppers
2 medium onions, chopped
1 clove garlic, minced
3 tablespoons olive oil
2 pounds ground beef
2 cooking apples, peeled and
  chopped
1 (16-ounce) can whole
  tomatoes, undrained and
  chopped

1 (3-ounce) jar pimiento-stuffed
  olives, drained and chopped
½ cup raisins
¼ cup pine nuts or slivered
  almonds, toasted
½ teaspoon salt
⅛ teaspoon ground cumin
⅛ teaspoon ground cinnamon

Cut off tops of peppers, and remove seeds and membranes. Cook peppers in boiling water to cover in a Dutch oven 10 minutes or until tender. Drain well, and set aside.

Sauté onion and garlic in oil in a large skillet over medium heat, stirring constantly, until tender. Add ground beef, and cook until meat is browned, stirring until meat crumbles. Drain.

Combine meat mixture, apple, and next 7 ingredients. Stuff reserved peppers with meat mixture; place in a greased 13- x 9- x 2-inch baking dish. Bake, uncovered, at 350° for 25 to 30 minutes or until thoroughly heated. Yield: 8 servings.   Susan Moss

"City" Dining
City of Hope National Medical Center
and Beckman Research Institute
New York, New York

Perfect Popover Pizza

1 pound lean ground beef
1 large onion, chopped
2 cups commercial spaghetti
  sauce with mushrooms
⅓ cup Chablis or other dry
  white wine
2 cups (8 ounces) shredded
  mozzarella cheese

1 cup milk
2 large eggs
1 tablespoon vegetable oil
1 cup all-purpose flour
½ cup grated Parmesan cheese

Brown ground beef and onion in a large skillet over medium heat, stirring until meat crumbles. Drain meat mixture, discarding drippings; return meat mixture to skillet. Add spaghetti sauce and wine; cook, uncovered, over low heat 8 minutes, stirring occasionally. Spoon into a lightly greased 13- x 9- x 2-inch baking dish. Sprinkle with mozzarella cheese, and set aside.

Combine milk, eggs, and oil in a medium bowl, beating with a wire whisk until blended. Gradually add flour, beating until smooth. Pour batter over ground beef mixture in baking dish; sprinkle with Parmesan cheese. Bake, uncovered, at 400° for 30 minutes or until puffed and golden. Cut into squares, and serve immediately. Yield: 6 servings.   Ruth Jordan

The Flavor of Mathews
The Mathews County Junior and Senior Woman's Club
Mathews, Virginia

Veal with Whole-Grain Mustard and Honey

2 tablespoons low-sodium
  teriyaki sauce
1 tablespoon coarse-grained
  mustard
1 tablespoon honey

1 teaspoon freshly ground
  pepper
8 (3-ounce) boneless veal loin
  chops
1 teaspoon vegetable oil

Combine first 4 ingredients in a small bowl, stirring well. Place veal chops in a large shallow dish. Pour marinade mixture over veal chops; cover and marinate in refrigerator 1 hour.

Remove veal chops from marinade, reserving marinade. Lightly brush veal chops with oil. Grill, covered, over medium-hot coals (350° to 400°) 3 to 4 minutes on each side or to desired degree of doneness, basting occasionally with reserved marinade. Yield: 4 servings.   James E. Griffin

Rhode Island Cooks
American Cancer Society, Rhode Island Division
Pawtucket, Rhode Island

Veal Française

1½ pounds veal cutlets	¼ cup Chablis or other dry
½ teaspoon salt	white wine
¼ teaspoon pepper	¼ cup butter or margarine,
1 to 1½ cups all-purpose flour	melted
1 to 2 large eggs, beaten	2 tablespoons lemon juice
½ cup butter or margarine,	1 tablespoon chopped fresh
melted	parsley
1 cup whipping cream	Garnish: lemon slices
½ cup chicken broth	

Place veal between 2 sheets of wax paper; flatten to ¼-inch thickness, using a meat mallet or rolling pin. Sprinkle with salt and pepper, and dredge in flour. Dip veal in beaten egg, and dredge again in flour.

Brown veal in ½ cup butter in a large skillet over medium-high heat 2 to 3 minutes on each side. Remove veal, reserving drippings in skillet; set aside, and keep warm.

Add whipping cream and next 4 ingredients to skillet; stir well. Bring just to a boil over medium heat, stirring occasionally. Return reserved veal to skillet; reduce heat, and simmer, uncovered, 5 minutes. Remove veal mixture to a serving platter. Sprinkle with chopped parsley. Garnish, if desired. Serve immediately. Yield: 6 servings.   Lucille Ricci

Angels & Friends Favorite Recipes II
Angels of Easter Seal
Youngstown, Ohio

Painter's Veal

To cut down on cleanup, wipe the skillet used for browning the veal cutlets with paper towels to remove the pan drippings, and then use the same skillet to sauté the vegetables.

6 (4-ounce) veal cutlets
2 tablespoons all-purpose flour
¼ cup vegetable oil
Paprika
2 cups sliced fresh mushrooms
2 medium onions, cut into
  ¼-inch-thick slices
3 tablespoons butter or
  margarine, melted

2 cups beef broth
½ cup Burgundy or other dry
  red wine
3 tablespoons chopped fresh
  chives
3 tablespoons chopped fresh
  parsley
¼ teaspoon pepper

Place veal between 2 sheets of wax paper; flatten to ¼-inch thickness, using a meat mallet or rolling pin. Cut veal into 1-inch pieces. Dredge veal in flour.

Brown veal in oil in a large skillet over medium heat; drain well. Place in a lightly greased 11- x 7- x 1½-inch baking dish. Sprinkle with paprika. Set aside.

Sauté mushrooms and onion in butter in a large skillet over medium heat, stirring constantly, until vegetables are tender. Add beef broth and remaining ingredients; stir well. Bring to a boil; cover, reduce heat, and simmer 3 to 5 minutes. Pour mushroom mixture over reserved veal. Cover and bake at 350° for 30 minutes. Yield: 4 servings.

Mark Hatton

YUMMM . . . Delicious & Fun Recipes
The YWCA of Ridgewood Children's Educational Services
Ridgewood, New Jersey

Stuffed Crown Roast of Lamb

1 (4- to 5-pound) crown roast
  of lamb
2 cloves garlic, slivered
1½ tablespoons fresh lemon
  juice
2 tablespoons salt, divided
½ teaspoon pepper
1 small eggplant (about
  1 pound)
3 tablespoons vegetable oil
  or olive oil, divided
½ cup minced onion
1 stalk celery, minced

1 pound lean ground lamb
1½ cups cooked long-grain
  rice or orzo
½ cup pine nuts, toasted
¼ cup raisins
¼ cup minced fresh parsley
8 kalamata olives, pitted and
  chopped
1 teaspoon grated lemon rind
¼ teaspoon ground cardamom
¼ teaspoon ground cinnamon
Salt and pepper to taste
Pitted kalamata olives

Make lengthwise slits through roast in several places with a sharp knife. Insert a sliver of garlic into each slit. Brush roast with lemon juice, and rub with 1 tablespoon salt and ½ teaspoon pepper. Place roast, bone ends up, in a shallow roasting pan lined with heavy-duty aluminum foil. Insert meat thermometer, making sure it does not touch fat or bone. Set aside.

Peel eggplant; cut into 1-inch cubes. Sprinkle with remaining 1 tablespoon salt, and let stand 15 minutes. Rinse eggplant, and pat dry with paper towels. Sauté eggplant in 2 tablespoons oil in a large skillet over medium-high heat, stirring constantly, until tender. Remove eggplant from skillet; set aside.

Sauté onion and celery in remaining 1 tablespoon oil in skillet over medium-high heat, stirring constantly, until tender. Add ground lamb, and cook until meat is browned, stirring until it crumbles; drain. Add reserved eggplant, rice, and next 7 ingredients to meat mixture. Add salt and pepper to taste; stir well. Spoon mixture into center of roast. Cover stuffing and exposed ends of ribs with aluminum foil. Bake at 350° for 1 hour and 15 minutes. Remove foil from stuffing; bake an additional 15 minutes or until meat thermometer registers 160° (medium). Remove foil; let stand 10 minutes. Transfer to a platter. Place pitted olives on exposed ends of ribs. Yield: 8 servings.   Korona Arniou Gemisti

The Complete Book of Greek Cooking
Recipe Club of St. Paul's Greek Orthodox Cathedral
Hempstead, New York

Peppercorn-Crusted Roast Lamb

Three types of peppercorns—white, green, and black—form the distinctive coating on this roasted leg of lamb. The black peppercorn is the strongest flavored of the three.

1 (6-pound) leg of lamb, boned and butterflied	½ cup Burgundy or other dry red wine
1 tablespoon white peppercorns, crushed	½ cup raspberry vinegar
1 tablespoon green peppercorns, crushed	¼ cup soy sauce
	8 cloves garlic, crushed
1 tablespoon black peppercorns, crushed	1 tablespoon chopped fresh rosemary
½ cup fresh mint leaves	2 tablespoons Dijon mustard

Place lamb in a large shallow dish. Combine crushed peppercorns in a small bowl; stir well. Reserve 2 tablespoons crushed peppercorn mixture. Combine remaining crushed peppercorn mixture, mint leaves, and next 5 ingredients; stir well. Pour marinade mixture over lamb. Cover and marinate in refrigerator 8 hours, turning occasionally.

Remove lamb from marinade, reserving marinade. Roll lamb, tying securely with heavy string at 2-inch intervals. Coat lamb with mustard; lightly pat reserved peppercorn mixture into mustard. Place lamb in a shallow roasting pan; pour reserved marinade around lamb. Insert meat thermometer into thickest part of lamb. Bake at 350° for 2 hours and 15 minutes or until meat thermometer registers 160° (medium), basting occasionally with pan juices. Let stand 20 minutes before slicing. Serve with pan juices. Yield: 6 to 8 servings.

The Pasquotank Plate
Christ Episcopal Churchwomen
Elizabeth City, North Carolina

Ginger-Thyme Pork Roast

1 tablespoon chopped fresh
  thyme
2½ teaspoons salt
1 teaspoon pepper
3 cloves garlic, divided
2 bay leaves, divided
¼ teaspoon ground ginger
1 (3- to 4-pound) rolled
  boneless pork loin roast
3 tablespoons vegetable oil
2 tablespoons butter or
  margarine
1 large onion, thinly sliced
1 large carrot, scraped and
  thinly sliced
4 fresh thyme sprigs
1 cup Chablis or other dry
  white wine
1 cup chicken broth
4 gingersnaps, crushed
¾ teaspoon ground ginger
¼ cup whipping cream
1 tablespoon minced fresh
  thyme
Garnish: fresh thyme sprigs

Position knife blade in food processor bowl; add chopped thyme, salt, pepper, 1 clove garlic, 1 bay leaf, and ¼ teaspoon ginger. Cover and pulse 5 times or until thyme is finely chopped.

Remove strings from roast. Rub roast with herb mixture. Place roast in a large heavy-duty, zip-top plastic bag. Seal bag securely. Place in a large bowl. Chill at least 8 hours.

Reroll roast, tying securely with heavy string at 2-inch intervals. Brown roast in oil in a large ovenproof Dutch oven over medium heat. Remove roast, discarding pan drippings. Set roast aside, and keep warm.

Wipe pan with paper towels. Melt butter in pan over medium heat. Add remaining 2 cloves garlic, remaining bay leaf, onion, carrot, and 4 thyme sprigs; cook, stirring constantly, 5 minutes. Return reserved roast to pan; insert meat thermometer into thickest part of roast. Cover and bake at 325° for 1 hour and 45 minutes or until meat thermometer registers 160° (medium).

Combine wine, broth, gingersnaps, and ¾ teaspoon ginger in a medium saucepan; cook over medium heat, stirring constantly, 8 minutes. Add whipping cream, and cook, stirring constantly, 8 minutes. Pour mixture through a wire-mesh strainer into a bowl; stir in minced thyme. Slice roast, and arrange on a serving platter. Garnish, if desired. Serve roast with warm sauce. Yield: 8 to 10 servings.

From Portland's Palate
The Junior League of Portland, Oregon

Pacific Rim Tenderloin

You can marinate the pork tenderloins in a large shallow dish if you don't have a zip-top plastic bag, but the bag is more convenient and makes cleanup a breeze.

4 (8-ounce) pork tenderloins
¼ cup soy sauce
2 tablespoons light brown
  sugar
2 tablespoons peanut oil
2 tablespoons dry sherry
1 tablespoon honey
1 teaspoon garlic salt
1 teaspoon ground cinnamon
½ cup firmly packed light
  brown sugar

½ cup pineapple juice
⅓ cup cider vinegar
¼ cup catsup
½ teaspoon garlic powder
2 tablespoons cornstarch
⅓ cup cold water
1 cup unsalted dry roasted
  peanuts, chopped

Place tenderloins in a large heavy-duty, zip-top plastic bag. Combine soy sauce and next 6 ingredients; stir well. Pour marinade mixture over tenderloins. Seal bag securely; place in a large bowl. Marinate in refrigerator 8 hours, turning occasionally.

Remove tenderloins from marinade, discarding marinade. Grill, covered, over medium-hot coals (350° to 400°) 20 to 30 minutes or until meat thermometer inserted in thickest part of tenderloins registers 160° (medium), turning occasionally.

Combine ½ cup brown sugar and next 4 ingredients in a small saucepan; stir well. Bring to a boil. Combine cornstarch and water, stirring until smooth. Stir cornstarch mixture into brown sugar mixture, and cook, stirring constantly, until slightly thickened.

Slice tenderloins, and place on a serving platter. Sprinkle with peanuts, and serve with warm sauce. Yield: 6 servings.

Above & Beyond Parsley
The Junior League of Kansas City, Missouri

Raspberry-Herb Pork Tenderloin

4 (8-ounce) pork tenderloins
½ cup raspberry vinegar
1 tablespoon Dijon mustard
1 tablespoon honey
2 cloves garlic, minced

½ teaspoon coarsely ground
  pepper
¼ teaspoon dried marjoram
¼ teaspoon rubbed sage
¼ teaspoon dried thyme

Place tenderloins in a large heavy-duty, zip-top plastic bag. Combine vinegar and remaining ingredients, stirring well. Pour marinade mixture over tenderloins. Seal bag securely; place in a large bowl. Marinate in refrigerator 8 hours, turning occasionally.

Remove tenderloins from marinade, reserving marinade. Grill, covered, over medium-hot coals (350° to 400°) 20 to 30 minutes or until meat thermometer inserted in thickest part of tenderloins registers 160° (medium), turning and basting frequently with reserved marinade. Yield: 6 to 8 servings.

Rogue River Rendezvous
The Junior Service League of Jackson County
Medford, Oregon

Curry-Spiced Pork Kabobs

4 (8-ounce) pork tenderloins,
  cut into 2-inch cubes
3 medium-size sweet red
  peppers, cut into 12 pieces
1 onion, cut into 6 wedges
½ cup commercial steak sauce

¼ cup vegetable oil
2 tablespoons curry powder
3 tablespoons catsup
1 teaspoon grated lemon rind
½ teaspoon salt
½ cup apple jelly, melted

Combine first 3 ingredients in a large heavy-duty, zip-top plastic bag. Combine steak sauce and next 5 ingredients; pour over tenderloin mixture. Seal bag securely; place in a bowl. Marinate in refrigerator at least 1 hour. Alternate tenderloin, pepper, and onion on six 10-inch metal skewers. Grill, covered, over medium-hot coals (350° to 400°) about 30 minutes or until done. Brush with jelly, and grill an additional minute. Yield: 6 servings.

RiverFeast: Still Celebrating Cincinnati
The Junior League of Cincinnati, Ohio

Pork Chops with Beer

2 tablespoons all-purpose flour
½ teaspoon salt
¼ teaspoon pepper
4 (1-inch-thick) rib pork chops
2 tablespoons vegetable oil

1 cup beer
1 cup beef broth
1 tablespoon prepared mustard
3 cloves garlic, crushed
½ teaspoon caraway seeds

Combine first 3 ingredients in a large heavy-duty, zip-top plastic bag; shake to mix. Add pork chops; shake well. Brown pork chops in oil in a large skillet over medium heat. Remove pork chops from skillet, discarding drippings. Set aside, and keep warm.

Combine beer, beef broth, mustard, garlic, and caraway seeds in skillet. Bring to a boil, stirring constantly. Reduce heat to medium; cook, stirring constantly, until reduced by half. Return pork chops to skillet. Cover, reduce heat, and simmer 45 minutes or until pork chops are tender, turning once. Remove pork chops to a serving platter; top with sauce. Yield: 4 servings.   Diana Noel

Country Cookbook
Our Lady's Guild of St. Christopher's Parish
Red Hook, New York

Pork Chops Calvados

Calvados, a dry apple-flavored brandy, is often used in chicken, veal, and pork dishes because the flavors complement one another well.

6 (1-inch-thick) pork loin
  chops, trimmed
¼ cup plus 2 tablespoons
  unsalted butter, melted
¾ teaspoon salt
¼ teaspoon pepper
4 cups (16 ounces) finely
  shredded Gruyère or Swiss
  cheese

3 tablespoons Dijon mustard
½ cup whipping cream,
  divided
¼ cup plus 2 tablespoons
  Calvados or other
  apple-flavored brandy
2 tablespoons chopped fresh
  parsley

Brown pork chops in melted butter in a large ovenproof skillet over medium-high heat. Sprinkle pork chops evenly with salt and pepper; cover and bake at 350° for 45 minutes.

Combine cheese, mustard, and 3 tablespoons whipping cream; spread mixture evenly over pork chops. Broil 5½ inches from heat (with electric oven door partially opened) 3 minutes or until cheese is lightly browned. Remove pork chops from skillet to a serving platter, reserving drippings in skillet. Set pork chops aside, and keep warm.

Add brandy to drippings; cook over high heat, deglazing skillet by scraping particles that cling to bottom. Reduce heat to medium-low. Add remaining ¼ cup plus 1 tablespoon whipping cream; cook, stirring constantly, 3 minutes or until slightly thickened. Pour sauce over pork chops; sprinkle with parsley. Yield: 6 servings.

Bone Appetite
San Diego Humane Society & SPCA Auxiliary
San Diego, California

Ham Balls with Mustard-Dill Sauce

1 pound ground ham
1 pound ground pork
½ cup corn flake crumbs
¼ cup finely chopped onion
2 large eggs, lightly beaten
1 teaspoon prepared mustard
⅛ teaspoon pepper
2 tablespoons butter or
  margarine

2 tablespoons all-purpose flour
1 cup milk
½ cup sour cream
1 tablespoon prepared mustard
½ teaspoon salt
¼ teaspoon dried dillweed

Combine first 7 ingredients in a bowl; stir well. Shape mixture into 24 meatballs. Place meatballs on a lightly greased rack in a roasting pan. Bake at 350° for 30 to 40 minutes or until done.

Melt butter in a heavy saucepan over low heat; add flour, stirring until smooth. Cook 1 minute, stirring constantly. Gradually add milk; cook over medium heat, stirring constantly, until mixture is thickened and bubbly. Gently stir in sour cream, mustard, salt, and dried dillweed; cook just until heated. Serve meatballs with warm sauce. Yield: 6 servings.   Anne Grisham Schultz

Recipes Worth Begging For
Friends of the Gastineau Humane Society
Juneau, Alaska

Sausage and Polenta

5½ cups water
1½ teaspoons salt
1½ cups yellow cornmeal
2 (7-ounce) jars roasted red
  peppers in oil, drained
1 medium onion, finely chopped
3 tablespoons vegetable oil,
  divided
2 teaspoons sugar

1 teaspoon salt
½ teaspoon dried oregano
¼ teaspoon dried basil
¾ pound small fresh
  mushrooms, sliced
1½ pounds hot Italian link
  sausage
¼ cup water
8 ounces Fontina cheese, sliced

Line a 13- x 9- x 2-inch baking dish with aluminum foil; set aside.

Combine 5½ cups water and 1½ teaspoons salt in a 4-quart saucepan; bring to a boil. Reduce heat to medium; gradually add cornmeal, stirring constantly with a wire whisk. Reduce heat to low; simmer, uncovered, 15 minutes or until very thick. Spread polenta evenly in prepared dish. Cover and chill 1 hour or until firm.

Place peppers in container of an electric blender; cover and process until smooth, stopping once to scrape down sides. Pour into a 4-cup liquid measuring cup; add water to make 2¼ cups.

Sauté onion in 1 tablespoon oil in a large skillet over medium-high heat, stirring constantly, until tender. Stir in reserved pepper mixture, sugar, 1 teaspoon salt, oregano, and basil. Bring to a boil; boil, stirring constantly, 1 minute. Set aside.

Sauté mushrooms in remaining 2 tablespoons oil in a skillet over medium heat, stirring constantly, until tender. Remove mushrooms from skillet; set aside. Add sausage and ¼ cup water to skillet; bring to a boil. Cover, reduce heat, and simmer 5 minutes. Uncover and cook an additional 20 minutes or until sausage is browned. Drain. Cut each sausage in half crosswise. Set aside.

Remove polenta from dish; cut into 3-inch rounds with a biscuit cutter. Spoon one-third of reserved pepper mixture into an un-greased 13- x 9- x 2-inch baking dish. Sprinkle leftover pieces of polenta around sides. Arrange rounds over pieces. Spoon reserved mushrooms and sausage into center of dish. Spoon remaining pepper mixture over mushrooms and sausage. Cover and bake at 375° for 40 to 50 minutes or until thoroughly heated. Uncover; top with cheese. Bake until cheese melts. Yield: 6 servings.

A Taste of New England
The Junior League of Worcester, Massachusetts

Pasta, Rice & Grains

You'll want to keep a good supply of pasta, rice, and grains in your pantry. These staples are equally at home on the breakfast, lunch, and dinner table.

Shrimp and Fresh Herb Linguine, page 196

Capellini with Veal and Tomatoes

1 (16-ounce) package capellini
2 slices bacon, cut into 1-inch
  pieces
1 large onion, thinly sliced
½ pound veal cutlets, cut into
  1-inch strips
2 tablespoons instant-blending
  flour
½ cup Chablis or other dry
  white wine
2 cloves garlic, minced
2 tablespoons extra virgin
  olive oil
½ teaspoon salt
½ teaspoon dried oregano
½ teaspoon dried thyme
5 medium tomatoes, cut into
  wedges
10 pitted ripe olives, cut in
  half
2 ounces prosciutto, cut into
  1-inch strips
2 tablespoons chopped fresh
  parsley

Cook pasta according to package directions; drain. Set aside, and keep warm.

Cook bacon in a large skillet over medium heat until transparent. Add onion; cook, stirring constantly, until bacon is crisp and onion is tender. Sprinkle veal with flour; add veal to skillet, and cook, stirring constantly, until veal is lightly browned. Stir in wine and next 5 ingredients. Bring to a boil; cover, reduce heat, and simmer 8 to 10 minutes or until veal is almost tender. Add tomato and olives; cover and simmer 5 to 7 minutes or until thoroughly heated. Add prosciutto; cover and let stand 2 minutes.

Serve veal mixture over reserved pasta; sprinkle with parsley. Yield: 6 servings.

Carol Monahan

Flavors of Cape Henlopen
Village Improvement Association
Rehoboth Beach, Delaware

Baked Mushroom Fettuccine

1 pound fresh mushrooms,
  sliced
¼ cup plus 2 tablespoons
  butter or margarine, melted
1 (15-ounce) carton ricotta
  cheese
½ cup grated Romano
  cheese
¾ cup milk
4 large eggs, beaten
1 (12-ounce) package
  fettuccine

Sauté mushrooms in butter in a skillet over medium-high heat, stirring constantly, until tender. Set aside. Combine cheeses, milk, and eggs; set aside.

Cook fettuccine according to package directions; drain. Combine fettuccine, mushrooms, and cheese mixture. Pour into a greased 13- x 9- x 2-inch baking dish. Cover and bake at 350° for 25 minutes or until heated. Let stand 10 minutes. Cut into squares. Serve immediately. Yield: 8 servings.   LaVerne Rains

McMahan Fire Department and Ladies Auxiliary Cookbook
McMahan Fire Department Ladies Auxiliary
Dale, Texas

River Country Pasta

Shiitake mushrooms are dark brown and have a rich, meaty flavor. You can substitute dried shiitake mushrooms for fresh, if desired. Rehydrate the dried mushrooms according to package directions.

1 (12-ounce) package
  fettuccine
2½ pounds fresh shiitake
  mushrooms
½ cup shredded or slivered
  cooked ham
¼ cup butter or margarine,
  melted

3½ cups whipping cream
¼ cup dry sherry
1¼ cups sliced green onions
½ cup chopped pecans
1 tablespoon chopped fresh
  parsley

Cook fettuccine according to package directions; drain. Set aside, and keep warm.

Slice mushrooms, discarding tough stems. Sauté mushrooms and ham in butter in a Dutch oven over medium-high heat, stirring constantly, 7 to 8 minutes or until tender. Set aside.

Combine whipping cream and sherry in a large skillet; bring to a boil. Reduce heat to medium, and cook until reduced by half (about 30 minutes). Stir in reserved mushroom mixture, green onions, pecans, and parsley. Add reserved fettuccine, and toss well. Serve immediately. Yield: 8 servings.

Above & Beyond Parsley
The Junior League of Kansas City, Missouri

Fusilli with Eggplant Sauce

Fusilli is a spaghetti-length pasta with a corkscrew shape.

1 medium eggplant, peeled
  and chopped
1 large onion, chopped
2 cloves garlic, minced
3 to 4 tablespoons olive oil
1 (28-ounce) can Italian-style
  tomatoes, undrained and
  chopped
¼ cup minced fresh flat-leaf
  parsley

½ teaspoon salt
½ teaspoon dried basil
½ teaspoon dried oregano
¼ teaspoon pepper
1 (16-ounce) package fusilli
3 to 4 tablespoons grated
  Romano cheese

Sauté eggplant, onion, and garlic in olive oil in a large skillet over medium-high heat, stirring constantly, 7 minutes or until tender. Add tomatoes and next 5 ingredients. Bring to a boil; reduce heat, and simmer, uncovered, 10 to 15 minutes, stirring frequently.

Cook fusilli according to package directions; drain. Place pasta in a large bowl. Add eggplant mixture and cheese; toss. Serve immediately. Yield: 8 servings.

Quilted Quisine
Paoli Memorial Hospital Auxiliary
Paoli, Pennsylvania

Chicken Lasagna

This Tomato Sauce also tastes great over plain cooked pasta.

3 pounds skinned and boned
  chicken breast halves
24 lasagna noodles, uncooked
Tomato Sauce
4 cups (16 ounces) shredded
  mozzarella cheese

2 cups grated Parmesan cheese
2 tablespoons chopped fresh
  parsley

Place chicken in an ungreased 13- x 9- x 2-inch baking dish. Bake at 375° for 30 to 35 minutes or until chicken is done. Let chicken cool, and coarsely chop meat. Set chicken aside.

Cook lasagna noodles according to package directions; drain well, and set aside.

Spoon ½ cup Tomato Sauce in bottom of a lightly greased 13- x 9- x 2-inch pan. Layer 4 lasagna noodles, 1½ cups chicken, 1½ cups Tomato Sauce, ¾ cup mozzarella cheese, and ⅓ cup Parmesan cheese in order listed. Repeat layers once, beginning with 4 lasagna noodles. Top with 4 lasagna noodles, 1 cup Tomato Sauce, ½ cup mozzarella cheese, ⅓ cup Parmesan cheese, and 1 tablespoon parsley. Repeat layering procedure with remaining ingredients in another lightly greased 13- x 9- x 2-inch pan. Cover and bake at 350° for 40 minutes. Uncover and bake an additional 5 minutes. Let stand 10 minutes before serving. Yield: 16 servings.

Tomato Sauce

1 cup diced onion
2 large cloves garlic, minced
¼ cup olive oil
1 (48-ounce) can crushed
 tomatoes, undrained
1 (10¾-ounce) can tomato
 puree
1 (6-ounce) can tomato paste
1 cup chopped zucchini
½ cup chopped green pepper
½ cup chopped sweet red
 pepper

2 to 3 bay leaves
2 tablespoons sugar
1 tablespoon fennel seeds
2 teaspoons dried basil
2 teaspoons dried oregano
½ teaspoon salt
½ teaspoon pepper
½ teaspoon dried crushed red
 pepper
½ cup Burgundy or other dry
 red wine
½ cup chopped fresh parsley

Sauté onion and garlic in olive oil in a large skillet over medium-high heat, stirring constantly, until tender. Add crushed tomatoes and next 13 ingredients; bring to a boil. Cover, reduce heat, and simmer 1 hour, stirring occasionally. Remove and discard bay leaves. Stir in wine and parsley. Cook until thoroughly heated. Yield: 9 cups.   Suzy Arnold

Newcomers' Favorites, International and Regional Recipes
Aiken Newcomers' Club
Aiken, South Carolina

Mushroom Lasagna

This recipe uses the expected noodles and cheese of a classic lasagna, but you'll find a difference in the sauce—it's a very rich white sauce loaded with sliced mushrooms.

1 (8-ounce) package lasagna
   noodles
1 pound sliced fresh
   mushrooms
2 cloves garlic, minced
¼ cup butter or margarine,
   melted
½ teaspoon salt
1 teaspoon lemon juice
¼ cup plus 1 tablespoon
   all-purpose flour

3 cups milk
½ cup chopped fresh parsley,
   divided
1 (15-ounce) carton ricotta
   cheese
2 cups (8 ounces) shredded
   mozzarella cheese
½ cup grated Parmesan cheese

Cook lasagna noodles according to package directions; drain well, and set aside.

Sauté mushrooms and garlic in melted butter in a large skillet over medium heat, stirring constantly, until tender. Stir in salt and lemon juice. Reduce heat to low. Add flour; cook 1 minute, stirring constantly. Gradually add milk; cook over medium heat, stirring constantly, until mixture is thickened and bubbly. Add ⅓ cup parsley, stirring well.

Spread 1 cup mushroom mixture in a lightly greased 13- x 9- x 2-inch baking dish. Layer one-third of lasagna noodles over mushroom mixture. Spread one-third of ricotta cheese evenly over lasagna noodles. Sprinkle one-third of mozzarella cheese over ricotta cheese. Spread 1 cup of mushroom mixture over mozzarella cheese. Sprinkle with one-third of Parmesan cheese. Repeat layers twice. Sprinkle with remaining parsley. Cover and bake at 350° for 30 minutes or until lasagna is hot and bubbly. Let stand 10 minutes before serving. Yield: 8 servings. Dahlia Knox

The Happy Cooker
Safeway, Inc.
Oakland, California

Vegetable-Cheese Lasagna

You won't miss the beef in this vegetable-packed lasagna.

3 cups thinly sliced fresh
    mushrooms
1 tablespoons plus 1 teaspoon
    butter or margarine, melted
1 cup chopped onion
6 cloves garlic, minced
1 tablespoon plus 1 teaspoon
    olive oil
1 (15-ounce) can tomato sauce
1 cup Italian-style tomatoes,
    drained and diced
1½ teaspoons salt, divided
1 teaspoon dried basil

1 teaspoon dried oregano
½ teaspoon pepper, divided
1 bay leaf
1 (8-ounce) package lasagna
    noodles
2 (10-ounce) packages frozen
    chopped spinach, thawed
    and drained
2 cups part-skim ricotta cheese
1 large egg, beaten
2¾ cups (11 ounces) shredded
    Monterey Jack cheese

Sauté mushrooms in butter in a large skillet over medium-high heat, stirring constantly, until tender. Remove from heat; set aside.

Sauté onion and garlic in oil in a saucepan over medium-high heat, stirring constantly, until tender. Add tomato sauce, tomatoes, ¾ teaspoon salt, basil, oregano, ¼ teaspoon pepper, and bay leaf. Bring to a boil; cover, reduce heat, and simmer 25 minutes, stirring occasionally. Remove bay leaf. Set tomato mixture aside.

Cook lasagna noodles according to package directions; drain well, and set aside.

Combine remaining ¾ teaspoon salt, remaining ¼ teaspoon pepper, spinach, ricotta cheese, and egg; stir well. Set aside.

Spread one-third of reserved tomato mixture in bottom of a lightly greased 13- x 9- x 2-inch baking dish. Layer half of lasagna noodles, half of spinach mixture, and half of mushrooms in order listed. Top with one-third tomato mixture and half of Monterey Jack cheese. Top with remaining lasagna noodles, spinach mixture, mushrooms, tomato mixture, and Monterey Jack cheese in order listed. Cover and bake at 350° for 40 minutes; uncover and bake an additional 10 minutes. Let stand 15 minutes before serving. Yield: 8 servings.

Leslie Hungerford

M.D. Anderson Volunteers Cooking for Fun
University of Texas M.D. Anderson Cancer Center
Houston, Texas

Sesame Linguine

Chili oil is made by steeping fiery dried red chile pepper pods in oil.

12 ounces linguine, uncooked
¼ cup dark sesame oil
¼ cup soy sauce
1 teaspoon chili oil

½ teaspoon minced garlic
½ cup minced watercress
Salt and pepper to taste
2 to 3 green onions, chopped

Cook pasta according to package directions; drain. Rinse pasta with cold water; drain well. Place pasta in a large bowl.

Combine sesame oil and next 3 ingredients; stir well. Stir in watercress. Pour watercress mixture over pasta, and toss gently. Add salt and pepper to taste. Cover and chill 8 hours. Sprinkle with green onions just before serving. Yield: 8 to 10 servings.

For Goodness Taste
The Junior League of Rochester, New York

Shrimp and Fresh Herb Linguine

12 ounces linguine, uncooked
1 tablespoon unsalted butter
or margarine
1 pound unpeeled medium-size
fresh shrimp
3 tablespoons olive oil
1 tablespoon unsalted butter
or margarine
⅓ cup chopped shallots
8 cloves garlic, minced

⅔ cup clam juice
½ cup Chablis or other dry
white wine
¼ cup plus 1 tablespoon
unsalted butter or margarine
½ cup chopped fresh parsley
¼ cup chopped fresh dill
1 teaspoon pepper
½ teaspoon salt

Cook linguine according to package directions; drain. Combine linguine and 1 tablespoon butter; toss. Set aside; keep warm.

Peel and devein shrimp. Sauté shrimp in olive oil in a large skillet over medium-high heat, stirring constantly, 5 minutes or until shrimp turn pink. Remove shrimp from skillet with a slotted spoon, reserving drippings in skillet; set shrimp aside.

Melt 1 tablespoon butter in skillet. Add shallot and garlic, and sauté over medium-high heat, stirring constantly, until tender. Add clam juice and wine; cook, stirring constantly, 8 minutes or until reduced by half. Reduce heat; add ¼ cup plus 1 tablespoon butter, stirring until butter melts. Stir in reserved shrimp, parsley, dill, pepper, and salt; cook until heated. Spoon shrimp mixture over reserved pasta; toss. Yield: 6 servings.　　　　　　　　Kitty Egan

Taste & Share the Goodness of Door County
St. Rosalia's Ladies Sodality of St. Rosalia's Catholic Church
Sister Bay, Wisconsin

Linguine with Scallops in Parchment

Parchment paper is a heavy, grease- and moisture-resistant paper that seals in the natural juices of foods that are cooked in it.

2½ cups whipping cream
1 cup chopped sun-dried
　tomatoes (without salt or oil)
1 large tomato, peeled,
　seeded, and chopped
2 tablespoons minced fresh
　rosemary
¼ teaspoon salt

¼ teaspoon pepper
12 ounces linguine, uncooked
½ cup unsalted butter or
　margarine
1 pound sea scallops, cut in
　half horizontally
Dried crushed red pepper to
　taste

Cut 6 (15- x 10-inch) rectangles of parchment paper; fold in half lengthwise. Trim each rectangle into a heart shape. Place parchment hearts on an ungreased baking sheet; open out flat.

Combine first 6 ingredients in a saucepan; bring to a boil. Reduce heat; cook, uncovered, 25 minutes. Set sauce aside.

Cook linguine according to package directions; drain. Place in a bowl; add butter, and toss. Add reserved sauce and scallops; toss.

Place one-sixth of linguine mixture on half of each parchment heart near the crease. Fold paper edges over to seal. Starting with rounded edges of hearts, pleat and crimp edges of parchment to make an airtight seal. Bake at 400° for 15 minutes or until bags are puffed and lightly browned. Place on serving plates. Cut an opening in the top of each packet, and fold paper back. Sprinkle with red pepper to taste. Serve immediately. Yield: 6 servings.

The Pasquotank Plate
Christ Episcopal Churchwomen
Elizabeth City, North Carolina

Timballo with Cheese Sauce

Timballo is a mixture of spaghetti, sausage, eggs, and cheese that's baked in a springform pan to create its molded appearance.

¼ cup fine, dry breadcrumbs,
  divided
1 (16-ounce) package
  spaghetti, broken in half
⅓ cup butter or margarine
2 pounds bulk pork sausage
½ pound fresh mushrooms,
  sliced
3 tablespoons finely chopped
  onion
⅓ cup sliced pimiento-stuffed
  olives (optional)

1 cup (4 ounces) shredded
  mozzarella cheese
½ cup grated Parmesan cheese
2 large eggs, beaten
2 tablespoons chopped fresh
  parsley
½ teaspoon salt
¼ teaspoon pepper
Cheese Sauce

Coat the bottom and sides of a buttered 10-inch springform pan with 3 tablespoons breadcrumbs. Set aside.

Cook spaghetti according to package directions; drain. Place in a large bowl; add butter, tossing until butter melts. Set aside.

Brown sausage in a large skillet, stirring until it crumbles. Remove sausage, reserving 2 tablespoons drippings in skillet. Set sausage aside. Sauté mushrooms and onion in drippings over medium-high heat, stirring constantly, until tender.

Combine reserved spaghetti, reserved sausage, mushroom mixture, olives, if desired, and next 6 ingredients; stir well.

Pour spaghetti mixture into prepared pan. Sprinkle with remaining 1 tablespoon breadcrumbs. Cover and bake at 375° for 45 minutes. Let stand 5 minutes. Carefully remove sides of springform pan. Serve with warm Cheese Sauce. Yield: 8 servings.

Cheese Sauce

¼ cup butter or margarine
¼ cup all-purpose flour
2 cups milk
¼ cup grated Parmesan cheese

1 tablespoon chopped fresh
  parsley
¾ teaspoon salt

Melt butter in a heavy saucepan over low heat; add flour, stirring until smooth. Cook 1 minute, stirring constantly. Gradually add milk; cook over medium heat, stirring constantly, until mixture is thickened and bubbly. Stir in Parmesan cheese, parsley, and salt. Yield: 2¼ cups.   Barbara Matzdorf

Feeding Our Flock
Cross of Christ Lutheran Church
Crown Point, Indiana

French Spaghetti

1 (16-ounce) package thin
  spaghetti
1 medium onion, chopped
2 tablespoons butter or
  margarine, melted
2 (14½-ounce) cans stewed
  tomatoes, undrained
1 teaspoon salt
1 (4½-ounce) jar sliced
  mushrooms, drained

1 (2¼-ounce) can sliced ripe
  olives, drained
3 tablespoons butter or
  margarine
3 tablespoons all-purpose flour
1 cup whipping cream
½ cup milk
¾ cup grated Parmesan cheese

Cook spaghetti according to package directions; drain well, and set aside.

Sauté onion in 2 tablespoons butter in a large skillet over medium-high heat, stirring constantly, until tender. Add tomatoes and salt; cook, uncovered, over medium heat 10 minutes, stirring occasionally. Stir in mushrooms and olives. Set aside.

Melt 3 tablespoons butter in a heavy saucepan over low heat; add flour, stirring until smooth. Cook 1 minute, stirring constantly. Gradually add whipping cream and milk; cook over medium heat, stirring constantly, until mixture is thickened and bubbly.

Place half of spaghetti in a lightly greased 13- x 9- x 2-inch baking dish. Pour half of reserved tomato mixture over spaghetti layer. Pour half of whipped cream mixture over tomato mixture, and sprinkle with half of Parmesan cheese. Repeat layers once. Cover and bake at 350° for 20 minutes. Uncover and bake an additional 10 minutes. Yield: 8 servings.   Anne Thomas

Concordia Seminary Cookbook 1992-1993
Concordia Seminary Women's Association
Clayton, Missouri

Tortellini with Tomato Vinaigrette

Sun-dried tomatoes add concentrated tomato flavor to this vinaigrette.

1 cup sun-dried tomatoes
  (without salt or oil)
½ cup red wine vinegar
1 tablespoon sugar
3 tablespoons Dijon mustard
1 teaspoon crushed garlic
½ teaspoon salt
½ teaspoon freshly ground
  pepper
½ cup olive oil
½ cup coarsely chopped fresh
  basil

4 cups water
½ teaspoon salt
18 ounces fresh tricolored
  cheese-filled tortellini,
  uncooked
1¼ cups julienne-sliced fresh
  basil, divided
1 cup diced fresh plum
  tomatoes
Salt and freshly ground pepper
  to taste
¼ cup grated Parmesan cheese

Place sun-dried tomatoes in a bowl; add boiling water to cover. Let stand 10 minutes; drain.

Position knife blade in food processor bowl; add tomatoes, vinegar, and next 5 ingredients. Cover and process 20 seconds or until smooth, stopping once to scrape down sides. With processor running, gradually pour olive oil through food chute; process 10 seconds or until smooth. Stir in chopped basil; set aside.

Bring 4 cups water and ½ teaspoon salt to a boil in a large saucepan. Add tortellini; cook, uncovered, over medium heat 5 minutes or until tender. Drain; let cool.

Combine reserved tomato mixture and tortellini in a large bowl, and toss gently. Add 1 cup julienne-sliced basil and diced tomato; stir well. Add salt and pepper to taste. Sprinkle with remaining ¼ cup julienne-sliced basil and cheese. Cover and chill thoroughly. Yield: 6 servings.

Pearl Roseman

California Kosher
Women's League of Adat Ari El Synagogue
North Hollywood, California

Risotto Bravo!

Arborio rice is traditionally used for making risotto because it has a higher starch content than most rices. It provides the creamy texture desired of this classic Italian dish.

1 cup Chablis or other dry white wine
1 (⅞-ounce) package dried porcini mushrooms
6 to 8 cups chicken broth
1½ cups chopped onion
3 tablespoons olive oil
2 cups Arborio or other short-grain rice, uncooked
2 cups shredded smoked or poached chicken
8 oil-packed sun-dried tomatoes, drained and chopped
¼ teaspoon salt
¼ teaspoon freshly ground pepper
Freshly grated Parmesan cheese

Bring wine to a boil in a small saucepan; stir in mushrooms. Remove from heat, and set aside.

Bring chicken broth to a boil in a large saucepan; cover, reduce heat to low, and keep warm.

Sauté onion in olive oil in a Dutch oven over medium heat, stirring constantly, until tender. Add rice; cook, stirring constantly, 2 minutes. Add 1 cup reserved chicken broth; cook over medium-high heat, stirring constantly, until most of the liquid is absorbed. Continue adding chicken broth, 1 cup at a time, and cook, stirring constantly, until 4 cups of chicken broth have been added and absorbed. Add reserved mushroom mixture, chicken, and tomatoes. Continue adding chicken broth, 1 cup at a time, and cook, stirring constantly, until mixture is creamy and rice is tender. (The entire process should take 30 to 35 minutes.) Stir in salt and pepper. Sprinkle with Parmesan cheese. Serve immediately. Yield: 4 to 6 servings.

Mrs. Peter Davison

Edgewood Cooks
Edgewood Auxiliary
San Francisco, California

Seafood Risotto

1 pound unpeeled medium-size fresh shrimp
7 to 8 cups chicken broth
2½ cups chopped onion, divided
¼ cup butter or margarine, melted
¾ cup extra virgin olive oil, divided
1 (1-pound) package Arborio or other short-grain rice
1 cup Chablis or other dry white wine, divided
3 cloves garlic, minced
¼ cup butter or margarine, melted
3 (6½-ounce) cans chopped clams, undrained
1 cup sliced fresh mushrooms
½ cup chopped fresh parsley
¼ teaspoon dried oregano
½ teaspoon salt
¼ teaspoon freshly ground pepper
⅓ cup freshly grated Parmesan cheese

Peel and devein shrimp; set aside.

Bring chicken broth to a boil in a large saucepan; cover, reduce heat to low, and keep warm.

Sauté 1½ cups onion in ¼ cup butter and ½ cup olive oil in a large skillet over medium-high heat, stirring constantly, until tender. Add rice and ½ cup wine; cook over medium-high heat, stirring constantly, until most of the liquid is absorbed. Add ½ cup reserved chicken broth; cook, stirring constantly, until most of the liquid is absorbed. Continue adding chicken broth, ½ cup at a time, and cook, stirring constantly, until mixture is creamy and rice is tender. Set aside, and keep warm.

Sauté remaining 1 cup onion and garlic in ¼ cup melted butter and remaining ¼ cup olive oil in a large skillet over medium-high heat, stirring constantly, until tender. Stir in remaining ½ cup wine, clams, clam liquid, and next 5 ingredients. Bring to a boil; reduce heat, and simmer, uncovered, 8 minutes. Return mixture to a boil; add reserved shrimp. Reduce heat, and simmer, uncovered, 5 minutes.

Add shrimp mixture to reserved rice mixture; cook, uncovered, over medium heat 1 to 2 minutes or until mixture is thoroughly heated. Sprinkle with Parmesan cheese. Serve immediately. Yield: 4 to 6 servings.

Sugar Snips & Asparagus Tips
Woman's Auxiliary of Infant Welfare Society of Chicago
Chicago, Illinois

Raisin and Almond Rice

⅓ cup finely chopped onion
¼ cup slivered almonds
1 tablespoon butter or
  margarine, melted
1½ cups chicken broth
1 cup long-grain rice,
  uncooked

1 tablespoon raisins
1 tablespoon golden raisins
¼ teaspoon salt
⅛ teaspoon freshly ground
  pepper

Sauté onion and almonds in butter in a medium saucepan over medium-high heat, stirring constantly, until onion is tender and almonds are lightly browned. Stir in chicken broth and remaining ingredients; bring to a boil. Cover, reduce heat, and simmer 20 minutes or until rice is tender and liquid is absorbed. Yield: 4 to 6 servings.   Victoria Majoras

Five Star Sensations
Auxiliary of University Hospitals of Cleveland
Shaker Heights, Ohio

Cashew Rice Pilaf

⅓ cup finely chopped onion
¼ cup butter or margarine,
  melted
2 cups chicken broth
1 cup long-grain rice,
  uncooked

½ teaspoon salt
½ cup chopped cashews
¼ cup chopped fresh parsley

Sauté onion in butter in a large skillet over medium-high heat, stirring constantly, until tender. Add chicken broth, rice, and salt; bring to a boil. Cover, reduce heat, and simmer 25 minutes or until rice is tender and liquid is absorbed. Remove from heat, and stir in cashews and parsley. Yield: 6 servings.

Fiddlers Canyon Ward Cookbook
Fiddlers Canyon Ward Relief Society
Cedar City, Utah

Sesame Fried Rice

Fried rice offers a clever way to use leftover meat. You can substitute diced cooked pork, beef, or ham for the chicken in this recipe.

2 cups diced cooked chicken
2 tablespoons vegetable oil
1 cup long-grain rice, uncooked
1 (14½-ounce) can ready-to-serve chicken broth

½ cup water
¼ cup soy sauce
¼ cup sesame seeds, toasted
4 green onions, sliced

Sauté chicken in oil in a large skillet over medium-high heat, stirring constantly, until lightly browned. Reduce heat to medium-low; add rice, and sauté, stirring constantly, until rice is golden. Add chicken broth, water, soy sauce, and sesame seeds; stir well. Bring to a boil; cover, reduce heat, and simmer 20 to 25 minutes or until rice is tender and liquid is absorbed. Remove from heat, and stir in green onions. Yield: 6 to 8 servings.

Food for Thought: "A Seasoned Celebration"
Unitarian-Universalist Fellowship of Athens
Athens, Georgia

Spicy Chick-Peas and Rice

The natural tan color of brown rice comes from the bran layers that remain on the grain after processing.

1 medium onion, chopped
1 clove garlic, minced
2 tablespoons olive oil
2 cups cooked long-grain brown rice
1 (16-ounce) can chick-peas (garbanzo beans), drained
½ cup water

2 tablespoons chopped fresh parsley
½ teaspoon salt
½ teaspoon dried basil
½ teaspoon dried marjoram
¼ teaspoon ground cumin
¼ teaspoon ground turmeric
⅛ teaspoon freshly ground pepper

Sauté onion and garlic in oil in a large skillet over medium-high heat, stirring constantly, until tender. Stir in rice and remaining ingredients. Cover, reduce heat, and simmer 15 to 20 minutes, stirring occasionally. Yield: 6 to 8 servings.   Susan Joseph

A Jewish Family Cookbook
Valley Beth Shalom Nursery School
Encino, California

Apricots and Wild Rice

Wild rice is actually the nutty-flavored seed of a long-grain marsh grass. It's expensive, and so is often used in combination with grains like the pearl barley in this recipe.

¾ cup wild rice, uncooked
3 cups chicken broth
½ cup pearl barley, uncooked
½ cup chopped dried apricots

¼ cup currants
1 tablespoon butter or
 margarine
⅓ cup sliced almonds, toasted

Combine wild rice and chicken broth in a medium saucepan. Bring to a boil; cover, reduce heat, and simmer 10 minutes. Remove from heat; stir in barley, apricots, currants, and butter.

Pour mixture into an ungreased 1½-quart casserole. Cover and bake at 325° for 30 minutes. Uncover and stir mixture gently. Cover and bake an additional 30 minutes or until rice and barley are tender and liquid is absorbed. Gently stir in almonds. Yield: 6 servings.

Still Gathering: A Centennial Celebration
Auxiliary to the American Osteopathic Association
Chicago, Illinois

Chippewa Wild Rice

3 cups water
1 teaspoon salt
1 cup wild rice, uncooked
4 slices bacon, cut into very
  thin strips
6 large eggs, beaten

½ teaspoon salt
¼ teaspoon pepper
⅓ cup butter or margarine,
  melted
2 tablespoons minced fresh
  chives

Bring water and 1 teaspoon salt to a boil in a medium saucepan; stir in wild rice. Cover, reduce heat, and simmer 50 to 60 minutes or until rice is tender and liquid is absorbed. Set aside; keep warm.

Cook bacon in a large skillet until crisp; remove bacon, reserving drippings. Set bacon and drippings aside.

Return 1 tablespoon drippings to skillet. Combine eggs, ½ teaspoon salt, and pepper; pour egg mixture into skillet. Cook over medium heat 8 minutes or until almost set and bottom is lightly browned. Gently flip, and cook until bottom is lightly browned. Remove from skillet; cut into very thin strips.

Combine reserved rice, reserved bacon, remaining reserved bacon drippings, egg strips, butter, and chives; toss gently. Serve immediately. Yield: 4 servings.

Gourmet Wonders of the World
Sixth Grade Class of Savage Elementary School
Savage, Montana

Pecan-Wild Rice Pilaf

3 cups chicken broth
1 cup wild rice, uncooked
3⅓ cups water
1¾ cups wheat pilaf, uncooked
1 cup chopped pecans
1 cup currants
¾ cup thinly sliced green
  onions

½ cup chopped fresh mint
½ cup chopped fresh parsley
2 tablespoons grated orange
  rind
1 tablespoon orange juice
2 tablespoons olive oil
¼ teaspoon freshly ground
  pepper

Bring chicken broth to a boil in a medium saucepan; stir in rice. Cover, reduce heat, and simmer 50 to 60 minutes or until rice is tender and liquid is absorbed. Set aside, and keep warm.

Bring water to a boil in a medium saucepan; stir in wheat pilaf. Cover, reduce heat, and simmer 15 minutes or until wheat pilaf is tender and liquid is absorbed.

Combine reserved wild rice, wheat pilaf, pecans, and remaining ingredients in a large bowl; stir well. Serve warm or at room temperature. Yield: 12 servings.   Camilla Turner

Cooking with Class, A Second Helping
Charlotte Latin School
Charlotte, North Carolina

Wheat and Barley Bowl

Wheat kernels that have been steamed, dried, and then crushed are called bulgur. When cooked, bulgur has a tender yet chewy texture. Here it's teamed with another hardy grain, barley, for a wholesome side-dish combination.

¾ cup barley, uncooked
3 tablespoons butter or
  margarine, melted
3 cups water
2 teaspoons beef-flavored
  bouillon granules
½ teaspoon salt
¼ teaspoon pepper
¼ cup bulgur wheat, uncooked

2 cups shredded fresh spinach
  leaves
1 large tomato, cut into
  wedges
½ cup sliced green onions
¼ cup minced fresh parsley
1 tablespoon lemon juice
¼ cup unsalted sunflower
  kernels

Sauté barley in butter in a large skillet over medium-high heat, stirring constantly, 5 to 10 minutes or until lightly browned. Add water and next 3 ingredients; bring to a boil. Cover, reduce heat, and simmer 40 minutes. Stir in bulgur wheat; cover and simmer 15 minutes. Add spinach, tomato, green onions, parsley, and lemon juice; cook just until thoroughly heated. Sprinkle with sunflower kernels. Serve immediately. Yield: 8 to 10 servings.

Celebrate!
The Junior League of Sacramento, California

Couscous with Peas and Mint

Couscous is a quick-cooking grain product made from ground semolina.

1½ cups chicken broth
2 tablespoons butter or
  margarine
1 (10-ounce) package frozen
  English peas
1 cup couscous, uncooked

2 tablespoons minced fresh
  mint
½ teaspoon salt
¼ teaspoon freshly ground
  pepper

Combine broth and butter in a medium saucepan; bring to a boil. Add peas and couscous; stir well. Return to a boil, stirring occasionally. Cover, remove from heat, and let stand 5 minutes or until liquid is absorbed. Stir in mint, salt, and pepper. Serve immediately. Yield: 4 servings.

Culinary Arts, Volume II
Society of the Arts of Allentown Art Museum
Allentown, Pennsylvania

Danse Macabre Deviled Grits

12 slices bacon
3 cups water
1 teaspoon salt
1 cup quick-cooking grits,
  uncooked

1 teaspoon grated orange rind
1 cup orange juice
¼ cup butter or margarine
4 large eggs, lightly beaten
2 tablespoons brown sugar

Partially cook bacon in a large skillet until almost crisp; set aside.
Combine water and salt in a medium saucepan; bring to a boil. Slowly stir in grits; cook, stirring constantly, 3 minutes. Remove from heat. Add orange rind and next 3 ingredients; stir well. Pour grits mixture into a lightly greased 10- x 6- x 2-inch baking dish.
Top with reserved bacon, and sprinkle with brown sugar. Bake, uncovered, at 350° for 40 to 45 minutes or until a knife inserted in center comes out clean. Yield: 6 servings.   Linda Thompson

Rhapsody of Recipes
Chattanooga Symphony Youth Orchestra
Chattanooga, Tennessee

Pies & Pastries

*There's nothing quite as American as apple pie,
but don't miss the rich nut pies, refreshing frozen pies, delicate
tarts, and flaky strudel also in this chapter.*

Festive Cranberry-Mince Pie, page 212

New-Fashioned Apple Pie

The best apples for cooking include Granny Smith, Jonathan, Winesap, and Rome Beauty. They retain their texture and flavor better than apple varieties recommended for eating like Red Delicious.

½ cup raisins
3 tablespoons Grand Marnier or other orange-flavored liqueur
Pastry for double-crust 9-inch pie
¼ cup plus 2 tablespoons sugar
¼ cup plus 2 tablespoons firmly packed brown sugar
1 tablespoon cornstarch
1 tablespoon lemon juice
1 teaspoon ground cinnamon
6 cups peeled, sliced cooking apples
3 tablespoons butter or margarine
1 egg yolk, beaten
2 tablespoons water

Combine raisins and Grand Marnier in a small bowl; let stand 5 minutes.

Roll half of pastry to ⅛-inch thickness on a lightly floured surface. Place in a 9-inch pieplate; set aside.

Combine sugars, cornstarch, lemon juice, and cinnamon in a large bowl; stir well. Add apple slices, and toss well to coat. Stir in reserved raisin mixture. Spoon apple mixture into pastry shell. Dot with butter.

Roll remaining pastry to ⅛-inch thickness; transfer to top of pie. Trim off excess pastry along edges. Fold edges under, and crimp. Cut slits in top to allow steam to escape. Combine egg yolk and water; brush over pastry. Bake at 450° for 15 minutes. Reduce oven temperature to 350°, and bake an additional 35 minutes. Cool on a wire rack. Yield: one 9-inch pie.

New England Pioneer Pantry
The Merrimack Valley Future Pioneers
North Andover, Massachusetts

Apples and Cream Crumb Pie

1 cup sugar
¼ cup all-purpose flour
1½ cups sour cream
1 large egg, lightly beaten
2 teaspoons vanilla extract
½ teaspoon salt

3 pounds cooking apples,
  peeled and cut into thin
  wedges
Cinnamon Pastry Shell
Streusel Topping

Combine first 6 ingredients; stir in apple. Spoon into pastry shell. Cover edges of pastry with strips of aluminum foil to prevent excessive browning. Bake at 450° for 15 minutes. Reduce oven temperature to 350°; bake 50 minutes. Remove foil; stir filling. Spoon topping over filling. Bake 20 to 25 minutes or until apples are tender. Serve warm. Yield: one 10-inch pie.

Cinnamon Pastry Shell

1¾ cups all-purpose flour
¼ cup sugar
1 teaspoon ground cinnamon

½ teaspoon salt
⅔ cup butter or margarine
3 to 4 tablespoons cold water

Combine first 4 ingredients; cut in butter with pastry blender until mixture is crumbly. Sprinkle cold water (1 tablespoon at a time) evenly over surface; stir with a fork until dry ingredients are moistened. Shape into a ball. Roll into a 12-inch circle on a floured surface. Place in a 10-inch pieplate; trim off excess along edges. Fold edges under; crimp. Yield: one 10-inch pastry shell.

Streusel Topping

½ cup all-purpose flour
⅓ cup sugar
⅓ cup firmly packed brown
  sugar

1 tablespoon ground cinnamon
¼ teaspoon salt
½ cup butter or margarine
1 cup coarsely chopped walnuts

Combine first 5 ingredients; cut in butter with pastry blender until mixture is crumbly. Stir in walnuts. Yield: 1¾ cups.

The Best of Sunset Boulevard
University Synagogue Sisterhood
Los Angeles, California

Caramel Crunch Apple Pie

28 caramels (about 8 ounces)   ¾ cup all-purpose flour
2 tablespoons water   ⅓ cup sugar
4 medium-size cooking apples,   ½ teaspoon ground cinnamon
  peeled and thinly sliced   ⅓ cup butter or margarine
1 unbaked 9-inch pastry shell   ½ cup chopped walnuts

Combine caramels and water in top of a double boiler; bring water in bottom to a boil. Reduce heat to low; cook until caramels melt, stirring occasionally.

Arrange half of apple slices in pastry shell; drizzle with half of melted caramel. Top with remaining apple slices, and drizzle with remaining melted caramel.

Combine flour, sugar, and cinnamon; cut in butter with pastry blender until mixture is crumbly. Stir in walnuts, and sprinkle over apple mixture. Bake at 375° for 40 to 45 minutes or until lightly browned. (Cover edges of pastry with strips of aluminum foil to prevent excessive browning after 30 minutes, if necessary.) Serve warm. Yield: one 9-inch pie.   Jill Harding

Family Style Cookbook
Northern Door Child Care Center
Sister Bay, Wisconsin

Festive Cranberry-Mince Pie

If you prefer, you can make this pie with a decorative lattice crust.

Pastry for double-crust 9-inch   1 (27-ounce) jar mincemeat
  pie   1 to 2 teaspoons grated orange
⅔ cup sugar   rind
2 tablespoons cornstarch   1 egg yolk, beaten
⅔ cup cold water   2 tablespoons water
1½ cups fresh cranberries

Roll half of pastry to ⅛-inch thickness on a lightly floured surface. Place in a 9-inch pieplate; set aside.

Combine sugar and cornstarch in a medium saucepan; stir well. Add ⅔ cup water, stirring well. Cook over medium heat, stirring constantly, until mixture is thickened and bubbly. Add cranberries.

Bring to a boil; reduce heat, and simmer, uncovered, 5 to 10 minutes or until cranberry skins pop, stirring frequently. Set aside, and let cool.

Combine mincemeat and orange rind; spoon into pastry shell. Top with reserved cranberry mixture.

Roll remaining half of pastry to ⅛-inch thickness; transfer to top of pie. Trim off excess pastry along edges. Fold edges under, and crimp. Cut slits in top to allow steam to escape. Combine egg yolk and 2 tablespoons water; brush over pastry. Bake at 425° for 30 minutes or until golden. Cool on a wire rack. Yield: one 9-inch pie.

The Tasty Palette Cookbook
South County Art Association
St. Louis, Missouri

Peach Praline Pie

If fresh peaches aren't available, you can substitute 2 (16-ounce) packages of frozen sliced peaches. Thaw the frozen peaches before cooking with them.

¾ cup sugar
3 tablespoons all-purpose flour
4 cups peeled, sliced fresh
  peaches
1½ tablespoons lemon juice
⅓ cup firmly packed brown
  sugar
¼ cup all-purpose flour
3 tablespoons butter or
  margarine
½ cup chopped pecans
1 unbaked 9-inch pastry shell

Combine ¾ cup sugar and 3 tablespoons flour in a large bowl. Add peaches and lemon juice; stir well, and set aside.

Combine brown sugar and ¼ cup flour in a bowl. Cut in butter with pastry blender until mixture is crumbly. Stir in pecans.

Sprinkle one-third of pecan mixture in bottom of pastry shell. Spoon reserved peach mixture evenly into pastry shell, and sprinkle with remaining pecan mixture. Bake at 400° for 40 minutes or until peaches are tender. Let pie cool on a wire rack. Yield: one 9-inch pie.   Sister Mary (Kenneth) Zirbes

Franciscan Centennial Cookbook
Franciscan Sisters
Little Falls, Minnesota

Fresh Pineapple Pie

Pastry for double-crust 9-inch
  pie
2 large eggs, beaten
1½ cups sugar
2 tablespoons all-purpose flour
1 tablespoon grated lemon rind
1 tablespoon lemon juice
⅛ teaspoon salt
3 cups coarsely chopped fresh
  pineapple

Roll half of pastry to ⅛-inch thickness on a lightly floured surface. Place in a 9-inch pieplate; set aside.

Combine eggs and next 5 ingredients in a large bowl; stir well. Stir in pineapple. Pour pineapple mixture into pastry shell.

Roll remaining pastry to ⅛-inch thickness; transfer pastry to top of pie. Trim off excess pastry along edges. Fold edges under, and crimp. Cut slits in top of pastry to allow steam to escape. Bake at 425° for 45 minutes. Cover pie with aluminum foil to prevent excessive browning after 30 minutes. Cool on a wire rack. Yield: one 9-inch pie. Erma McGowan

The Taste of St. Louis
St. Louis Catholic Church
Miami, Florida

Green Tomato Pie

Pastry for double-crust 9-inch
  pie
1¾ pounds green tomatoes,
  thinly sliced
1¼ cups sugar
3 tablespoons all-purpose flour
¼ teaspoon salt
¼ teaspoon ground nutmeg
Dash of ground cloves
1 tablespoon plus 1 teaspoon
  grated lemon rind
3 tablespoons fresh lemon
  juice
2 tablespoons water
2 tablespoons butter or
  margarine

Roll half of pastry to ⅛-inch thickness on a lightly floured surface. Place in a 9-inch pieplate; set aside.

Place green tomato slices in a shallow dish. Add boiling water to cover, and let stand 5 minutes. Drain well, and set aside.

Combine sugar, flour, salt, nutmeg, and cloves; stir well, and set aside. Combine lemon rind, lemon juice, and water in a small bowl; set aside.

Place half of reserved green tomato slices in pastry shell; sprinkle with half of reserved sugar mixture. Pour half of reserved lemon juice mixture over sugar mixture. Dot with 1 tablespoon butter. Repeat layers once.

Roll remaining half of pastry to ⅛-inch thickness; cut into ½-inch strips. Arrange pastry strips in a lattice design over green tomato mixture. Trim off excess pastry along edges. Fold edges under, and crimp. Bake at 425° for 50 minutes. Cool on a wire rack. Yield: one 9-inch pie.   Marie F. Tellier

St. Gregory the Great Parish Jubilee Cookbook
St. Gregory the Great Parish
Lebanon, Pennsylvania

Kettle Morraine Nut Pie

The American Club is an historic hotel in Kohler, Wisconsin. Immigrants who settled in that state often used nuts for flavor in their baked goods.

1 cup sugar	½ cup sliced almonds
1 cup dark corn syrup	½ cup pecan halves
4 large eggs, lightly beaten	½ cup walnut pieces
3 tablespoons cornstarch	1 unbaked 9-inch pastry shell
3 tablespoons butter or margarine, melted	

Combine first 4 ingredients in a large bowl, stirring with a wire whisk until blended. Stir in butter. Add nuts, and stir well.

Pour nut mixture into unbaked pastry shell. Bake at 350° for 50 to 55 minutes or until a knife inserted in center comes out clean. Cover edges of pastry with strips of aluminum foil to prevent excessive browning after 30 minutes. Cool on a wire rack. Yield: one 9-inch pie.   The American Club

Recipes from Historic Hotels
National Trust for Historic Preservation
Washington, DC

Macadamia Nut Pie

Hawaii is one of the largest exporters of macadamia nuts. Try them in this tropical adaptation of Southern pecan pie.

1 cup light corn syrup
¾ cup plus 2 tablespoons
  sugar
3 large eggs, lightly beaten
2 tablespoons butter or
  margarine, melted

1½ teaspoons vanilla extract
1½ cups finely chopped
  macadamia nuts
1 unbaked 9-inch pastry shell

Combine first 5 ingredients in a large bowl; stir well. Stir in macadamia nuts. Pour mixture into pastry shell. Bake at 325° for 1 hour and 5 minutes or until set. Cool on a wire rack. Yield: one 9-inch pie.

Carl Haupt

A Collection of Favorite Recipes
Po'okela Church
Makawao, Hawaii

Peanut Butter Cream Pie

This meringue-topped pie melts in your mouth. Be sure to spread the meringue while the filling is hot, and seal it to the edge of the pastry to prevent it from shrinking and weeping.

¾ cup sifted powdered sugar
⅓ cup creamy peanut butter
⅔ cup sugar
3 tablespoons cornstarch
1 tablespoon all-purpose flour
½ teaspoon salt
3 cups milk
3 egg yolks

2 tablespoons butter or
  margarine
1 teaspoon vanilla extract
1 baked 9-inch pastry shell
3 egg whites
¼ teaspoon cream of tartar
¼ cup sugar

Place powdered sugar in a small bowl; cut in peanut butter with pastry blender until mixture is crumbly. Set aside.

Combine ⅔ cup sugar and next 3 ingredients in top of a double boiler; stir well. Gradually add milk, egg yolks, butter, and vanilla, stirring well. Bring water to a boil; reduce heat to low, and cook, stirring constantly, 20 minutes or until mixture is thickened. Remove from heat.

Sprinkle two-thirds of reserved peanut butter mixture in bottom of pastry shell; top with hot custard mixture. Beat egg whites and cream of tartar at high speed of an electric mixer until foamy. Gradually add ¼ cup sugar, 1 tablespoon at a time, beating until stiff peaks form and sugar dissolves (2 to 4 minutes). Immediately spread meringue over hot filling, sealing to edge of pastry. Sprinkle remaining peanut butter mixture over meringue. Bake at 325° for 30 minutes or until golden. Cool completely on a wire rack. Yield: one 9-inch pie.   Estelle Gibbs

Home Cooking with SMRMC
Southwest Mississippi Regional Medical Center Auxiliary
McComb, Mississippi

Walnut-Rum Pie

The title of this pie leaves out one very important flavor—chocolate!

1 unbaked 9-inch pastry shell
¾ cup sugar
½ cup all-purpose flour
½ cup butter or margarine, melted
2 large eggs, beaten

1 cup semisweet chocolate morsels
1 cup coarsely chopped walnuts
2 tablespoons dark rum
Whipped cream

Prick bottom of pastry shell with a fork. Bake at 400° for 5 minutes, and set aside.

Combine sugar, flour, butter, and eggs in a medium bowl; stir well. Stir in chocolate morsels, walnuts, and rum. Pour mixture into pastry shell. Bake at 350° for 30 minutes. Cool on a wire rack. Serve with whipped cream. Yield: one 9-inch pie.

From Your Neighbor's Kitchen
Friends of Riverton Park
Riverton, New Jersey

Chocolate Chip Pie

This crustless pie resembles a big, super-thick chocolate chip cookie. Serve it with scoops of vanilla or butter pecan ice cream.

2 cups all-purpose flour
1 tablespoon baking powder
¼ teaspoon salt
1½ cups firmly packed light brown sugar
½ cup butter or margarine, melted

2 large eggs, beaten
1 tablespoon vanilla extract
1 (12-ounce) package semisweet chocolate morsels
½ cup chopped walnuts or pecans

Combine first 4 ingredients in a medium bowl. Add butter, eggs, and vanilla; stir well. Stir in chocolate morsels and walnuts. Spoon into a greased 9-inch pieplate. Bake at 350° for 35 to 40 minutes or until a knife inserted in center comes out clean. Cool on a wire rack. Yield: one 9-inch pie.   Marty Craine

The Global Gourmet
Multicultural Awareness Council of Nova University
Ft. Lauderdale, Florida

Alaskan Grapefruit Pie

32 large marshmallows
½ cup grapefruit juice, divided
1 cup whipping cream, whipped

2½ cups fresh grapefruit sections
1 baked 9-inch pastry shell
¼ cup flaked coconut, toasted

Combine marshmallows and ¼ cup grapefruit juice in a large heavy saucepan. Cook over medium-low heat, stirring frequently, until marshmallows melt. Remove from heat; let cool.

Stir remaining ¼ cup grapefruit juice into cooled marshmallow mixture. Fold in whipped cream and grapefruit sections. Pour into pastry shell. Cover and chill at least 3 hours. Sprinkle with coconut just before serving. Yield: one 9-inch pie.

Culinary Masterpieces
Birmingham Museum of Art
Birmingham, Alabama

Chocolate Truffle Pie

Traditionally, truffles are small round chocolate candies noted for their incredibly rich and creamy texture. This pie's silky smooth chocolate filling inspires this recipe title.

16 ounces semisweet chocolate morsels
½ cup butter or margarine
2 tablespoons Kahlúa or other coffee-flavored liqueur
4 large eggs
¼ cup sugar

1 teaspoon vanilla extract
⅛ teaspoon salt
¼ cup all-purpose flour
2 cups whipping cream
½ teaspoon vanilla extract
¼ cup sifted powdered sugar

Grease a 9-inch springform pan, and line with parchment paper or wax paper; grease paper. Set aside.

Combine chocolate morsels and butter in top of a double boiler; bring water to a boil. Reduce heat to low; cook until chocolate and butter melt, stirring occasionally. Remove from heat; add liqueur, beating with a wire whisk until blended. Set aside, and let cool.

Combine eggs, ¼ cup sugar, 1 teaspoon vanilla, and salt in a large mixing bowl. Beat at high speed of an electric mixer 5 minutes or until mixture triples in volume. Sprinkle flour over egg mixture, and gently fold in. Fold in reserved chocolate mixture. (Batter will decrease in volume.)

Pour batter into prepared pan. Bake at 400° for 10 to 12 minutes or until center is firm but not set. (Do not overbake.) Cool to room temperature in pan on a wire rack. Cover and chill at least 8 hours.

To serve, carefully remove sides of springform pan. Beat whipping cream and ½ teaspoon vanilla until foamy; gradually add sifted powdered sugar, beating until soft peaks form. Gently spoon whipped cream mixture into a decorator bag fitted with desired tip. Decoratively pipe whipped cream mixture on top of pie. Yield: one 9-inch pie.

Barb Millar

ACORD Cookbook I
Avonworth Municipal Authority
Pittsburgh, Pennsylvania

Magnificent Mocha Pie

The crust of this pie is actually a baked meringue that contains graham cracker crumbs, chocolate, and pecans.

1 cup sugar
1 teaspoon baking powder
5 egg whites
Dash of salt
1¼ cups graham cracker
  crumbs
4 ounces sweet baking
  chocolate, grated
⅔ cup chopped pecans,
  toasted

2 teaspoons vanilla extract,
  divided
2 teaspoons instant coffee
  granules
½ teaspoon water
1 cup whipping cream
¼ cup sifted powdered sugar
2 ounces sweet baking
  chocolate, grated

Combine 1 cup sugar and baking powder in a small bowl; stir well, and set aside.

Beat egg whites and salt at high speed of an electric mixer until foamy. Gradually add reserved sugar mixture, 1 tablespoon at a time, beating until stiff peaks form and sugar dissolves (2 to 4 minutes). Gently fold in graham cracker crumbs, 4 ounces grated chocolate, pecans, and 1 teaspoon vanilla. Spoon into a buttered 10-inch pieplate. Bake at 350° for 35 minutes or until lightly browned. Cool completely on a wire rack.

Combine remaining 1 teaspoon vanilla, coffee granules, and water, stirring until coffee granules dissolve. Combine coffee mixture, whipping cream, and powdered sugar in a large mixing bowl; cover and chill at least 2 hours.

Beat whipping cream mixture until stiff peaks form; spoon into center of pie. Spread evenly, leaving a 1-inch border around edge of pie. Sprinkle with 2 ounces grated chocolate. Cover and chill 1 hour. Yield: one 10-inch pie.

Family & Company
The Junior League of Binghamton, New York

Joanie's Mocha Crunch Angel Pie

The sugar syrup in this recipe must be cooked to the firm ball stage to cook the egg whites in this pie. A candy thermometer is a handy kitchen tool for making sure that the sugar syrup has reached the desired temperature.

1⅓ cups chocolate wafer
  crumbs
½ cup blanched almonds,
  finely chopped
⅓ cup butter or margarine,
  melted
2 tablespoons sugar
¼ teaspoon ground cinnamon
1 cup sugar

½ cup water
3 egg whites
1 tablespoon instant coffee
  granules
Dash of salt
2 cups whipping cream,
  whipped
½ cup slivered almonds
Garnish: chocolate curls

Combine first 5 ingredients; stir well. Firmly press crumb mixture in bottom and up sides of a greased 9-inch pieplate; chill.

Combine 1 cup sugar and water in a small saucepan; cook over medium heat, stirring constantly, until sugar dissolves. Bring to a boil, and cook, without stirring, until mixture reaches firm ball stage or candy thermometer registers 242°.

Beat egg whites in a large mixing bowl at high speed of an electric mixer until stiff peaks form. Pour hot sugar mixture in a very thin stream over beaten egg white while beating constantly at high speed until mixture is cool and holds its shape. Add coffee granules and salt; beat well. Fold in whipped cream and slivered almonds. Spoon mixture into prepared crust. Garnish, if desired. Cover and freeze until firm. Let stand at room temperature 10 minutes before serving. Yield: one 9-inch pie.

A Full Measure
Long Beach League for John Tracy Clinic
Long Beach, California

Frozen Cranberry Velvet Pie

Embellish the whipped cream garnish of this frozen pie by topping it with fresh cranberries or a few of the whole cranberries from the canned whole-berry cranberry sauce.

1¼ cups vanilla wafer crumbs
¼ cup plus 2 tablespoons
  butter or margarine, melted
1 cup whipping cream
¼ cup sugar
½ teaspoon vanilla extract

1 (8-ounce) package cream
  cheese, softened
1 (16-ounce) can whole-berry
  cranberry sauce
Garnish: whipped cream

Combine vanilla wafer crumbs and butter; stir well. Firmly press crumb mixture in bottom and up sides of a 9-inch pieplate; chill.

Beat 1 cup whipping cream until foamy; gradually add sugar, beating until soft peaks form. Stir in vanilla.

Beat cream cheese in a large mixing bowl at medium speed of an electric mixer until creamy. Add whipped cream mixture, and beat until smooth. Gently fold in cranberry sauce.

Spoon cranberry sauce mixture into chilled crust, spreading evenly. Cover and freeze until firm. Let pie stand at room temperature 10 minutes before serving. Garnish, if desired. Yield: one 9-inch pie.   Mary Louise Brooks

The Nineteenth Century Woman's Club Historical Centennial Cookbook
Nineteenth Century Woman's Club
Oak Park, Illinois

Apple Tart Tatin

This upside-down apple tart with a caramel topping was created by two French sisters who made their living baking the unique pastry. It takes its name from theirs—Tatin.

¾ cup sugar
3 tablespoons butter or
  margarine
5 to 6 cups peeled, thinly
  sliced Golden Delicious
  apples

1½ tablespoons lemon juice
½ teaspoon ground cinnamon
1 teaspoon vanilla extract
Dash of ground nutmeg
Pastry

Combine sugar and butter in a heavy saucepan; cook over medium heat, stirring constantly with a wooden spoon, until sugar melts and turns a light golden brown (about 13 minutes). Pour caramelized sugar into a 9-inch pieplate; set aside.

Combine apple slices and next 4 ingredients in a large bowl; toss gently. Arrange apple mixture over caramelized sugar in pieplate.

Roll Pastry to ⅛-inch thickness on a lightly floured surface. Place on top of apple mixture. Trim off excess along edges (do not seal edges). Bake at 400° for 45 minutes. (Cover edges of Pastry with strips of aluminum foil to prevent excessive browning, if necessary.) Cool 20 minutes on a wire rack. Invert tart onto a serving plate. Serve warm with ice cream. Yield: one 9-inch tart.

Pastry

1 cup all-purpose flour
1 tablespoon sugar
1 teaspoon salt

¼ cup butter or margarine
2 to 3 tablespoons shortening
2 to 3 tablespoons cold water

Combine first 3 ingredients in a medium bowl; stir well. Cut in butter and shortening with pastry blender until mixture is crumbly. Sprinkle cold water (1 tablespoon at a time) evenly over surface of dry ingredients; stir with a fork until dry ingredients are moistened. Shape pastry mixture into a ball; chill. Yield: enough pastry for one 9-inch tart.
Anne Vossenberg

From the Heart Classic Recipes
Sacred Heart Hospital Auxiliary
Bluebell, Pennsylvania

Chocolate Truffle Tart

¼ cup plus 2 tablespoons
  butter or margarine,
  softened
½ cup sugar
¾ cup all-purpose flour
⅓ cup cocoa

⅛ teaspoon salt
½ teaspoon vanilla extract
1¼ cups whipping cream
1 (12-ounce) package
  semisweet chocolate morsels
Garnish: white chocolate curls

Beat butter and sugar at medium speed of an electric mixer until creamy. Add flour, cocoa, salt, and vanilla, beating until mixture is crumbly. Firmly press mixture in bottom and 1 inch up sides of a greased 10-inch springform pan. Bake at 350° for 10 minutes. Cool completely on a wire rack.

Cook whipping cream in a medium saucepan over low heat just until whipping cream comes to a boil. Remove from heat; add chocolate morsels, stirring until mixture is smooth. Cool until slightly thickened. Pour into prepared crust. Cover and chill 2 hours or until firm. Garnish, if desired. Yield: one 10-inch tart.

A Cleveland Collection
The Junior League of Cleveland, Ohio

Pecan Lace Tart

Melted semisweet chocolate is drizzled on the top of this rich pecan tart to give it a delicate lacy appearance.

1⅓ cups all-purpose flour
1 tablespoon plus 1 teaspoon
  sugar
¼ teaspoon salt
¾ cup unsalted butter or
  margarine
3 to 4 tablespoons cold water
3 (1-ounce) squares semisweet
  chocolate, divided
1⅓ cups sugar

1 cup whipping cream
⅓ cup water
1½ teaspoons vanilla extract
1 large egg
1 egg yolk
1⅔ cups chopped pecans,
  toasted
¼ cup unsalted butter or
  margarine, melted

Combine flour, 1 tablespoon plus 1 teaspoon sugar, and salt in a medium bowl; cut in ¾ cup butter with pastry blender until mixture is crumbly. Sprinkle cold water (1 tablespoon at a time) evenly over surface; stir with a fork until dry ingredients are moistened. Shape into a ball; chill at least 1 hour.

Roll pastry into a 12-inch circle on a lightly floured surface. Fit into a buttered 11-inch tart pan with removable bottom; chill until firm. Prick bottom of pastry with a fork. Line with parchment paper; butter parchment paper, and fill with dried beans or pie weights. Bake at 375° for 8 minutes. Remove beans and parchment paper; bake an additional 16 to 18 minutes or until lightly browned. Cool completely in pan on a wire rack.

Place 2 chocolate squares in top of a double boiler; bring water to a boil. Reduce heat to low; cook until chocolate melts, stirring occasionally. Spread melted chocolate over bottom of prepared pastry. Set aside.

Combine 1⅓ cups sugar, whipping cream, and ⅓ cup water in a large heavy saucepan. Bring to a boil over medium heat, stirring constantly. Cover and cook 2 to 3 minutes to wash down sugar crystals from sides of pan. Uncover and cook until mixture reaches firm ball stage or candy thermometer registers 246°. Remove from heat; let cool 10 minutes. Stir in vanilla.

Beat egg and egg yolk with a wire whisk. Gradually stir about one-fourth of hot mixture into egg; add to remaining hot mixture, stirring constantly. Stir in pecans and ¼ cup melted butter. Pour into prepared pastry. Place tart pan on an ungreased baking sheet. Bake at 400° for 15 minutes. Reduce oven temperature to 375°, and bake an additional 10 minutes. Cool in pan on wire rack 30 minutes.

Place remaining chocolate square in top of a double boiler; bring water to a boil. Reduce heat to low; cook until chocolate melts, stirring occasionally. Remove from heat, and let cool slightly.

Spoon melted chocolate into a small zip-top plastic bag; seal bag securely. Snip a tiny hole in 1 corner of bag with scissors. Pipe melted chocolate in a decorative design on top of tart. Carefully remove tart from pan. Serve at room temperature. Yield: one 11-inch tart.

Dining Al Fresco
Wolf Trap Associates
Vienna, Virginia

Ambrosia Crumble

1½ cups shredded coconut, divided
1 cup all-purpose flour
1 cup sugar, divided
½ cup firmly packed brown sugar
½ cup unsalted butter or margarine
½ fresh pineapple, cut into 1-inch cubes (about 2 cups)
3 large navel oranges, peeled and sectioned
3 large bananas, cut into ½-inch-thick slices
2 tablespoons fresh lemon juice

Combine 1 cup coconut, flour, ¾ cup sugar, and brown sugar; cut in butter with pastry blender until mixture is crumbly. Set aside.

Combine remaining ½ cup coconut, remaining ¼ cup sugar, pineapple, orange, banana, and lemon juice; toss well. Place fruit mixture in a buttered 13- x 9- x 2-inch baking dish; sprinkle with reserved flour mixture. Bake at 350° for 45 minutes or until golden. Serve warm with vanilla ice cream. Yield: 12 servings.

Gracious Goodness, Charleston!
Bishop England High School Endowment Fund
Charleston, South Carolina

Apple Twists

Apple Twists are tender wedges of apples wrapped in flaky strips of pastry. Serve them warm with vanilla or cinnamon ice cream.

1½ cups all-purpose flour
1 teaspoon salt
½ cup shortening
4 to 5 tablespoons cold water
4 large cooking apples
⅓ cup butter or margarine, melted
½ cup sugar
2 teaspoons ground cinnamon
1¼ cups water

Combine flour and salt; cut in shortening with pastry blender until mixture is crumbly. Sprinkle cold water (1 tablespoon at a time) evenly over surface; stir with a fork until dry ingredients are moistened. Shape into a ball; chill.

Peel and core apples; cut each apple into 8 wedges. Set aside.

Roll pastry into a 10- x 16-inch rectangle on a floured surface. Cut into 32 (10- x ½-inch) strips. Wrap 1 strip diagonally around each wedge. Arrange in a greased 13- x 9- x 2-inch pan. Brush with butter. Combine sugar and cinnamon; sprinkle over wedges. Pour water around wedges. Bake at 400° for 35 to 40 minutes or until apples are tender and pastry is lightly browned. Serve warm with ice cream. Yield: 8 servings. Norma Fletcher

First United Methodist Church Centennial Cookbook, 1993
United Methodist Women of First United Methodist Church
Casper, Wyoming

Apple-Cheddar Strudels

6 medium-size cooking apples, peeled and chopped
1 cup (4 ounces) shredded Cheddar cheese
½ cup chopped walnuts
½ cup fine, dry breadcrumbs
½ cup honey
1 teaspoon grated lemon rind
2 tablespoons fresh lemon juice
1 teaspoon ground cinnamon
Dash of salt
½ (16-ounce) package frozen phyllo pastry, thawed
½ cup butter or margarine, melted
½ cup fine, dry breadcrumbs or toasted wheat germ

Combine first 9 ingredients in a large bowl; stir well. Set aside.

Work with 1 sheet of phyllo at a time, keeping remaining sheets covered with a slightly damp towel. Layer 5 sheets of phyllo on wax paper, brushing each with butter and sprinkling with about 2½ teaspoons breadcrumbs. Spread half of apple mixture down long side of phyllo stack to within 1 inch of sides. Fold sides over mixture. Roll up phyllo, starting at long side. Repeat procedure with remaining phyllo, butter, breadcrumbs, and apple mixture.

Place strudels in an ungreased 15- x 10- x 1-inch jellyroll pan. Brush strudels with any remaining melted butter. Make diagonal slits about ¼ inch deep, 1 inch apart, across top of each strudel with a sharp knife. Bake at 375° for 35 to 40 minutes or until browned. Serve strudels warm with ice cream or whipped cream. Yield: two 14-inch strudels. Katherine Dichter

Palate Pleasers
The Women's Auxiliary of the Hebrew Rehabilitation Center
for Aged
Boston, Massachusetts

Citrus Blossoms

Delicate phyllo pastry squares form the petals of these "blossoms." The pastries are filled with a tart lime curd and accented with fresh berries.

2 cups sugar
1 cup unsalted butter or margarine
2 tablespoons grated lime rind
1 cup fresh lime juice
6 large eggs, lightly beaten
4 egg yolks, lightly beaten

½ (16-ounce) package frozen phyllo pastry, thawed
½ cup unsalted butter or margarine, melted
½ pint fresh blueberries, raspberries, or blackberries
Garnish: fresh mint leaves

Combine first 4 ingredients in top of a double boiler; bring water to a boil. Reduce heat to low; cook, stirring constantly, until butter melts. Combine eggs and egg yolks. Gradually stir about one-fourth of hot mixture into eggs; add to remaining hot mixture, stirring constantly. Cook over medium-low heat, stirring constantly, until mixture thickens and coats a metal spoon (about 15 to 20 minutes). Remove from heat; let cool. Place lime mixture in a glass or plastic container; cover and chill.

Work with 1 sheet of phyllo at a time, keeping remaining sheets covered with a slightly damp towel. Place 1 sheet of phyllo on work surface; brush with melted butter. Place second sheet of phyllo on top of first sheet; brush with butter. Cut stack of phyllo into 12 squares. Press 1 phyllo square into each of 12 (2½-inch) muffin cups. Repeat procedure twice, using 4 sheets of phyllo and melted butter, and rotating muffin pan slightly each time a phyllo square is added to form "petals." Repeat procedure with remaining phyllo and butter, filling an additional muffin pan. Bake at 375° for 8 minutes or until golden. Carefully remove phyllo cups from pans, and cool completely on wire racks.

To serve, spoon 1 rounded tablespoon reserved lime mixture into each phyllo cup; top with berries. Garnish, if desired. Serve immediately. Yield: 2 dozen.

Above & Beyond Parsley
The Junior League of Kansas City, Missouri

Poultry

Whether it's crispy fried chicken, elegant roasted Cornish hens, or grilled turkey steaks, poultry is a popular entrée that can be prepared in many tempting ways.

Roasted Lemon Chicken, page 230

Roasted Lemon Chicken

1 (3½-pound) roasting chicken
2 small lemons
⅓ cup olive oil
3 tablespoons fresh lemon
  juice
2 tablespoons butter or
  margarine, melted

2 cloves garlic, minced
1 tablespoon plus 1 teaspoon
  minced fresh thyme
½ teaspoon salt
½ teaspoon freshly ground
  pepper
Garnish: fresh parsley sprigs

Remove giblets, and rinse chicken with cold water; pat dry.

Punch holes in lemon rind with a wooden pick. Cut lemons in half. Place lemon halves in cavity of chicken. Truss chicken; place chicken, breast side up, on a lightly greased rack in a shallow roasting pan. Insert meat thermometer into breast of chicken, making sure it does not touch bone.

Combine oil and next 6 ingredients in a small bowl, stirring well. Brush chicken with ¼ cup oil mixture. Bake, uncovered, at 375° for 1½ hours or until meat thermometer registers 170°, brushing occasionally with remaining oil mixture. Remove chicken to a serving platter. Garnish, if desired. Yield: 4 servings.

Still Gathering: A Centennial Celebration
Auxiliary to the American Osteopathic Association
Chicago, Illinois

Roast Chicken with Black Pepper Glaze

8 to 10 cloves garlic
2 teaspoons fresh lemon juice
1 tablespoon plus 2 teaspoons
  extra virgin olive oil, divided
2 (3½-pound) broiler-fryers

2 lemons, cut in half
¼ teaspoon salt
1 to 2 tablespoons freshly
  ground pepper
Curly endive

Position knife blade in food processor bowl; add garlic, lemon juice, and 2 teaspoons olive oil. Cover and process 30 seconds, stopping once to scrape down sides; set garlic paste aside.

Remove giblets, and rinse chickens thoroughly with cold water; pat dry. Gently separate chicken skin from legs, thighs, and breasts. Spread reserved garlic paste under skin. Place chickens on a lightly greased rack, breast side up; rub remaining 1 tablespoon olive oil over chickens. Squeeze lemon halves over chickens. Place lemon halves in chicken cavities. Lift wing tips up and over back of each chicken, tucking wing tips under chicken. Secure with wooden picks, and tie leg ends together with string. Sprinkle with salt and pepper. Cover and chill 30 minutes.

Place chickens on rack in a shallow roasting pan. Add water to roasting pan to depth of ½ inch. Insert a meat thermometer into breast of each chicken, making sure it does not touch bone. Bake, uncovered, at 375° for 1 hour and 20 minutes or until meat thermometers register 170°. Place on serving platter lined with curly endive. Yield: 8 servings.

Sugar Snips & Asparagus Tips
Woman's Auxiliary of Infant Welfare Society of Chicago
Chicago, Illinois

"Great Expectations" Roast Chicken

2 tablespoons olive oil
2 tablespoons lemon juice
2 tablespoons balsamic vinegar
1 tablespoon butter or
  margarine, melted
1 teaspoon seasoned salt

1 teaspoon fines herbes
1 clove garlic, minced
½ to ¾ pound whole fresh
  mushrooms
1 (3- to 3½-pound) broiler-
  fryer

Combine first 7 ingredients in a small saucepan; bring to a boil, stirring frequently. Remove from heat. Dip mushrooms into vinegar mixture; set mushrooms and vinegar mixture aside.

Remove giblets, and rinse chicken with cold water; pat dry. Place on a lightly greased rack in a shallow roasting pan. Insert meat thermometer into breast of chicken, making sure it does not touch bone. Baste with reserved vinegar mixture. Bake, uncovered, at 375° for 55 minutes, basting every 20 minutes with vinegar mixture. Add reserved mushrooms to pan; baste with any remaining vinegar mixture. Bake an additional 20 minutes or until meat thermometer registers 170°. Yield: 4 servings.   Judy Walters

Carol & Friends, A Taste of North County
Carol & Friends Steering Committee of the Carol Cox Re-Entry
Women's Scholarship Fund at CSU-San Marcos
San Marcos, California

Broiled Chicken with Vinegar and Honey

1 (2½- to 3-pound) broiler-
  fryer
3 tablespoons cider vinegar
1 tablespoon honey
2 cloves garlic, minced
2 teaspoons peeled, minced
  gingerroot

2 teaspoons low-sodium soy
  sauce
1 teaspoon Dijon or spicy
  brown mustard

Remove giblets, and rinse chicken with cold water; pat dry. Cut chicken in half lengthwise, using an electric knife. Place, skin side down, on a lightly greased rack in a shallow roasting pan.

Combine vinegar and remaining ingredients in container of an electric blender or food processor; cover and process until smooth, stopping once to scrape down sides. Brush chicken with vinegar mixture. Set remaining vinegar mixture aside.

Broil 5½ inches from heat (with electric oven door partially opened) 10 minutes. Turn; broil an additional 5 minutes. Reduce oven temperature to 400°. Bake, uncovered, for 30 to 35 minutes or until done, basting occasionally with vinegar mixture. (Cover chicken with aluminum foil to prevent excessive browning after 20 minutes, if necessary.) Yield: 4 servings.   Mary Mathews Bebech

Thymely Treasures
Hubbard Historical Society
Hubbard, Ohio

Amaretto Chicken

3 tablespoons all-purpose
  flour
1½ teaspoons salt
1½ teaspoons ground white
  pepper
1½ teaspoons garlic salt
1½ teaspoons paprika
1 (2½- to 3-pound) broiler-
  fryer, cut up

3 tablespoons butter or
  margarine, melted
1 tablespoon vegetable oil
1 cup amaretto
½ cup water
1 (6-ounce) can frozen orange
  juice concentrate, thawed
  and undiluted
1 tablespoon Dijon mustard

Combine first 5 ingredients in a shallow dish; stir well. Dredge chicken in flour mixture. Brown chicken in butter and oil in a large skillet over medium-high heat.

Remove chicken to an ungreased 13- x 9- x 2-inch baking dish, reserving drippings in skillet. Add amaretto and remaining ingredients to skillet; stir well. Bring to a boil; boil, stirring constantly, 2 minutes or until slightly thickened. Pour amaretto mixture over chicken. Cover and bake at 325° for 40 minutes or until chicken is done. Yield: 4 servings.   Carol Hayes

A Collection of Excellent Recipes
Olathe Medical Center
Olathe, Kansas

Lemon Baked Chicken

Fresh lemon juice blends with pineapple, catsup, brown sugar, and soy sauce to give this baked chicken a sweet and sour twist.

1 (2½-pound) broiler-fryer, cut up	⅓ cup catsup
¼ teaspoon salt	⅓ cup fresh lemon juice
¼ teaspoon pepper	2 tablespoons brown sugar
3 tablespoons vegetable oil	1 tablespoon Dijon mustard
1 medium onion, chopped	2 teaspoons soy sauce
½ cup chopped celery	1 teaspoon grated lemon rind
1 (8-ounce) can crushed pineapple, drained	½ teaspoon salt

Sprinkle chicken with ¼ teaspoon salt and pepper. Brown chicken in oil in a large skillet. Remove chicken to a lightly greased 13- x 9- x 2-inch baking dish, reserving drippings in skillet.

Sauté onion and celery in drippings over medium-high heat, stirring constantly, until tender. Add pineapple and remaining ingredients; stir well. Bring to a boil over medium heat; pour over chicken. Bake, uncovered, at 350° for 50 minutes or until chicken is done. Yield: 4 servings.   Lois Jellema

Kitchen Operations
Windham Community Memorial Hospital Auxiliary
Willimantic, Connecticut

Herbed Chicken Casserole

*Three classic herbs—marjoram, oregano, and rosemary—team up with white
wine to add wonderful flavor interest to this chicken casserole.*

1 teaspoon dried marjoram
1 teaspoon dried oregano
1 teaspoon dried rosemary,
  crushed
2 (3-pound) broiler-fryers,
  cut up and skinned

2 tablespoons butter or
  margarine, melted
¾ cup Chablis or other dry
  white wine
⅓ cup lemon juice

Combine first 3 ingredients; sprinkle herb mixture evenly over
chicken. Brown chicken, in batches, in butter in a large skillet over
medium-high heat.

Place chicken in a lightly greased 5-quart baking dish. Combine
wine and lemon juice; stir well. Pour wine mixture over chicken.
Cover and bake at 375° for 45 minutes or until chicken is done.
Yield: 8 servings.

Barbara Matthews

The Happy Cooker
Safeway, Inc.
Oakland, California

Roast Chicken with Rosemary, Thyme, and Lemon

*Rosemary and thyme are members of the mint family. Rosemary's flavor hints
of lemon and pine, while thyme has a pungent clove-like taste.*

5 to 6 pounds chicken pieces
  (breasts, legs, thighs, wings)
¼ cup olive oil
1½ pounds new potatoes, cut
  into ½-inch-wide wedges
1 teaspoon salt
½ teaspoon freshly ground
  pepper
¼ cup plus 3 tablespoons
  lemon juice

2 tablespoons red wine vinegar
12 large fresh thyme sprigs
10 large fresh rosemary sprigs
2 lemons, cut into ⅛-inch-thick
  slices
Garnishes: lemon wedges,
  fresh thyme sprigs, fresh
  rosemary sprigs

Brown chicken, in batches, in oil in a large skillet over medium-high heat. Remove chicken to a large shallow roasting pan. Place potato wedges around chicken; sprinkle with salt and pepper.

Combine lemon juice and vinegar; pour over chicken and potatoes. Top with 12 thyme sprigs, 10 rosemary sprigs, and lemon slices. Bake, uncovered, at 400° for 45 to 50 minutes or until chicken is done and potatoes are tender.

Remove and discard herb sprigs and lemon slices. Remove chicken and potatoes to a warm serving platter. Garnish, if desired. Yield: 6 to 8 servings.   Terri Nunziato

Angels & Friends Favorite Recipes II
Angels of Easter Seal
Youngstown, Ohio

Grilled Margarita Chicken

Fresh lime juice, tequila, orange-flavored liqueur, and salt—all the ingredients in a margarita—give this grilled chicken its playful title.

⅔ cup olive oil
½ cup fresh lime juice
¼ cup tequila
¼ cup chopped fresh cilantro
2 tablespoons Triple Sec or
 other orange-flavored liqueur

½ teaspoon salt
8 skinned and boned chicken
 breast halves

Combine first 6 ingredients in a medium bowl, stirring until blended. Pour olive oil mixture into an ungreased 13- x 9- x 2-inch baking dish. Add chicken, turning to coat. Cover and marinate in refrigerator 1 hour.

Remove chicken from marinade, reserving marinade. Grill, covered, over medium-hot coals (350° to 400°) 10 minutes on each side or until chicken is done, turning and basting occasionally with reserved marinade. Yield: 8 servings.

Desert Treasures
The Junior League of Phoenix, Arizona

Jalapeño Southern Fried Chicken

5 cups buttermilk
2 large cloves garlic, minced
2 medium jalapeño peppers,
  seeded and minced, divided
5 to 6 pounds chicken breast
  halves
1½ cups self-rising flour
2 teaspoons grated orange rind
1 teaspoon salt

½ teaspoon dried basil
¼ teaspoon ground red
  pepper
½ cup butter or margarine
½ cup honey
Vegetable oil
Garnish: jalapeño pepper
  slices

Combine buttermilk, garlic, and half of minced jalapeño peppers. Place chicken in a large bowl; pour marinade mixture over chicken. Cover and marinate in refrigerator 1½ to 2 hours.

Combine flour and next 4 ingredients; stir well. Remove chicken from marinade, discarding marinade. Dredge chicken in flour mixture. Place chicken on wax paper; let stand at room temperature 20 minutes.

Melt butter in a small saucepan over low heat. Add remaining minced jalapeño pepper, and cook 1 minute. Stir in honey. Bring to a boil; reduce heat, and simmer, uncovered, 15 minutes. Remove from heat; set sauce aside, and keep warm.

Pour oil to depth of ¾ inch into a large heavy skillet; heat to 325°. Fry chicken, in batches, in hot oil over medium-high heat 5 to 7 minutes on each side or until chicken is done. Drain on paper towels. Remove chicken to a serving platter. Garnish, if desired. Serve with reserved sauce. Yield: 10 to 12 servings.

Heart & Soul
The Junior League of Memphis, Tennessee

Parslied Potato-Crusted Chicken Breasts

Serve this chicken immediately to keep the potato coating from becoming soggy.

4 skinned and boned chicken
  breast halves
¼ cup all-purpose flour
1 large baking potato (about 1
  pound), peeled and shredded

2 large eggs, beaten
¼ cup minced fresh parsley
1 teaspoon salt
¼ teaspoon pepper
2 tablespoons olive oil

Dredge chicken in flour. Press shredded potato between paper towels to remove excess moisture. Combine potato, eggs, parsley, salt, and pepper in a bowl; stir well. Pat potato mixture onto both sides of chicken.

Cook chicken in hot olive oil in a large skillet over medium heat 10 minutes on each side or until done. Serve immediately. Yield: 4 servings.

Specialties of the House
Kenmore Association
Fredericksburg, Virginia

Hot, Hot Chicken in Garlic Sauce

3 pounds skinned and boned chicken breast halves
¼ cup canola or other vegetable oil, divided
6 to 7 dried red chile pepper pods
3 stalks celery, thinly sliced diagonally
1 (8-ounce) can sliced water chestnuts, drained
½ cup fresh broccoli flowerets, thinly sliced
½ cup diagonally sliced carrot
5 cloves garlic, thinly sliced
1 teaspoon peeled, minced gingerroot
1 green onion, cut into 1-inch pieces
¾ cup rice wine
¼ cup chili paste (optional)

Cut chicken lengthwise into ¼-inch strips. Set chicken aside.

Pour oil around top of preheated wok, coating sides; heat at medium-high (375°) for 2 minutes. Add chile pepper pods, and stir-fry 2 to 3 minutes. Remove chile pepper pods from wok; set aside. Add reserved chicken, and stir-fry 7 minutes or until lightly browned. Remove chicken from wok; drain well, and set aside. Add celery and next 5 ingredients to wok, and stir-fry 3 to 5 minutes.

Add reserved chile pepper pods, reserved chicken, and green onion to wok. Combine wine and chili paste, if desired; add to wok, and stir-fry until thoroughly heated. Serve over hot cooked brown rice or pasta. Yield: 4 servings.   Denise LeMay

Some Like It Hot
The Bement School
Deerfield, Massachusetts

Kung Pao Chicken

A hot and spicy flavor and a peanut topping are traditional to Kung Pao Chicken. If you like, stir-fry a few additional dried red chile pepper pods for an even hotter flavor.

¼ cup water
1½ tablespoons sugar
1 tablespoon cornstarch
1 teaspoon pepper
2 tablespoons soy sauce
2 teaspoons white vinegar
1 teaspoon dry sherry
1 teaspoon vegetable oil
¼ teaspoon hot sauce
3 tablespoons vegetable oil
2 dried red chile pepper pods
2 tablespoons peeled, chopped
  gingerroot

1 pound skinned and boned
  chicken breasts, cut into
  1-inch pieces
1 cup chopped green pepper
1 cup chopped green onions
¾ cup chopped celery
½ cup sliced fresh mushrooms
1 clove garlic, minced
1 cup salted roasted peanuts
  or cashews
Hot cooked rice

Combine first 9 ingredients in a small bowl; stir well. Set soy sauce mixture aside.

Pour 3 tablespoons oil around top of preheated wok, coating sides; heat at medium-high (375°) for 2 minutes. Add chile pepper pods, and stir-fry 1 minute. Remove and discard chile pepper pods. Add chopped gingerroot, and stir-fry 1 minute. Remove and discard gingerroot.

Add chicken, and stir-fry 5 to 6 minutes or until done. Remove chicken from wok; set aside. Add green pepper and next 4 ingredients; stir-fry 2 minutes or until crisp-tender. Stir in reserved chicken and peanuts. Add reserved soy sauce mixture, and stir-fry until thickened. Serve over rice. Yield: 4 servings.   Don Jensen

Home at the Range with Wyoming B.I.L.'s
Chapter Y of P.E.O. Sisterhood
Casper, Wyoming

Anne's Hot Chicken Casserole

If you prefer mildly seasoned foods, don't be put off by the name of this dish. This flavorful chicken and vegetable mixture is hot in temperature rather than spice level.

5 pounds assorted chicken
  pieces plus giblets
2 stalks celery with leaves
1 carrot, cut into 1-inch pieces
1 small onion, quartered
1 teaspoon salt
¼ teaspoon pepper
1¼ cups sliced fresh
  mushrooms
1 medium onion, minced

1 (8-ounce) can sliced water
  chestnuts, drained
1 (2-ounce) jar sliced pimiento,
  drained
1 cup slivered almonds
1 cup mayonnaise
1 cup salad dressing
¼ teaspoon salt
⅛ teaspoon pepper
½ to ¾ cup corn flake crumbs

Combine first 6 ingredients in a large Dutch oven; add water to cover. Bring to a boil; cover, reduce heat, and simmer 1 hour or until chicken is done. Remove chicken from broth, reserving broth. Let chicken cool; skin, bone, and coarsely chop meat. Set chicken aside. Pour reserved broth through a wire-mesh strainer into a bowl, discarding giblets and vegetables. Reserve broth for another use.

Combine chopped chicken, mushrooms, and next 8 ingredients in a large bowl; stir well. Spoon chicken mixture into a lightly greased 2-quart casserole; sprinkle with corn flake crumbs. Bake, uncovered, at 350° for 1 hour or until thoroughly heated. Yield: 6 to 8 servings.   Anne Kauzlarich

Cooking with Diplomacy
Association of American Foreign Service Women
Washington, DC

Cornish Hens
with Orange-Honey Sauce

These rice-stuffed Cornish hens are special enough for company. The Orange-Honey Sauce glazes the hens for an attractive appearance.

4 (1½-pound) Cornish hens
½ teaspoon salt
2 cups hot cooked rice
1 large orange, peeled, seeded,
  and coarsely chopped
2 cups canned ready-to-serve
  chicken broth

½ cup orange juice
⅓ cup honey
¼ cup cornstarch
2 tablespoons lemon juice
½ teaspoon grated orange rind

Remove giblets, and rinse hens thoroughly with cold water; pat dry. Sprinkle cavities of hens with salt. Lift wingtips up and over back of hens, tucking wingtips under hens.

Combine rice and chopped orange; stuff hens lightly with rice mixture, and close cavities. Secure with wooden picks, and tie leg ends together with string.

Combine chicken broth and remaining ingredients in a medium saucepan; cook over medium heat, stirring constantly, until thickened and bubbly.

Place hens, breast side up, on a lightly greased rack in a shallow roasting pan. Brush hens with chicken broth mixture. Cover and bake at 400° for 30 minutes. Uncover and bake an additional 30 minutes or until done, basting with broth mixture every 10 minutes. Yield: 4 servings. Rosie Stuart

Our Daily Bread
Women's Club of Our Lady of Mt. Carmel
Carmel, Indiana

Cornish Hens with Walnut Stuffing and Wine Sauce

6 slices bacon
1 cup chopped onion
1 cup chopped green pepper
3 cups dry white bread cubes
1 cup chopped walnuts
1½ teaspoons salt
½ teaspoon dried thyme
½ teaspoon rubbed sage

6 (1- to 1½-pound) Cornish hens
Basting Sauce
3 tablespoons all-purpose flour
1 cup Chablis or other dry
  white wine
1 cup currant jelly
1 teaspoon salt
1 teaspoon dry mustard

Cook bacon in a large skillet until crisp; remove bacon, reserving 3 tablespoons drippings in skillet. Crumble bacon, and set aside. Sauté onion and green pepper in drippings over medium-high heat, stirring constantly, until tender. Add reserved bacon, bread cubes, and next 4 ingredients, tossing gently.

Remove giblets, and rinse hens with cold water; pat dry. Stuff with bread cube mixture; close cavities. Secure with wooden picks, and tie leg ends with string. Place, breast side up, on a greased rack in a shallow roasting pan. Brush with Basting Sauce. Bake at 400° for 1 hour or until done, basting occasionally with Basting Sauce.

Remove hens to a serving platter. Set aside, and keep warm. Drain drippings, reserving ⅔ cup drippings. Place flour in a heavy saucepan; gradually add reserved drippings, stirring until smooth. Cook over low heat, stirring constantly, 1 minute. Gradually add wine; cook over medium heat, stirring constantly, until thickened and bubbly. Stir in jelly, 1 teaspoon salt, and mustard, and cook until thoroughly heated. Serve hens with sauce. Yield: 6 servings.

Basting Sauce

½ cup butter, melted
½ cup Chablis or other dry
  white wine

1½ teaspoons salt
1 clove garlic, crushed
½ teaspoon rubbed sage

Combine all ingredients; stir well. Yield: 1 cup.   Diane Neuser

The Library Cookbook
Friends of the Kent Library
Carmel, New York

Herbed Roast Turkey

1 (10- to 12-pound) turkey
¼ teaspoon salt
⅛ teaspoon pepper
1 small cooking apple,
  quartered
1 carrot, cut into 1-inch pieces
1 stalk celery, cut into 1-inch
  pieces
½ cup unsalted butter or
  margarine
4 ounces garlic and herb
  cream cheese, softened
1 tablespoon finely chopped
  fresh basil
1 tablespoon finely chopped
  fresh parsley

2 teaspoons finely chopped
  fresh chives
2 teaspoons finely chopped
  fresh sage
2 teaspoons finely chopped
  fresh thyme
2 cloves garlic, minced
2 tablespoons cognac
¼ teaspoon salt
⅛ teaspoon pepper
1 lemon, thinly sliced
1 tablespoon cornstarch
2 tablespoons cold water
1 tablespoon Madeira

Remove giblets, and rinse turkey thoroughly with cold water; pat dry. Sprinkle cavity with ¼ teaspoon salt and ⅛ teaspoon pepper. Combine apple, carrot, and celery; stuff cavity with apple mixture. Tie ends of legs to tail with cord or tuck them under flap of skin around tail. Lift wingtips up and over back, and tuck under bird. Place turkey on a lightly greased rack in a roasting pan, breast side up. Set aside.

Combine butter and next 10 ingredients; stir well. Gently separate skin from breast and thighs of turkey. Spread cheese mixture under skin on breast and thighs. Insert lemon slices under skin. Insert meat thermometer into meaty portion of thigh, making sure it does not touch bone.

Cover and bake at 425° for 25 minutes. Reduce oven temperature to 350°; bake 2½ hours or until meat thermometer registers 180°. When turkey is two-thirds done, cut the cord or band of skin holding the drumstick ends to the tail; this will ensure that the inside of the thighs is cooked. Turkey is done when drumsticks are easy to move up and down. Increase oven temperature to 425°; uncover and bake 10 minutes or until skin is crisp and browned. Remove turkey to a serving platter, reserving pan drippings. Let turkey stand 15 minutes before carving.

Place reserved pan drippings in a medium saucepan. Combine cornstarch and water, and stir well. Add cornstarch mixture to pan drippings, stirring until blended. Cook over medium heat, stirring constantly, until mixture is thickened. Stir in Madeira, and cook until thoroughly heated. Serve turkey with gravy. Yield: 10 servings.

Hospitality: A Cookbook Celebrating Boston's North Shore
Salem Hospital Aid Association
Salem, Massachusetts

Turkey Breast with Herb Sauce

If the turkey breast starts to get too brown, cover it with aluminum foil.

½ cup butter or margarine, melted	1 teaspoon paprika
	2 cloves garlic, crushed
¼ cup Chablis or other dry white wine	1 (4½- to 5-pound) turkey breast
1¼ teaspoons dried rosemary	2 teaspoons cornstarch
1 teaspoon salt	2 tablespoons cold water

Combine first 6 ingredients; stir well, and set aside.

Place turkey breast, skin side up, on a lightly greased rack in a shallow roasting pan. Insert meat thermometer into thickest part of breast, making sure it does not touch bone. Brush turkey with one-fourth of reserved butter mixture, and bake, uncovered, at 325° for 1 hour. Brush turkey with half of remaining butter mixture, and bake an additional 30 minutes. Brush turkey with remaining butter mixture, and bake an additional hour or until meat thermometer registers 170°. (Cover turkey with aluminum foil to prevent excessive browning, if necessary.)

Remove turkey to a serving platter, reserving pan drippings. Set turkey aside, and keep warm. Add enough water to pan drippings to make 2 cups; place in a medium saucepan. Combine cornstarch and water; stir well. Add cornstarch mixture to pan drippings, stirring well. Bring to a boil over medium heat. Boil, stirring constantly, 1 minute or until slightly thickened. Serve turkey with sauce. Yield: 8 to 10 servings.   Mrs. Frances deWilton

A Cook's Tour of the Bayou Country
Churchwomen of the Southwest Deanery of the Episcopal
Diocese of Louisiana
Franklin, Louisiana

Grilled Turkey Steak

1 pound turkey tenderloin
  steaks (1 inch thick)
½ cup Chablis or other dry
  white wine

¼ cup soy sauce
1 tablespoon vegetable oil
1 clove garlic, crushed

Place turkey steaks in a shallow dish. Combine wine and remaining ingredients in a jar; cover tightly, and shake vigorously. Pour marinade mixture over turkey steaks. Cover and marinate in refrigerator 2 hours.

Remove turkey steaks from marinade, reserving marinade. Grill, covered, over medium-hot coals (350° to 400°) 10 to 12 minutes on each side or until meat thermometer inserted in thickest part of turkey steaks registers 170°, basting frequently with reserved marinade. Yield: 4 servings.

Blooming Good
National Council of State Garden Clubs
St. Louis, Missouri

Turkey Cutlets with Tarragon and Wine

1 large onion, thinly sliced
1 clove garlic, minced
¼ cup butter or margarine,
  melted
½ pound fresh mushrooms,
  diced
¼ cup all-purpose flour
½ teaspoon salt
¼ teaspoon pepper

2 pounds turkey breast cutlets
2 tablespoons vegetable oil
1 tablespoon dried tarragon
½ cup Chablis or other dry
  white wine
3 tablespoons fresh lemon
  juice
2 tablespoons finely chopped
  fresh parsley

Sauté onion and garlic in butter in a large skillet over medium heat, stirring constantly, until almost tender. Add mushrooms, and sauté, stirring constantly, until tender. Drain, reserving drippings in skillet; set vegetables aside.

Combine flour, salt, and pepper; stir well. Dredge turkey in flour mixture. Brown turkey in drippings and oil 2 minutes on each side;

sprinkle with tarragon just before turning. Pour wine and lemon juice over turkey; add reserved vegetable mixture, and simmer, uncovered, 5 minutes or until turkey is done. Sprinkle with parsley. Yield: 4 to 6 servings. Linda Nuccio

Country Cookbook
Our Lady's Guild of St. Christopher's Parish
Red Hook, New York

Turkey Patties Oriental

1¼ **pounds fresh ground turkey**
⅓ **cup fine, dry breadcrumbs**
1 **large egg**
¾ **teaspoon garlic salt**
1 **tablespoon vegetable oil**
1 **cup chicken broth**
1 **tablespoon soy sauce**
2 **teaspoons cornstarch**
1 **teaspoon sugar**
1 **teaspoon white vinegar**

⅛ **teaspoon ground white pepper**
2 **stalks celery, thinly sliced diagonally**
1 **medium onion, thinly sliced**
1 **medium-size green pepper, cut into ¾-inch pieces**
2 **medium tomatoes, cut into wedges**
½ **teaspoon salt**
¼ **teaspoon pepper**

Combine first 4 ingredients in a medium bowl, stirring well. Shape turkey mixture into 4 (¾-inch-thick) patties. Brown patties in oil in a large skillet over medium heat, turning once.

Combine chicken broth and next 5 ingredients; stir well. Pour chicken broth mixture over patties; bring to a boil over medium-high heat, stirring occasionally. Add celery, onion, and green pepper; cover, reduce heat, and simmer 6 minutes. Add tomato, salt, and pepper; cook 2 to 3 minutes or until turkey is done. Yield: 4 servings. Charlotte Bolla

Gethsemane Lutheran Church Centennial Cookbook
Gethsemane Churchwomen
Hopkins, Minnesota

Turkey Pot Pie with Cornbread Crust

Yellow cornmeal can be substituted for the white cornmeal if it's not available in your area of the country.

2 cups water
2 large carrots, scraped and thinly sliced
1 large baking potato, peeled and diced
2 medium onions, thinly sliced
¼ cup plus 2 tablespoons unsalted butter or margarine, melted
¼ cup plus 2 tablespoons all-purpose flour
4 cups turkey or chicken broth
¾ teaspoon salt

¾ teaspoon ground white pepper
4 cups diced, cooked turkey
1 cup frozen lima beans, thawed
1 cup all-purpose flour
1 cup white cornmeal
1 tablespoon baking powder
1 teaspoon salt
2 tablespoons sugar
1 large egg, lightly beaten
1 cup plus 1 tablespoon milk
3 tablespoons vegetable oil

Combine water, carrot, and potato in a large saucepan; bring to a boil. Cover, reduce heat, and simmer until vegetables are tender. Drain; set vegetables aside.

Sauté onion in butter in a large skillet over medium heat, stirring constantly, until tender. Reduce heat to low. Add ¼ cup plus 2 tablespoons flour; cook, stirring constantly, 1 minute. Gradually add broth; cook over medium heat, stirring constantly, until mixture is thickened and bubbly. Stir in ¾ teaspoon salt and white pepper. Remove from heat, and set aside.

Place one-third of turkey in a lightly greased 13- x 9- x 2-inch baking dish. Combine reserved vegetables and lima beans; sprinkle one-third of vegetable mixture over turkey. Repeat layers twice, and set aside.

Combine 1 cup flour, cornmeal, baking powder, salt, and sugar in a large bowl; stir well. Combine egg, milk, and oil; add to dry ingredients, stirring just until dry ingredients are moistened. Pour batter over turkey mixture. Bake, uncovered, at 425° for 35 to 40 minutes or until lightly browned and thoroughly heated. Yield: 8 servings.

Rosie's Place Recipes
Rosie's Place
Boston, Massachusetts

Salads

*In this chapter, you'll find salads of every variety—
from simply dressed greens crowned with crispy croutons
to fresh fruit with a saucy dressing!*

Tossed Green Sesame-Crouton Salad, page 257

Cider Salad

Carrots and Golden Delicious apples give this gelatin salad some crunch.

2 cups apple cider
1 (3-ounce) package lemon-
  flavored gelatin
⅛ teaspoon salt
2 cups finely grated carrot

1 cup unpeeled diced Golden
  Delicious apple
½ cup raisins
1 tablespoon white vinegar

Bring cider to a boil. Combine boiling cider, gelatin, and salt, stirring 2 minutes or until gelatin and salt dissolve. Chill until the consistency of unbeaten egg white.

Fold in carrot, apple, raisins, and vinegar; pour mixture into a lightly oiled 6-cup mold. Cover and chill until firm. Unmold onto a serving plate. Yield: 8 servings.   Lucile Matheson

Fabulous Fare
Women's Fellowship of Center Harbor Congregational Church
Center Harbor, New Hampshire

Orange Sherbet Gelatin

2 (3-ounce) packages orange-
  flavored gelatin
1 cup boiling water
1 pint orange sherbet,
  softened

1 cup whipping cream,
  whipped
1 (11-ounce) can mandarin
  oranges, drained

Combine gelatin and boiling water, stirring 2 minutes or until gelatin dissolves; let cool. Add sherbet, stirring until blended. Fold in whipped cream and oranges.

Spoon mixture into a lightly oiled 6-cup mold. Cover and chill until firm. Unmold onto a serving plate. Yield: 8 servings.

Simply Heavenly
Woman's Synodical Union of the Associate Reformed
Presbyterian Church
Greenville, South Carolina

Fresh Apple Salad

Stir the toasted pecans into the salad just before serving to keep them crisp.

1 (20-ounce) can pineapple
  chunks, undrained
¼ cup sugar
¼ cup butter or margarine
1 tablespoon lemon juice
2 tablespoons cornstarch
2 tablespoons cold water
1 cup mayonnaise

8 cups unpeeled, chopped
  McIntosh or other tart
  apples (about 6 large)
2 cups seedless green grapes
1 to 2 teaspoons poppy seeds
1½ cups coarsely chopped
  pecans, toasted

Drain pineapple chunks, reserving juice; set pineapple aside.

Combine pineapple juice, sugar, butter, and lemon juice in a small saucepan; cook over medium heat, stirring constantly, until mixture comes to a boil. Combine cornstarch and water; stir well. Stir cornstarch mixture into juice mixture. Cook over medium heat, stirring constantly, until mixture is thickened and bubbly. Remove from heat; cover and chill. Stir in mayonnaise.

Combine reserved pineapple chunks, apple, grapes, and poppy seeds in a large bowl; toss well. Pour mayonnaise mixture over fruit mixture; toss well. Cover and chill thoroughly. Stir in pecans just before serving. Yield: 12 servings.   Carol Heckman

Favorites from First
First Lutheran Churchwomen
St. James, Minnesota

Overnight Layered Fruit Salad

This fruit version of the ever popular Seven-Layer Salad should be made at least 8 hours ahead of time.

2 cups shredded iceberg
  lettuce
2 navel oranges
2 Golden Delicious apples,
  unpeeled and thinly sliced

2 cups seedless green grapes
⅓ cup mayonnaise
⅓ cup sour cream
1 cup (4 ounces) shredded
  mild Cheddar cheese

Place shredded lettuce in a deep 2-quart glass serving bowl. Peel and section oranges, reserving juice. Combine apple slices and orange juice; toss to coat. Layer apple slices over lettuce; top with orange sections and grapes.

Combine mayonnaise and sour cream in a small bowl; stir well. Spread mayonnaise mixture over salad, sealing to edge of bowl. Sprinkle with cheese. Cover and chill at least 8 hours. Yield: 6 servings.

Jack Reynolds

When the Master Gardener Cooks
Seminole County Master Gardeners
Sanford, Florida

Red Onion and Orange Salad

6 large navel oranges, peeled
  and thinly sliced
1 large purple onion, thinly
  sliced and separated into
  rings

Fresh cilantro or parsley sprigs
½ cup honey
¼ cup rice vinegar
1 tablespoon caraway seeds

Arrange orange slices and onion slices overlapping alternately on a large serving platter. Insert fresh cilantro sprigs among the slices. Combine honey, vinegar, and caraway seeds in a small bowl, stirring well. Pour dressing over salad. Cover and chill 3 hours. Yield: 6 servings.

Southwest Cooks! The Tradition of Native American Cuisines
Southwest Museum
Los Angeles, California

Black Bean and Corn Salad with Cumin Dressing

Frozen corn can be substituted for the fresh corn in this trendy Southwestern salad. If frozen corn is used, omit the blanching procedure.

½ pound dried black beans
2 quarts water
1 teaspoon salt
½ teaspoon dried oregano
¼ teaspoon ground cumin
1 clove garlic, minced

Cumin Dressing
1½ cups fresh cut corn
¾ cup chopped purple onion
½ cup chopped sweet red
  pepper

Wash and sort beans. Bring 2 quarts water to a boil in a Dutch oven; add beans. Cover and remove from heat. Let stand 1 hour. Add salt, oregano, cumin, and garlic; stir well. Bring to a boil; cover, reduce heat, and simmer 35 minutes or until beans are tender. Drain.

Combine beans and Cumin Dressing in a large bowl, tossing well. Cover and chill at least 8 hours, stirring occasionally.

Cook corn in boiling water to cover 3 minutes; drain. Plunge into ice water; drain well. Add corn, onion, and chopped red pepper to chilled bean mixture; toss well. Cover and chill thoroughly. Yield: 10 servings.

Cumin Dressing

⅓ cup olive oil
1 tablespoon red wine vinegar
1 teaspoon balsamic vinegar
1 teaspoon cider vinegar
¼ to ½ teaspoon salt

½ teaspoon ground cumin
¼ to ½ teaspoon sugar
⅛ teaspoon ground red
  pepper

Combine all ingredients in a jar. Cover tightly, and shake vigorously. Yield: about ½ cup.

Linda Y. Turner

Five Star Sensations
Auxiliary of University Hospitals of Cleveland
Shaker Heights, Ohio

Delectable Broccoli Salad

¾ cup raisins
1 cup warm water
4 to 5 cups fresh broccoli
   flowerets, cut into bite-size
   pieces
8 slices bacon, cooked and
   crumbled

½ cup thinly sliced celery
½ cup sunflower kernels,
   toasted
1 cup mayonnaise
¼ cup sugar
2 tablespoons balsamic vinegar
1 teaspoon curry powder

Combine raisins and warm water in a small bowl, and let stand 5 minutes; drain. Combine raisins, broccoli, and next 3 ingredients in a large bowl; toss well. Combine mayonnaise, sugar, vinegar, and curry powder in a small bowl; stir well. Spoon dressing mixture over broccoli mixture; toss gently. Serve immediately. Yield: 10 servings.   Jim and Sue Huffer

Culinary Masterpieces
Birmingham Museum of Art
Birmingham, Alabama

Red, White, and Green Salad

2½ cups fresh broccoli
   flowerets
2½ cups fresh cauliflower
   flowerets
1 cup chopped tomato
½ cup chopped green onions

½ cup sour cream
½ cup mayonnaise or salad
   dressing
⅛ teaspoon salt
⅛ teaspoon pepper
Lettuce leaves

Combine first 4 ingredients in a large bowl; toss gently. Combine sour cream, mayonnaise, salt, and pepper, stirring well. Pour dressing mixture over broccoli mixture; toss gently. Cover and chill 3 to 4 hours. Serve salad in a lettuce-lined salad bowl. Yield: 10 to 12 servings.   Sharon Yarborough

Enon's Best Kept Secret II
Enon Baptist Church
Jayess, Mississippi

Chick-Pea Salad

You can chill this salad up to 8 hours to allow flavors more time to blend.

2 (19-ounce) cans chick-peas
  (garbanzo beans), drained
2 medium tomatoes, seeded
  and diced
¼ cup chopped green pepper
¼ cup chopped sweet red
  pepper
¼ cup kalamata olives, pitted
  and halved
¼ cup chopped fresh parsley
4 green onions, chopped
1 tablespoon chopped fresh
  oregano
½ cup olive oil
3 tablespoons balsamic vinegar
¼ teaspoon salt
⅛ teaspoon pepper

Combine first 8 ingredients in a bowl; toss. Set aside. Combine oil and remaining ingredients in a jar. Cover tightly, and shake vigorously. Pour dressing over chick-pea mixture; toss. Serve at room temperature. Yield: 10 to 12 servings.   Ann Coffey

Starlight and Moonbeams
Babies' Alumni of Hilton Head Hospital
Hilton Head Island, South Carolina

Jicama Salad

2 small zucchini, cut into very
  thin strips
1 small jicama (about ½
  pound), peeled and cut into
  very thin strips
1 small sweet red pepper, cut
  into very thin strips
1 small sweet yellow pepper,
  cut into very thin strips
1 small carrot, scraped and cut
  into very thin strips
¼ cup peanut oil
3 tablespoons lime juice
½ teaspoon salt
¼ teaspoon ground red
  pepper

Combine all ingredients in a bowl; toss. Cover and chill. Serve with a slotted spoon. Yield: 6 to 8 servings.   Selma Gold

M.D. Anderson Volunteers Cooking for Fun
University of Texas M.D. Anderson Cancer Center
Houston, Texas

Roasted Pepper Trio

2 medium-size sweet red
  peppers
2 medium-size sweet yellow
  peppers
2 medium-size green peppers
⅓ cup olive oil
1 teaspoon salt
1½ tablespoons chopped fresh
  chives

½ teaspoon minced garlic
½ teaspoon salt
¼ cup plus 2 tablespoons olive
  oil
2 tablespoons red wine vinegar
2 teaspoons Dijon mustard
½ teaspoon sugar
⅛ teaspoon hot sauce

Cut peppers in half lengthwise; remove and discard seeds and membranes. Place peppers, skin side up, on 2 ungreased baking sheets; flatten peppers with palm of hand. Drizzle ⅓ cup olive oil evenly over peppers; sprinkle with 1 teaspoon salt.

Broil peppers 5½ inches from heat (with electric oven door partially opened) 15 to 20 minutes or until skins of peppers are charred. Place peppers in ice water; let stand until cool. Remove peppers from water; peel and discard skins. Slice peppers into 1-inch-wide strips. Place peppers on a serving platter; sprinkle with chives, and set aside.

Combine garlic and ½ teaspoon salt in a bowl; mash to form a paste. Combine garlic paste, ¼ cup plus 2 tablespoons olive oil, and remaining ingredients in a jar. Cover tightly, and shake vigorously. Pour dressing over reserved peppers. Yield: 6 servings.

Rogue River Rendezvous
The Junior Service League of Jackson County
Medford, Oregon

Layered Egg and Potato Salad

2 pounds new potatoes,
  unpeeled
⅔ cup olive oil
½ cup thinly sliced green
  onions
2 tablespoons red wine vinegar
1 clove garlic, minced
1½ teaspoons salt

½ teaspoon sugar
½ teaspoon paprika
½ teaspoon pepper
½ cup chopped fresh parsley
8 large hard-cooked eggs,
  sliced
1 (2-ounce) jar diced pimiento,
  drained

Cook potatoes in boiling water to cover 25 to 30 minutes or until tender; drain and let cool slightly. Peel potatoes, and cut crosswise into ¼-inch-thick slices. Place potato slices in a bowl.

Combine olive oil and next 7 ingredients in a small bowl, stirring with a wire whisk until blended. Pour dressing mixture over warm potatoes; toss gently. Cover and chill at least 4 hours.

Drain potatoes, reserving dressing mixture. Layer half each of potato slices, parsley, egg slices, and dressing mixture in a shallow 2½-quart serving bowl in order listed. Repeat layers once. Sprinkle with pimiento. Cover and chill thoroughly. Yield: 8 servings.

Blooming Good
National Council of State Garden Clubs
St. Louis, Missouri

Egg Salad Accordions

This pretty salad takes its name from the fanned appearance of these egg salad-stuffed tomatoes.

4 medium tomatoes
6 large hard-cooked eggs, chopped
¼ cup finely chopped celery
¼ cup finely chopped green pepper
¼ cup mayonnaise or salad dressing

2 tablespoons thinly sliced green onions
2 tablespoons prepared mustard
½ teaspoon salt
Dash of pepper
Garnish: fresh parsley sprigs

Place tomatoes on work surface, stem side down. Cut each tomato into 6 slices, cutting to, but not through, stem end. Spread slices apart slightly; cover and chill.

Combine egg and next 7 ingredients; stir well. Cover and chill thoroughly. To serve, spoon egg mixture evenly between tomato slices. Garnish, if desired. Yield: 4 servings.   Mary Lee Doney

Rhapsody of Recipes
Chattanooga Symphony Youth Orchestra
Chattanooga, Tennessee

Feta Cheese, Apple, and Spiced Pecan Salad

These Spiced Pecans can do double duty as a crunchy salad topper or as a savory appetizer or snack.

1 head Boston lettuce, torn
1 head red leaf lettuce, torn
1 Red Delicious apple, unpeeled and finely chopped
8 ounces feta cheese, crumbled
Spiced Pecans
½ cup olive oil

2 tablespoons white wine vinegar
1 tablespoon plus 1 teaspoon Dijon mustard
¼ teaspoon salt
⅛ teaspoon freshly ground pepper

Combine lettuces, apple, cheese, and Spiced Pecans in a large bowl; toss gently, and set aside.

Combine olive oil, vinegar, mustard, salt, and pepper in a jar. Cover tightly, and shake vigorously. Pour dressing mixture over lettuce mixture; toss gently. Serve immediately. Yield: 8 servings.

Spiced Pecans

3 tablespoons unsalted butter or margarine, melted
1 teaspoon salt
1 teaspoon ground cinnamon

¼ teaspoon ground red pepper
Dash of hot sauce
1⅔ cups pecan halves

Combine first 5 ingredients in a medium bowl; add pecans, stirring to coat.

Spread in a single layer on an ungreased baking sheet. Bake at 300° for 15 minutes, stirring once. Cool completely on baking sheet on a wire rack. Yield: 1⅔ cups.   Janet Maxwell Roseland

A Taste of Twin Pines
Twin Pines Alumni of Twin Pines Cooperative House
West Lafayette, Indiana

Tossed Green Sesame-Crouton Salad

2 cups (¾-inch) French
  baguette cubes
2 tablespoons sesame seeds
2 tablespoons butter or
  margarine, melted
12 cups mixed salad greens
¼ cup vegetable oil
3 tablespoons tarragon vinegar

½ to 1 teaspoon salt
½ teaspoon pepper
½ teaspoon dry mustard
¼ teaspoon sugar
½ teaspoon minced garlic
½ teaspoon lemon juice
¼ teaspoon Worcestershire
  sauce

Sauté bread cubes and sesame seeds in butter in a large skillet over medium heat, stirring constantly, until golden. Set aside.

Place salad greens in a large bowl. Combine oil and next 8 ingredients in a jar. Cover tightly, and shake vigorously. Pour over salad greens; toss. Top with reserved croutons and sesame seeds. Yield: 8 servings.
Dorothy Hudgins

The Flavor of Mathews
The Mathews County Junior and Senior Woman's Club
Mathews, Virginia

Mixed Reds

The edible red nasturtiums used as a garnish add a peppery flavor.

1 head red leaf lettuce, torn
½ head radicchio, torn
¼ cup shredded red cabbage
2 radishes, thinly sliced
3 tablespoons pomegranate
  seeds
¼ cup olive oil

2 tablespoons red wine vinegar
1 tablespoon raspberry vinegar
½ teaspoon Dijon mustard
¼ teaspoon salt
⅛ teaspoon pepper
Garnish: edible red
  nasturtiums

Combine first 5 ingredients in a large bowl; toss. Set aside.

Combine olive oil and next 5 ingredients in a jar. Cover tightly, and shake vigorously. Pour dressing over salad mixture; toss gently. Garnish, if desired. Serve immediately. Yield: 6 servings.

Settings: From Our Past to Your Presentation
The Junior League of Philadelphia, Pennsylvania

Spinach-Pear Salad

½ cup olive oil
¼ small onion
2 tablespoons grated Parmesan cheese
2 tablespoons cider vinegar
½ to 1 teaspoon salt
½ teaspoon Worcestershire sauce
¼ teaspoon sugar
¼ teaspoon dry mustard
¼ teaspoon dried basil
⅛ teaspoon pepper
1 (10-ounce) package fresh spinach
2 pears, peeled and thinly sliced
¼ cup golden raisins
¼ cup pecan halves, toasted

Position knife blade in food processor bowl; add first 10 ingredients. Cover and process until well blended, stopping once to scrape down sides. Set dressing aside.

Remove and discard stems from spinach. Wash spinach, and pat dry with paper towels. Combine spinach, pear, raisins, and pecans in a large bowl. Pour reserved dressing over salad, and toss gently. Serve immediately. Yield: 8 servings.   Bonnie Lloyd

June Fete Fare
The Women's Board of Abington Memorial Hospital
Abington, Pennsylvania

Strawberry and Spinach Salad with Pecans

If you have any dressing left over, you'll enjoy it drizzled over fresh fruit.

2 tablespoons butter or margarine
1½ cups pecan halves
1 cup sugar
1 pound fresh spinach
2 cups thinly sliced celery
1 pint fresh strawberries, hulled and halved
Dressing

Melt butter in a large heavy skillet over medium heat. Add pecans and sugar; stir well. Cook over medium heat, stirring constantly, 7 to 8 minutes or until sugar is caramel colored. Remove pecans with a slotted spoon, and spread in a single layer on a sheet of lightly greased wax paper. Let cool completely.

Remove and discard stems from spinach. Wash spinach, and pat dry with paper towels. Combine spinach, celery, and strawberries in a large bowl. Pour 1 cup Dressing over salad mixture; toss gently. Add reserved pecans; toss gently. Serve immediately with remaining Dressing. Yield: 4 to 6 servings.

Dressing

⅔ cup white vinegar
½ cup sugar
3 to 4 green onions,
  chopped

2 teaspoons salt
2 teaspoons dry mustard
2 cups vegetable oil
3 tablespoons poppy seeds

Combine first 5 ingredients in container of an electric blender; cover and process until smooth, stopping once to scrape down sides. With blender on high, gradually add oil in a slow, steady stream. Process until thick and smooth, stopping once to scrape down sides. Transfer dressing mixture to a bowl; stir in poppy seeds. Cover and chill. Yield: 2¾ cups.

A Cleveland Collection
The Junior League of Cleveland, Ohio

Carrot and Pineapple Coleslaw

2 cups shredded cabbage
1 (15¼-ounce) can pineapple
  chunks, drained
1 cup shredded carrot
⅓ cup slivered almonds,
  toasted

⅔ cup mayonnaise
⅔ cup sour cream
1 tablespoon lemon juice
1 teaspoon sugar
1 teaspoon grated onion
⅛ teaspoon salt

Combine cabbage, pineapple chunks, carrot, and almonds in a large bowl, and toss gently. Combine mayonnaise and remaining ingredients, stirring until smooth. Pour dressing mixture over cabbage mixture, and toss gently. Cover and chill thoroughly. Yield: 6 servings.

Sandy Kurtzer

United Methodist Church Cookbook
Haxtun United Methodist Church
Haxtun, Colorado

Honey Mustard Slaw

½ cup mayonnaise or salad
  dressing
½ cup sour cream
2 tablespoons honey
1 to 2 tablespoons Dijon
  mustard
3 cups coarsely shredded
  cabbage

2 cups coarsely shredded
  romaine lettuce
2 cups peeled, shredded
  jicama
¼ cup sliced green onions
½ cup coarsely chopped
  pecans, toasted

Combine first 4 ingredients in a small bowl, stirring well. Cover and chill thoroughly.

Combine cabbage, lettuce, jicama, and green onions in a large bowl; toss gently. Pour mayonnaise mixture over cabbage mixture; toss gently. Sprinkle with chopped pecans just before serving. Yield: 8 servings.

Gladys Morford

First United Methodist Church Centennial Cookbook, 1993
United Methodist Women of First United Methodist Church
Casper, Wyoming

Couscous Salad

⅔ cup raisins
⅔ cup boiling water
1½ cups chicken broth
⅛ teaspoon ground saffron
1½ cups couscous, uncooked
1½ cups diced celery
⅓ cup sliced green onions

⅓ cup pine nuts, toasted
¼ cup minced fresh parsley
¼ cup fresh lemon juice
½ teaspoon salt
¼ teaspoon pepper
¼ teaspoon ground cinnamon
½ cup olive oil

Place raisins in a small bowl; pour boiling water over raisins, and let stand 10 minutes. Drain and set aside.

Combine chicken broth and saffron in a medium saucepan; bring to a boil. Stir in couscous. Cover, remove from heat, and let stand 4 minutes or until liquid is absorbed.

Combine couscous, reserved raisins, celery, and next 3 ingredients in a large bowl; toss gently, and set aside.

Combine lemon juice, salt, pepper, and cinnamon in a bowl; stir well. Gradually add olive oil, beating constantly with a wire whisk until blended. Pour dressing mixture over couscous mixture; toss gently. Cover and chill thoroughly. Yield: 6 servings.

Classics of the American Midwest
Lancaster County Medical Auxiliary Foundation
Lincoln, Nebraska

Two Bean and Rice Salad

If you find yourself short of time, omit the Garlic Dressing and use a commercial Italian salad dressing instead. Using a low-fat dressing will make this salad a healthy choice.

3 cups cooked long-grain rice, chilled
1 (16-ounce) can pinto beans, drained
1 (15-ounce) can black beans, drained
1 (10-ounce) package frozen English peas, thawed
2 (4-ounce) cans chopped green chiles, drained
1 cup sliced celery
½ cup chopped purple onion
¼ cup chopped fresh cilantro
Garlic Dressing
Garnishes: fresh cilantro sprigs, whole green chiles

Combine first 8 ingredients in a large bowl, and toss gently. Pour Garlic Dressing over rice mixture, and toss gently. Cover and chill at least 8 hours. Garnish, if desired. Yield: 12 to 14 servings.

Garlic Dressing

⅓ cup white wine vinegar
¼ cup olive oil
½ teaspoon garlic powder
½ teaspoon pepper

Combine all ingredients in a jar. Cover tightly, and shake vigorously. Yield: ½ cup.
Margaret Lewis

Now We're Cookin'
Presbyterian Women of Northwood Presbyterian Church
Clearwater, Florida

Kitchen Sink Pasta Salad

8 ounces linguine, uncooked
8 ounces bow tie pasta,
  uncooked
8 ounces tricolored rotini,
  uncooked
8 ounces wagon wheel or shell
  macaroni, uncooked
2 large cucumbers, chopped
2 cups chopped green pepper
2 cups chopped celery
1 cup fresh broccoli
  flowerets
1 cup fresh cauliflower
  flowerets
1 cup chopped fresh parsley
½ pound salami, cubed
½ pound cooked ham, cut into
  very thin strips
8 ounces mozzarella cheese,
  cubed
1 cup grated Parmesan cheese
¾ cup chopped purple onion
1 (6-ounce) can medium pitted
  ripe olives, drained
½ cup sunflower kernels
½ cup toasted soybeans
2 teaspoons salt
1½ teaspoons pepper
Herb-Garlic Vinaigrette
3 tomatoes, coarsely chopped
3 large hard-cooked eggs,
  chopped

Cook pastas according to package directions; drain. Rinse with cold water; drain. Combine pastas and next 16 ingredients in a 2-gallon container; toss. Pour half of Herb-Garlic Vinaigrette over pasta mixture; toss. Cover and chill at least 8 hours. Cover and chill remaining vinaigrette.

To serve, pour remaining chilled vinaigrette over pasta salad; toss gently. Top salad with chopped tomato and egg. Yield: 24 servings.

Herb-Garlic Vinaigrette

2 cups olive oil
¾ cup red wine vinegar
2 tablespoons water
2 cloves garlic, minced
2½ teaspoons dried Italian
  seasoning
1 teaspoon sugar
¼ teaspoon salt
⅛ teaspoon pepper

Combine all ingredients in a jar. Cover tightly, and shake vigorously. Yield: 3 cups.

Classics of the American Midwest
Lancaster County Medical Auxiliary Foundation
Lincoln, Nebraska

Grilled Chicken Caesar Salad

As an alternative to grilling, place chicken on a lightly greased rack in a broiler pan, and broil it 5½ inches from heat (with electric oven door partially opened) 5 minutes on each side or until done.

2 slices rye bread, cut into
  ½-inch cubes
⅓ cup plus 1 tablespoon olive
  oil, divided
1 pound skinned and boned
  chicken breast halves
½ teaspoon salt, divided
½ teaspoon pepper, divided
4 anchovy fillets, chopped

2 teaspoons minced garlic
2 tablespoons lemon juice
1 tablespoon Dijon mustard
¼ teaspoon hot sauce
1 large head romaine lettuce,
  torn
3 tablespoons freshly grated
  Parmesan cheese

Sauté bread cubes in 1 tablespoon olive oil in large skillet over medium-high heat, stirring constantly, until lightly browned. Drain croutons on paper towels; set aside.

Sprinkle chicken with ¼ teaspoon salt and ¼ teaspoon pepper. Grill chicken, covered, over medium coals (300° to 350°) 5 minutes on each side or until done. Let cool 5 minutes; slice crosswise into ¼-inch-thick slices. Set chicken aside.

Combine remaining ¼ teaspoon salt, anchovy fillets, and garlic in a large bowl; mash to form a paste. Add remaining ¼ teaspoon pepper, lemon juice, mustard, and hot sauce; beat with a wire whisk until blended. Gradually add remaining ⅓ cup olive oil, beating constantly with a wire whisk until blended. Add reserved chicken, stirring to coat. Add lettuce, cheese, and reserved croutons; toss gently. Serve immediately. Yield: 4 servings.   Marylyn Gockeler

The Best of Friends
Friends of Waterloo Village
Bernardsville, New Jersey

Lemon-Artichoke Chicken Salad

The marinade from the artichoke hearts helps dress this chicken salad uniquely and quickly.

6 skinned and boned chicken breast halves
2 (6-ounce) jars marinated artichoke hearts, undrained
¾ cup chopped fresh parsley
6 to 8 slices bacon, cooked and crumbled
¼ cup plus 2 tablespoons fresh lemon juice
3 tablespoons olive oil

Place chicken in a large saucepan; add water to cover. Bring to a boil; cover, reduce heat, and simmer until chicken is done. Remove chicken from broth, discarding broth. Let chicken cool, and coarsely chop meat.

Combine chopped chicken and remaining ingredients in a large bowl, and stir well. Cover salad, and chill thoroughly. Yield: 4 to 6 servings.
                                                        Georgia Edwards

The Charlotte Central Cooks' Book
Charlotte Central School PTO
Charlotte, Vermont

Sesame-Pork Salad

If you prefer, you can use slivered cooked chicken in place of pork.

¼ pound snow pea pods, trimmed
3 cups cooked long-grain rice
1½ cups slivered cooked pork
1 medium cucumber, peeled, seeded, and cut into very thin strips
1 sweet red pepper, cut into very thin strips
½ cup sliced green onions
2 tablespoons sesame seeds, toasted
¼ cup chicken broth
3 tablespoons rice vinegar or white wine vinegar
3 tablespoons soy sauce
1 tablespoon peanut oil
1 teaspoon dark sesame oil

Cook snow peas in boiling water to cover 1 minute or until snow peas are crisp-tender; drain. Plunge snow peas into ice water; drain. Cut snow peas into very thin strips. Combine snow peas, rice, and next 5 ingredients in a large bowl, and toss gently.

Combine chicken broth and remaining ingredients in a jar. Cover tightly, and shake vigorously. Pour dressing mixture over rice mixture, and toss gently to coat. Cover and chill thoroughly. Yield: 4 servings.

Fiddlers Canyon Ward Cookbook
Fiddlers Canyon Ward Relief Society
Cedar City, Utah

Layered Tuna Salad with Dill

The cannellini beans called for in this main-dish salad are large, white Italian kidney beans.

½ cup olive oil
¼ cup chopped fresh dill
3 tablespoons fresh lemon juice
1 teaspoon minced garlic
¾ teaspoon salt
¼ teaspoon pepper
2 (6½-ounce) cans tuna in water, drained and flaked
1 (15-ounce) can cannellini beans, drained

1 (7-ounce) jar roasted red peppers, drained and cut into very thin strips
4 ounces feta cheese, crumbled
4 cups thinly sliced romaine lettuce
2 cups halved cherry tomatoes
1 cucumber, thinly sliced
¼ cup kalamata olives, pitted

Combine first 6 ingredients in a medium bowl; stir with a wire whisk until blended. Spoon 3 tablespoons dressing mixture into each of 2 small bowls; pour remaining dressing mixture into a medium bowl. Add tuna to dressing in 1 small bowl; toss gently, and set aside. Add beans to dressing in other small bowl; toss gently, and set aside. Add red peppers and feta cheese to dressing in medium bowl; toss gently, and set aside.

Place lettuce in a large bowl. Layer reserved bean mixture, tomatoes, reserved tuna mixture, cucumber, and red pepper mixture over lettuce in order listed. Sprinkle with olives. Serve immediately. Yield: 6 servings.   Robin Baker Dickson

Windows: Reflections of Taste
Brenau University Alumnae Association
Gainesville, Georgia

Plum Sauce Dressing

This salad dressing is made with a base of commercial plum sauce. With its Oriental flavor, it would be wonderful over any Chinese-inspired salad.

¼ cup plus 2 tablespoons rice vinegar
¼ cup peanut or vegetable oil
¼ cup sugar
¼ cup sesame seeds, toasted

¼ cup commercial plum sauce
2 tablespoons light sesame oil
2 teaspoons salt
1 teaspoon pepper

Combine all ingredients in a jar. Cover tightly, and shake vigorously. Chill. Shake well just before serving. Serve dressing over salad greens. Yield: about 1¼ cups.

Terry Lock

A Collection of Favorite Recipes
Po'okela Church
Makawao, Hawaii

Blue Cheese-Walnut Dressing

1⅓ cups mayonnaise
¾ cup sour cream
1 teaspoon dried dillweed
1 teaspoon Worcestershire sauce
½ teaspoon salt
½ teaspoon garlic powder

½ teaspoon dry mustard
½ teaspoon pepper
¾ cup coarsely chopped walnuts
4 ounces blue cheese, crumbled

Combine first 8 ingredients in a medium bowl, beating with a wire whisk until blended. Stir in chopped walnuts and blue cheese. Cover and chill at least 8 hours. Serve dressing over salad greens. Yield: 3 cups.

Diane Totherow

Cooking with Class, A Second Helping
Charlotte Latin School
Charlotte, North Carolina

Sauces & Condiments

Most sauces and condiments are made from just a few simple but flavor-packed ingredients. Vinegars, spices, and sweeteners are some of the taste-teasers used in these recipes.

Tomato-Pear Chutney, page 275

Apricot-Ginger Sauce

This sauce has a chunky texture. If you prefer, you can transfer the cooled sauce to the container of an electric blender, and cover and process until smooth. The yield will be slightly less.

2½ cups water
¼ cup sugar
8 ounces dried apricots, chopped

1 tablespoon chopped crystallized ginger
2 tablespoons apricot brandy

Combine water and sugar in a medium saucepan; stir well. Bring to a boil over medium heat. Add apricots and ginger; reduce heat, and simmer, uncovered, 15 minutes. Stir in brandy, and simmer 2 minutes. Serve warm with pork or ham, or chill and serve over ice cream. Yield: 2¾ cups.

Cooking with Herb Scents
Western Reserve Herb Society
Bay Village, Ohio

Lemon Fruit Sauce

Enjoy this quick and easy sauce as a dressing over fruit salad, as a dip for fresh fruit, or as a dessert sauce over pound cake.

1 (8-ounce) carton sour cream
½ cup sifted powdered sugar
1 teaspoon grated lemon rind

1 teaspoon fresh lemon juice
¼ teaspoon vanilla extract

Combine all ingredients in a small bowl, stirring with a wire whisk until blended. Cover and chill at least 8 hours. Yield: 1 cup.

California Sizzles
The Junior League of Pasadena, California

Maple-Cranberry Sauce

1 (12-ounce) package fresh
  cranberries
1 cup pure maple syrup
1 cup cranberry-raspberry
  drink

1 tablespoon grated orange
  rind
1 cup walnuts

Combine first 4 ingredients in a nonaluminum saucepan; bring to a boil. Reduce heat to medium, and cook 10 minutes or until cranberry skins pop and mixture is thickened, stirring frequently. Stir in walnuts. Remove from heat, and let cool. Cover and chill. Yield: 3½ cups.

Classics of the American Midwest
Lancaster County Medical Auxiliary Foundation
Lincoln, Nebraska

Pear-Honey Cranberry Sauce

Serve this colorful, honey-sweetened sauce over ice cream, pound cake, or as an accompaniment to turkey or pork.

½ cup sugar
½ cup water
2 medium pears, peeled and
  diced
1 (12-ounce) package fresh
  cranberries

1 cup honey
1 teaspoon grated lemon rind
2 teaspoons fresh lemon juice

Combine sugar and water in a large saucepan; stir well. Cook over medium-high heat, stirring constantly, until sugar dissolves. Reduce heat to medium. Stir in diced pear, and cook 3 minutes, stirring frequently. Add cranberries and honey, and cook 5 to 7 minutes or until cranberry skins pop. Remove from heat, and stir in grated lemon rind and lemon juice. Cover and chill thoroughly. Yield: 4 cups.

Cookin' with C.L.A.S.S.
Citizens League for Adult Special Services
Lawrence, Massachusetts

Rosy Fruit Sauce

This fruit sauce is made with a combination of apples, pears, and plums. It gets its rosy color from the Rome apples and plums.

1½ pounds Golden Delicious
  apples, unpeeled
1½ pounds Rome apples,
  unpeeled
2 ripe pears, unpeeled
2 ripe plums, unpeeled
3½ cups water

½ cup sugar
¼ cup firmly packed brown
  sugar
1 tablespoon fresh lemon juice
1 teaspoon ground cinnamon
1 teaspoon ground nutmeg
Dash of ground cloves

Wash and core apples and pears; pit plums. Cut each into 8 wedges. Combine fruit, water, and remaining ingredients in a Dutch oven; bring to a boil. Reduce heat, and cook, uncovered, 30 minutes or until tender, mashing occasionally with a potato masher.

Pour fruit mixture through a wire-mesh strainer into a large bowl, and discard skins. Serve sauce warm, or cover and chill. Yield: 6 cups.
Lore Kephart

Heavenly Hosts
Bryn Mawr Presbyterian Church
Bryn Mawr, Pennsylvania

Tangy Dipping Sauce

Creole mustard and horseradish supply the tang in this sauce.

1 (18-ounce) jar orange
  marmalade
¼ cup plus 1 tablespoon
  Creole mustard

¼ cup plus 1 tablespoon
  prepared horseradish

Combine all ingredients in a medium bowl; stir well. Store in the refrigerator. Serve at room temperature with chicken or pork. Yield: 2⅓ cups.
Sherri Wilson

Impressions: A Palette of Fine Memphis Dining
Auxiliary to the Memphis Dental Society
Memphis, Tennessee

Fort Sauce

Honey and hot sauce spike this mayonnaise-based sauce and add a sweet and hot flavor.

⅔ cup mayonnaise
2 tablespoons catsup
2 tablespoons honey
2 tablespoons grated onion
1 teaspoon curry powder

1 teaspoon lemon juice
1 teaspoon tarragon vinegar
6 to 7 drops of hot sauce
¼ teaspoon salt
⅛ teaspoon pepper

Combine all ingredients in a medium bowl; stir with a wire whisk until blended. Serve with chilled shrimp, cooked vegetables, or steamed artichokes. Yield: 1¼ cups. Pat Knight

Cooking in Paradise
Key West Power Squadron
Key West, Florida

Mango-Jicama Salsa

Be sure to wear protective gloves when seeding fresh jalapeño peppers. The seeds and membranes of the peppers contain irritating oils that can burn your skin and eyes.

2 cups peeled, diced jicama
1 cup chopped fresh mango
½ cup chopped onion
2 tablespoons chopped fresh cilantro

1 to 2 jalapeño peppers, seeded and minced
3 tablespoons fresh lemon juice

Combine all ingredients in a bowl; stir well. Cover and chill at least 2 hours. Serve with tortilla chips. Yield: 3 cups.

Some Like It Hot
The Junior League of McAllen, Texas

Peanut Sauce

1 cup salted roasted peanuts,
  ground
1 small onion, chopped
½ cup vegetable broth
3 tablespoons rice vinegar
2 tablespoons dry sherry

2 tablespoons soy sauce
1 teaspoon peeled, grated
  gingerroot
1 teaspoon chili powder
⅛ teaspoon ground red
  pepper

Position knife blade in food processor bowl; add all ingredients. Cover and process 20 seconds, stopping once to scrape down sides. Pour sauce mixture into a small saucepan; cook over low heat until sauce is thoroughly heated. Serve sauce over hot cooked pasta. Yield: 2 cups.
Robin Schrek

The Best of Friends
Friends of Waterloo Village
Bernardsville, New Jersey

Sun-Dried Tomato Pesto

Pesto is most often made with fresh basil, garlic, toasted pine nuts, Parmesan cheese, and olive oil. This sun-dried tomato version gives traditional pesto a new personality.

¼ cup pine nuts, toasted
¼ cup oil-packed sun-dried
  tomatoes, drained
2 cloves garlic
¼ cup plus 2 tablespoons
  olive oil

¼ cup freshly grated Asiago or
  Parmesan cheese
1 tablespoon tomato paste
½ teaspoon dried thyme

Position knife blade in food processor bowl; add first 3 ingredients. Cover and process 30 seconds or until tomatoes are finely chopped. Combine tomato mixture, olive oil, and remaining ingredients in a small bowl; stir well. Cover and chill up to 3 days. Serve over hot cooked pasta. Yield: ¾ cup.

Culinary Arts, Volume II
Society of the Arts of Allentown Art Museum
Allentown, Pennsylvania

Baked Aloha

Serve this pudding-like pineapple mixture with sliced cooked ham, pork roast, or poultry.

1 (20-ounce) can crushed
  pineapple, drained
1 cup sugar
¼ cup water
2 large eggs, beaten

2 tablespoons cornstarch
1 teaspoon vanilla extract
¼ teaspoon ground cinnamon
1 tablespoon butter or
  margarine

Combine first 6 ingredients in a medium bowl; stir well. Pour mixture into a lightly greased 1-quart casserole. Sprinkle with cinnamon, and dot with butter. Bake, uncovered, at 325° for 1 hour. Serve immediately. Yield: 6 servings.

For Goodness Taste
The Junior League of Rochester, New York

Florida Oranges in Red Wine

The vanilla bean is a slender pod that's actually the fruit of a type of orchid—the only variety of orchid that bears an edible fruit.

6 oranges
1 cup water
1 cup Burgundy or other dry
  red wine
¾ cup sugar

4 lemon slices
2 whole cloves
1 vanilla bean
1 (3-inch) stick cinnamon

Peel and seed oranges; cut horizontally into ¼-inch-thick slices. Place orange slices in a bowl, and set aside.

Combine water and remaining ingredients in a large saucepan; bring to a boil, stirring until sugar dissolves. Boil, uncovered, 15 minutes. Pour mixture through a wire-mesh strainer into a bowl, discarding lemon slices, cloves, vanilla bean, and cinnamon. Pour wine mixture over reserved orange slices. Serve warm or at room temperature. Yield: 4 to 6 servings.

Tampa Treasures
The Junior League of Tampa, Florida

Pumpkin-Apricot Butter

1 (29-ounce) can pumpkin
2 cups honey
1 (6-ounce) package dried
  apricots, finely chopped

1¼ cups water
¾ cup lemon juice
1 teaspoon vanilla extract

Combine pumpkin and honey in a saucepan; cook over medium heat until thoroughly heated, stirring occasionally. Add apricots and remaining ingredients. Bring to a boil; reduce heat, and simmer, uncovered, 55 to 60 minutes or until thickened. Spoon into jars; cover and store in the refrigerator. Yield: 6 half pints.

Steamboat Entertains
Steamboat Springs Winter Sports Club
Steamboat Springs, Colorado

Cranberry-Onion Confit

2 medium onions, thinly sliced
½ cup butter or margarine,
  melted
½ cup water
¼ cup plus 2 tablespoons
  grated orange rind
2 (12-ounce) packages fresh
  cranberries
3 cups cranberry juice cocktail

2 cups sugar
1 cup orange juice
1 teaspoon ground cinnamon
½ teaspoon ground ginger
⅛ teaspoon ground cardamom
⅛ teaspoon ground coriander
⅛ teaspoon ground nutmeg
1 cup chopped fresh basil

Sauté onion in butter in a large skillet over medium heat, stirring constantly, 25 minutes or until onion is caramelized. Set aside.

Bring water to a boil. Add orange rind; remove from heat. Cover and let stand 3 minutes. Drain and set aside.

Combine cranberries and next 8 ingredients in a Dutch oven. Bring to a boil; reduce heat, and simmer, uncovered, 1 hour, stirring occasionally. Let cool. Stir in onion, orange rind, and basil. Cover and chill at least 8 hours. Yield: 8 cups.   JoAnn Singer

Five Star Sensations
Auxiliary of University Hospitals of Cleveland
Shaker Heights, Ohio

Banana Chutney

Serve this chutney with cheese, or as a spread, or with curried dishes.

8 bananas, sliced
3 cups chopped onion
1 (8-ounce) package pitted
  dates, chopped
1½ cups white vinegar
2 cups water

1 cup sugar
¾ cup raisins
2 teaspoons ground ginger
1 teaspoon salt
1 teaspoon curry powder

Combine first 4 ingredients in a large saucepan; bring to a boil. Cover, reduce heat, and simmer 20 minutes. Add water and remaining ingredients, and cook, uncovered, 1 hour or until thickened. Spoon chutney into jars; cover and store in refrigerator. Yield: 8 half pints.   Mary Becker

When the Master Gardener Cooks
Seminole County Master Gardeners
Sanford, Florida

Tomato-Pear Chutney

1 (29-ounce) can pears,
  drained and diced
1 (28-ounce) can Italian-style
  tomatoes, undrained and
  chopped
½ (14-ounce) can Italian-style
  tomatoes, undrained and
  chopped
1 cup raisins

1 cup firmly packed brown
  sugar
1 large onion, chopped
½ cup cider vinegar
2 teaspoons ground cinnamon
1 teaspoon ground ginger
1 teaspoon mustard seeds
¼ teaspoon salt

Combine all ingredients in a large saucepan; stir well. Bring to a boil; reduce heat, and simmer, uncovered, 1 hour and 40 minutes or until thickened, stirring occasionally. Cover and chill at least 8 hours. Yield: 4½ cups.   Winnie Rudicil

All Saints' Cookbook
All Saints' Episcopal Churchwomen
Morristown, Tennessee

Marinated Green Peppers

You can toss these Marinated Green Peppers into salads, or add them to sandwiches, cooked vegetables, or scrambled eggs for extra flavor and color.

1 cup water
1 cup white wine vinegar
1 cup vegetable oil
3 cloves garlic, thinly sliced
1 tablespoon sugar
1 tablespoon salt

1½ teaspoons mustard seeds
½ teaspoon celery seeds
6 medium-size green peppers,
   cut into ¾-inch strips
2 medium onions, thinly sliced
   and separated into rings

Combine first 8 ingredients in a large saucepan; bring to a boil. Add pepper strips, and return to a boil. Boil 2 to 3 minutes or until pepper strips are crisp-tender. Remove from heat, and stir in onion. Pour into a large jar with a tight-fitting lid. Cover and chill at least 1 week. Store in refrigerator. Yield: 6 cups.

The Tasty Palette Cookbook
South County Art Association
St. Louis, Missouri

Garlic Spread

Slather Garlic Spread on toasted bagels or warm slices of French bread.

1 (8-ounce) package cream
   cheese, softened
¼ cup butter or margarine,
   softened
1 teaspoon minced fresh
   parsley

½ teaspoon crushed garlic
¼ teaspoon salt
¼ teaspoon coarsely ground
   pepper

Beat cream cheese and butter at medium speed of an electric mixer until creamy. Stir in parsley and remaining ingredients. Cover and chill thoroughly. Let stand at room temperature 30 minutes before serving. Yield: 1⅓ cups.   Pat Lee

Cross-Town Cooking
Women's Group of Assumption and Sacred Heart Parishes
Bellingham, Washington

Topping for French Bread

This simple topping of Parmesan cheese, mayonnaise, and green onions adds terrific flavor to slices of French bread.

½ cup grated Parmesan cheese
½ cup mayonnaise
¼ cup chopped green onions
  with tops

French bread, sliced

Combine all ingredients except French bread in a small bowl; stir well. To serve, spread topping on sliced French bread, and place on an ungreased baking sheet. Broil 5½ inches from heat (with electric oven door partially opened) until lightly browned. Serve warm. Yield: ¾ cup.   Anne Starkey

A Taste of History
University of North Alabama Women's Club
Florence, Alabama

Creamy Lemon Mayonnaise

Try this creamy mayonnaise dressing over a chef's salad or shrimp salad.

1 cup mayonnaise
1 teaspoon grated lemon rind
3 tablespoons lemon juice

⅓ cup whipping cream
3 tablespoons powdered sugar

Combine mayonnaise, lemon rind, and lemon juice in a small bowl; stir well. Beat whipping cream until foamy; gradually add sugar, beating until soft peaks form. Fold whipped cream into mayonnaise mixture. Serve immediately. Yield: 1¾ cups.

The Pasquotank Plate
Christ Episcopal Churchwomen
Elizabeth City, North Carolina

Gerry Cohen's Mustard

Spread some of this zippy mustard on your next sandwich for a real flavor impact. It's spiked with horseradish!

½ cup dry mustard
½ cup white vinegar
1 large egg, lightly beaten
½ cup sugar
2 tablespoons minced onion
2 tablespoons prepared
  horseradish

2½ teaspoons fresh lemon
  juice
⅛ teaspoon ground cloves
⅛ teaspoon ground red
  pepper

Combine mustard and vinegar in a glass bowl; cover and let stand at room temperature at least 8 hours.

Place mustard mixture in top of a double boiler; add egg and remaining ingredients, stirring well. Bring water to a boil; reduce heat, and simmer, uncovered, 1 hour, stirring occasionally (do not let mixture boil). Remove from heat; let cool. Spoon into a glass jar; cover and store in refrigerator. Yield: 1 cup.   Lisa Ekus

Some Like It Hot
The Bement School
Deerfield, Massachusetts

Mustard and Bourbon Marinade

½ cup firmly packed dark
  brown sugar
½ cup Dijon mustard
⅓ cup minced green onions
¼ cup plus 2 tablespoons
  bourbon

¼ cup soy sauce
2 teaspoons Worcestershire
  sauce

Combine all ingredients in a medium bowl, stirring with a wire whisk until blended. Use as a marinade and basting sauce for shrimp or chicken. Yield: 1½ cups.   Evelyn Sloan

Our Favorite Recipes
Unity Truth Center
Port Richey, Florida

Soups & Stews

*These hearty soups and stews make great family suppers
or casual entertaining fare, while the delicate cream soups create
elegant first courses for formal dinners.*

Cheesy Chowder, page 291

Cold Apple Soup

Serve this chilled apple soup as an appetizer or as a dessert soup. Orange-flavored liqueur adds pizazz.

6 medium cooking apples,
  peeled and sliced
2 cups apple juice
¼ cup fresh lemon juice
2 tablespoons sugar
1 teaspoon ground cinnamon
1 teaspoon vanilla extract
2 cups half-and-half

2 cups orange juice
1 medium cooking apple,
  unpeeled and shredded
3 tablespoons Cointreau or
  other orange-flavored liqueur
Garnishes: whipped cream,
  apple peel

Combine apple slices and apple juice in a medium saucepan. Bring to a boil; cover, reduce heat, and simmer 10 minutes or until tender. Remove from heat; stir in lemon juice, sugar, cinnamon, and vanilla. Cover and chill up to 8 hours.

Add half-and-half and orange juice to chilled apple mixture; stir well. Transfer half of chilled apple mixture to container of an electric blender; cover and process on high speed 1 minute or until smooth, stopping once to scrape down sides. Repeat procedure with remaining apple mixture. Stir in shredded apple and liqueur. To serve, ladle soup into individual soup bowls. Garnish, if desired. Yield: 11 cups.

Othello D. Ballenger

Palmetto Palate Cookbook
American Cancer Society, South Carolina Division
Columbia, South Carolina

Red Pepper Vichyssoise

If you prefer, you can substitute sour cream for the Crème Fraîche.

4 medium-size sweet red
  peppers
2 cups thinly sliced leeks
2 tablespoons butter or
  margarine, melted
4½ cups chicken broth
3 cups peeled, thinly sliced
  baking potatoes

1 cup whipping cream
¼ teaspoon salt
⅛ teaspoon ground white
  pepper
Crème Fraîche
Garnish: chopped fresh chives

Cut peppers into thirds; remove seeds and membranes. Place peppers in a large saucepan; add water to cover. Bring to a boil; reduce heat, and simmer, uncovered, 6 minutes. Drain; let cool. Remove and discard skin from peppers. Place peppers in container of an electric blender; cover and process until smooth, stopping once to scrape down sides. Cover and chill thoroughly.

Sauté leeks in butter in a Dutch oven over medium-high heat, stirring constantly, until tender. Add broth and potato. Bring to a boil; reduce heat, and simmer, partially covered, 30 minutes or until potato is tender. Place half of potato mixture in container of an electric blender; cover and process until smooth, stopping once to scrape down sides. Repeat procedure with remaining potato mixture. Stir in whipping cream, salt, and pepper. Cover and chill thoroughly.

Combine pepper mixture and potato mixture; stir well. To serve, ladle soup into individual soup bowls. Top each serving with a dollop of Crème Fraîche. Garnish, if desired. Yield: 8 cups.

Crème Fraîche

2 tablespoons buttermilk   1 cup whipping cream

Combine buttermilk and whipping cream; cover and let stand at room temperature 8 hours. Yield: 1 cup.

Some Like It Hot
The Junior League of McAllen, Texas

Chilled Tomato and Yogurt Soup

1½ cups chopped onion
2 tablespoons butter or
    margarine, melted
3 cups peeled, seeded, and
    chopped tomatoes
2 cups peeled, seeded, and
    chopped cucumber

2 cups chicken broth
1 teaspoon dried basil
2 cups plain yogurt
½ teaspoon salt
Garnish: chopped fresh mint

Sauté onion in butter in a large saucepan over medium heat, stirring constantly, until tender. Add tomato and next 3 ingredients. Bring to a boil; reduce heat, and simmer, uncovered, 30 minutes, stirring frequently.

Transfer half of tomato mixture to container of an electric blender; cover and process until smooth, stopping once to scrape down sides. Repeat procedure with remaining mixture. Stir in yogurt and salt. Cover and chill. To serve, ladle into individual soup bowls. Garnish, if desired. Yield: 8 cups.   Gene Maston

Heavenly Morsels from Hell's Kitchen
Metro Baptist Church
New York, New York

Cream of Green Bean Soup

Potatoes thicken this soup instead of flour or cornstarch. If the soup gets too thick, add the greater amount of whipping cream called for.

6 green onions, sliced
6 shallots, chopped
1 clove garlic, minced
3 tablespoons butter or
    margarine, melted
2 medium baking potatoes,
    peeled and diced

4 cups chicken broth
2 pounds fresh green beans,
    cut into 2-inch pieces
½ to 1 cup whipping cream
1 tablespoon lemon juice
½ teaspoon dried tarragon
¼ teaspoon pepper

Sauté green onions, shallot, and garlic in butter in a medium skillet over medium heat, stirring constantly, until tender. Set aside.

Cook potato in boiling water to cover 15 minutes or until tender; drain well, and set aside. Bring chicken broth to a boil in a large saucepan; add green beans, and cook 30 to 35 minutes or until tender. Add reserved green onions mixture and potato; stir well.

Transfer half of green bean mixture to container of an electric blender; cover and process until smooth, stopping once to scrape down sides. Repeat procedure with remaining green bean mixture. Return pureed mixture to pan; bring to a boil. Reduce heat; stir in whipping cream, lemon juice, and tarragon. Cook until thoroughly heated. To serve, ladle soup into individual soup bowls, and sprinkle with pepper. Yield: 7 cups.   Elaine Perry

Flavors of Cape Henlopen
Village Improvement Association
Rehoboth Beach, Delaware

New Mexican Soup

Refried beans give this spicy soup its thick and creamy texture and green chiles its flavor punch. For a Tex-Mex interpretation of a soup and salad lunch, add a taco on the side.

4 slices bacon, diced
¾ cup chopped onion
¾ cup chopped celery
1 clove garlic, minced
1 (16-ounce) can refried beans
1 (14½-ounce) can ready-to-serve chicken broth

1 (4-ounce) can chopped green chiles, undrained
¼ teaspoon chili powder
¼ teaspoon pepper
Shredded Cheddar cheese
Crushed tortilla chips

Cook bacon in a large saucepan until crisp; remove bacon, reserving drippings in saucepan. Set bacon aside.

Sauté onion, celery, and garlic in drippings over medium heat, stirring constantly, until tender. Add refried beans and next 4 ingredients; stir well. Bring to a boil; reduce heat, and simmer, uncovered, 10 minutes.

To serve, ladle soup into individual soup bowls. Sprinkle each serving with reserved bacon, and top with cheese and crushed tortilla chips. Yield: 4¾ cups.

Southwest Seasons Cookbook
Casa Angelica Auxiliary
Albuquerque, New Mexico

Roasted Garlic and Leek Soup

When garlic is roasted, it takes on a more mellow flavor and buttery texture. You can even use roasted garlic as a spread for French bread. Just press the puree from the roasted cloves onto bread slices and spread.

4 large heads garlic, unpeeled
¼ cup olive oil
4 medium leeks
1 medium onion, chopped
¼ cup plus 2 tablespoons butter or margarine, melted
¼ cup plus 2 tablespoons all-purpose flour

4 cups chicken broth
⅓ cup dry sherry
1 cup whipping cream
1 tablespoon fresh lemon juice
Salt and ground white pepper to taste
Garnish: chopped fresh chives

Gently peel papery outer skin from garlic, leaving heads intact. Remove and discard ¼ inch from top of each garlic head. Place garlic in a small shallow baking dish; drizzle with olive oil. Bake, uncovered, at 350° for 1 hour or until tender. Remove from oven, and let cool. Press garlic cloves to release garlic; discard papery skin. Chop garlic, and set aside.

Remove and discard root, tough outer leaves, and top of leek to where dark green becomes pale. Chop leek. Sauté leek, reserved chopped garlic, and onion in butter in a large saucepan over medium-high heat, stirring constantly, until tender. Reduce heat to low; add flour. Cook 1 minute, stirring constantly. Add chicken broth and sherry; bring to a boil, stirring constantly. Reduce heat, and simmer, uncovered, 20 minutes, stirring occasionally. Remove from heat, and let cool slightly.

Position knife blade in food processor bowl. Pour leek mixture into container; cover and process until smooth, stopping once to scrape down sides. Return leek mixture to pan. Stir in whipping cream; simmer, uncovered, over low heat 10 minutes, stirring occasionally. Add lemon juice and salt and pepper to taste. To serve, ladle soup into individual soup bowls. Garnish, if desired. Yield: 6 cups.

Still Gathering: A Centennial Celebration
Auxiliary to the American Osteopathic Association
Chicago, Illinois

Moroccan Lentil Soup

Red lentils are smaller, rounder, and lack the seed coat of brown lentils. If red lentils aren't available in your area, you can substitute brown lentils.

6 large fresh spinach leaves
1 medium onion, chopped
2 tablespoons olive oil
1 carrot, scraped and sliced
2 cloves garlic, minced
6 cups chicken broth
1 cup red lentils
1 cup peeled, seeded, and
 chopped tomato
4 green onions, sliced
¼ cup chopped fresh parsley
¼ cup chopped fresh cilantro

1 bay leaf
2 teaspoons ground ginger
2 teaspoons ground turmeric
2 teaspoons paprika
1 teaspoon ground cumin
1 teaspoon ground cinnamon
½ teaspoon pepper
¼ teaspoon salt
½ cup fine egg noodles,
 uncooked
½ cup plain yogurt

Remove stems from spinach; wash leaves thoroughly, and pat dry. Cut into thin strips; set aside.

Sauté onion in olive oil in a large saucepan over medium-high heat, stirring constantly, until tender. Add sliced carrot and garlic, and sauté, stirring constantly, until crisp-tender. Add chicken broth and next 13 ingredients; bring to a boil. Partially cover, reduce heat, and simmer 20 minutes or until lentils are tender. Stir in reserved spinach and noodles; cook, partially covered, 7 minutes or until noodles are done. Remove and discard bay leaf.

To serve, ladle soup into individual soup bowls. Top each serving with a dollop of yogurt. Yield: 7½ cups.

Celebrate!
The Junior League of Sacramento, California

Colorful Potato Soup

1 medium onion, finely
  chopped
2 tablespoons butter or
  margarine, melted
4 chicken-flavored bouillon
  cubes
4 cups boiling water
1 (14½-ounce) can ready-to-
  serve chicken broth

3 cups peeled, diced baking
  potatoes (about 2 pounds)
1 cup grated carrot
1 to 1½ teaspoons salt
¼ teaspoon pepper
2 tablespoons all-purpose flour
1 (8-ounce) carton sour cream
2 tablespoons chopped fresh
  parsley

Sauté onion in butter in a Dutch oven over medium heat, stirring constantly, until tender. Dissolve bouillon cubes in boiling water. Add bouillon and broth to pan; bring to a boil. Add potato; cover, reduce heat, and simmer 15 minutes. Stir in carrot, salt, and pepper; cover and simmer 15 minutes or until potato is tender.

Combine flour and 2 tablespoons cooking liquid, stirring with a wire whisk until smooth. Stir flour mixture into soup mixture; cook, stirring constantly, until thickened and bubbly. Reduce heat to low; stir in sour cream and parsley. Cook just until thoroughly heated. Yield: 8 cups.

Pat Quinn

Now You're Cookin'
Our Lady of Perpetual Help Church
Glenview, Illinois

Pumpkin-Vegetable Soup

Canned pumpkin enhances the taste and texture of this autumn-inspired version of vegetable soup.

1½ cups chopped onion
2 tablespoons butter, melted
3 cups canned ready-to-serve
  chicken broth
1 (19-ounce) can chick-peas
  (garbanzo beans), drained
1 cup peeled, diced baking
  potato
1 cup sliced carrot

1 cup frozen whole kernel corn
1 cup frozen lima beans
½ cup sliced celery
1 (16-ounce) can pumpkin
½ teaspoon salt
¼ teaspoon ground nutmeg
⅛ teaspoon ground white
  pepper
1 cup whipping cream

Sauté onion in butter in a saucepan over medium heat, stirring constantly, until tender. Add broth and next 6 ingredients; bring to a boil. Cover, reduce heat, and simmer 15 minutes or until vegetables are tender. Stir in pumpkin, salt, nutmeg, and white pepper; simmer 5 minutes. Stir in whipping cream; cook until heated. Yield: 11 cups.   Rose Marie Fowler

Exclusively Pumpkin Cookbook
Coventry Historical Society
Coventry, Connecticut

Green Chile, Chicken, and Corn Soup

1 medium onion	2 Anaheim chiles
2 whole cloves	2¾ cups fresh cut corn (about
5 cups beef broth	4 ears)
3 cups chicken broth	1 avocado, sliced
3 chicken breast halves,	2 medium tomatoes, chopped
skinned	Garnishes: sour cream, fresh
2 large baking potatoes, peeled	cilantro sprigs
and diced	

Stud onion with cloves. Combine onion, broths, chicken, and potato in a Dutch oven; bring to a boil. Cover, reduce heat, and simmer 20 minutes or until potato is tender. Remove onion. Remove chicken from broth, reserving broth in pan. Let cool; bone chicken, and chop meat. Return chicken to pan; set aside.

Cut chiles in half lengthwise; remove seeds and membranes. Place chiles, skin side up, on an ungreased baking sheet; flatten with palm of hand. Broil 3 inches from heat (with electric oven door partially opened) 6 minutes or until charred. Place chiles in ice water; peel and discard skins. Coarsely chop chiles, and add to reserved broth mixture. Stir in corn; bring to a boil. Reduce heat, and simmer, uncovered, 4 minutes or until corn is tender.

To serve, ladle soup into individual soup bowls. Top each serving with avocado slices and chopped tomato. Garnish, if desired. Yield: 12¾ cups.

Southwest Cooks! The Tradition of Native American Cuisines
Southwest Museum
Los Angeles, California

Chicken-Mushroom Soup with Barley

Barley is a hardy grain that can be traced back to the Stone Age. Pearl barley, often used in soups and stews, has the bran removed and has been steamed and polished.

3 pounds assorted chicken
  pieces, skinned
2½ quarts water
1½ cups sliced celery
½ cup chopped onion
2 carrots, scraped and sliced
1 bay leaf

2½ teaspoons salt
1 teaspoon dried thyme
¼ teaspoon pepper
1 pound fresh mushrooms,
  sliced
¾ cup pearl barley, uncooked

Combine first 9 ingredients in a Dutch oven. Bring to a boil; cover, reduce heat, and simmer 1 hour or until chicken is done. Drain, reserving chicken, vegetables, and broth. Bone chicken; chop meat, and set aside.

Return reserved vegetables and broth to pan; add mushrooms and barley, stirring well. Bring to a boil; cover, reduce heat, and simmer 30 minutes. Stir in reserved chicken, and simmer an additional 10 minutes or until barley is tender. Remove and discard bay leaf. Yield: 11 cups.

Orel Borgeson

Food for Family, Friends and Fellowship
Covenant Women Ministries of Forest Park Covenant Church
Muskegon, Michigan

Chicken-Vegetable Soup, Thai Style

1 large carrot, scraped and
  diagonally sliced
1 stalk celery, diagonally
  sliced
½ cup chopped onion
2 cloves garlic, minced
2 tablespoons peanut oil
6 cups chicken broth

2 cups chopped cooked
  chicken breast
1 (14-ounce) can coconut milk
1 medium baking potato,
  peeled and diced
¾ cup chunky peanut butter
¼ to ½ teaspoon dried
  crushed red pepper

Sauté carrot, celery, onion, and garlic in oil in a Dutch oven over medium-high heat, stirring constantly, until tender. Stir in broth and remaining ingredients; bring to a boil. Reduce heat, and simmer, uncovered, 20 to 30 minutes or until potato is tender. Yield: 10 cups.

Rogue River Rendezvous
The Junior Service League of Jackson County
Medford, Oregon

Eggplant Soup

Eggplant becomes bitter tasting with age. For the best flavor, choose a firm, smooth-skinned eggplant that feels heavy for its size. The flesh of eggplant discolors quickly, so cut it just before using.

1 pound Italian sausage	1 teaspoon salt
2 tablespoons olive oil	1 teaspoon sugar
1 medium onion, chopped	1 teaspoon dried basil
2 cloves garlic, minced	1 teaspoon dried oregano
1 medium eggplant, peeled and diced	$\frac{1}{2}$ to 1 cup Burgundy or other dry red wine
8 large tomatoes, peeled and quartered	$\frac{1}{2}$ cup elbow macaroni, uncooked
3 medium zucchini, diced	$\frac{1}{4}$ teaspoon pepper
3 carrots, scraped and diced	Freshly grated Parmesan cheese
2 stalks celery, diced	
4 cups beef broth	

Brown sausage in a large Dutch oven over medium heat, stirring until it crumbles; drain.

Return sausage to pan. Add olive oil, onion, and garlic. Cook over medium-high heat, stirring constantly, until onion is tender. Add eggplant; cook, stirring constantly, 3 minutes. Add tomato and next 8 ingredients; bring to a boil. Reduce heat, and simmer, uncovered, 2 hours. Stir in wine, macaroni, and pepper; cook 15 to 20 minutes or until pasta is done.

To serve, ladle soup into individual soup bowls. Top each serving with Parmesan cheese. Yield: 18 cups.   Katherine Meade

The Cradle of Aviation Cookbook
Glenn H. Curtiss Museum
Hammondsport, New York

Basque Potato Soup

1 pound smoked sausage,
  sliced
1 cup chopped onion
2 (16-ounce) cans whole
  tomatoes, undrained and
  chopped
2 cups water
2 beef-flavored bouillon cubes
1 bay leaf
½ teaspoon dried thyme
6 medium baking potatoes,
  peeled and diced

1 cup diagonally sliced celery
1 cup sliced carrot
½ cup Burgundy or other dry
  red wine
2 tablespoons chopped celery
  leaves
2 cups shredded cabbage
1 tablespoon lemon juice
Salt and pepper to taste

Cook sausage and onion in a large Dutch oven 5 minutes, stirring frequently; drain well. Return sausage mixture to pan; add tomatoes and next 4 ingredients. Bring to a boil; cover, reduce heat, and simmer 15 minutes. Stir in potato and next 4 ingredients; simmer 20 minutes. Add cabbage, and simmer an additional 20 minutes. Remove and discard bay leaf. Stir in lemon juice and salt and pepper to taste. Yield: 11 cups.

Virginia Celebrates
The Council of the Virginia Museum of Fine Arts
Richmond, Virginia

Smoked Barley Soup

For soup with a thinner consistency, stir in an extra cup of half-and-half.

4 (14½-ounce) cans ready-to-
  serve chicken broth
¾ pound meaty smoked ham
  hocks
1 cup pearl barley, uncooked
3 large baking potatoes, peeled
  and diced

2 carrots, scraped and diced
1 medium onion, chopped
1 clove garlic, minced
1 cup half-and-half
Salt and pepper to taste

Combine chicken broth and ham hocks in a Dutch oven. Bring to a boil; reduce heat, and simmer, uncovered, 40 minutes or until meat is tender. Remove meat from bone; coarsely chop meat, and return to broth.

Add barley and next 4 ingredients; bring to a boil. Reduce heat, and simmer, uncovered, 50 minutes or until barley and vegetables are tender. Stir in half-and-half. Add salt and pepper to taste, and cook until thoroughly heated. Yield: 11 cups.   Beverly Fawcett

We're Really Cookin' Now!
Epsilon Sigma Alpha of Oklahoma
McAlester, Oklahoma

Cheesy Chowder

This chowder gets its creamy texture from melted process American cheese. Be careful if you're inclined to substitute cheeses. Not all melt as smoothly as the process variety.

1 cup peeled, chopped baking
  potato
½ cup chopped carrot
½ cup chopped celery
½ cup chopped onion
½ cup chopped green pepper
¼ cup butter or margarine,
  melted

3 cups chicken broth
Dash of ground white pepper
2 cups milk
½ cup all-purpose flour
3 cups (12 ounces) shredded
  process American cheese
1 tablespoon minced fresh
  parsley

Sauté first 5 ingredients in butter in a Dutch oven over medium-high heat, stirring constantly, until crisp-tender. Add chicken broth and pepper; bring to a boil. Cover, reduce heat, and simmer 30 minutes.

Combine milk and flour, stirring until smooth; add to broth mixture, stirring constantly. Stir in cheese and parsley. Cook over medium heat 20 minutes or until thickened, stirring frequently. Yield: 7½ cups.   Bonnie Grodahl

Batter's Up!
Rembrandt Area Craft Club
Rembrandt, Iowa

Mushroom Chowder

We suggest sprinkling additional Parmesan cheese on top of each serving.

½ cup chopped onion
¼ cup butter or margarine,
    melted
1 pound fresh mushrooms,
    sliced
1½ cups water
1 cup peeled, diced baking
    potato

1 cup finely chopped celery
½ cup diced carrot
1½ teaspoons salt
⅛ teaspoon pepper
1 tablespoon all-purpose flour
2 tablespoons water
1 cup milk
¼ cup grated Parmesan cheese

Sauté onion in butter in a large saucepan over medium-high heat, stirring constantly, until tender. Add mushrooms and next 6 ingredients; bring to a boil. Cover, reduce heat, and simmer 15 to 20 minutes or until vegetables are tender.

Combine flour and 2 tablespoons water; stir well. Add to vegetable mixture; cook, stirring constantly, until thickened. Stir in milk and cheese; cook just until thoroughly heated, stirring frequently (do not boil). Yield: 6 cups.   Linda L. Books

Now We're Cookin'
Presbyterian Women of Northwood Presbyterian Church
Clearwater, Florida

Tuna-Cheese Chowder

2 medium carrots, scraped
    and shredded
1 medium onion, finely
    chopped
¼ cup butter or margarine,
    melted
¼ cup all-purpose flour
2 cups milk
2 cups chicken broth

1 cup (4 ounces) shredded
    process American cheese
1 (6⅛-ounce) can tuna in
    water, drained and flaked
½ teaspoon celery seeds
½ teaspoon Worcestershire
    sauce
¼ teaspoon salt
Garnish: chopped fresh chives

Sauté carrot and onion in butter in a large saucepan over medium heat, stirring constantly, until tender. Reduce heat to low; add flour, stirring until blended. Cook 1 minute, stirring constantly. Gradually add milk and broth; cook over medium heat, stirring constantly, until thickened and bubbly. Reduce heat to low. Add cheese and next 4 ingredients; cook, stirring constantly, just until cheese melts. To serve, ladle soup into individual soup bowls. Garnish, if desired. Yield: 5¼ cups. Tondi Tillman

Family Style Cookbook
Northern Door Child Care Center
Sister Bay, Wisconsin

Chicken in a Pot, Japanese Style

If you can't find fresh black Chinese or shiitake mushrooms at your grocery store, you can substitute 2 ounces of dried mushrooms that have been rehydrated according to package directions.

6 ounces Japanese noodles
  (soba or udon), uncooked
8 cups chicken broth
12 ounces skinned and boned
  chicken breast halves, cut
  into 2-inch pieces
1 cup thinly sliced carrot
9 fresh black Chinese or
  shiitake mushrooms, halved
6 large Napa cabbage leaves,
  cut into 2-inch squares

1 (8-ounce) can bamboo
  shoots, drained
3 green onions, cut into 2-inch
  pieces
12 ounces firm tofu, drained
  and cut into 1-inch cubes
1 tablespoon dry sherry
Dash of pepper
1 tablespoon soy sauce
  (optional)
½ cup chopped fresh parsley

Cook noodles according to package directions; drain. Set aside. Bring chicken broth to a boil in a large Dutch oven over medium-high heat. Add chicken and carrot; reduce heat, and simmer, uncovered, 15 minutes. Stir in mushrooms and next 3 ingredients; simmer, uncovered, 5 minutes. Add reserved noodles, tofu, sherry, pepper, and soy sauce, if desired. Simmer, uncovered, an additional 10 minutes or until mixture is thoroughly heated. To serve, ladle into individual soup bowls; sprinkle with parsley. Yield: 13 cups. Eleanor Gold Hirsch

California Kosher
Women's League of Adat Ari El Synagogue
North Hollywood, California

Black Bean-Turkey Chili

2 medium onions, chopped
1 sweet red pepper, finely
  chopped
6 cloves garlic, minced
2 tablespoons olive oil
2 pounds fresh ground turkey
1 pound Italian turkey sausage,
  sliced
2 (15-ounce) cans black beans,
  drained
1 (28-ounce) can Italian-style
  tomatoes, undrained and
  chopped

1 (14-ounce) can Italian-style
  tomatoes, undrained and
  chopped
1 (12-ounce) can tomato paste
2 (4-ounce) cans chopped
  green chiles, undrained
1 cup beer
3 tablespoons chili powder
1 tablespoon dried basil
1 tablespoon dried oregano
1 teaspoon salt
½ teaspoon pepper
¼ cup chopped fresh cilantro

Sauté onion, red pepper, and garlic in olive oil in a large skillet over medium-high heat, stirring constantly, until vegetables are tender. Add ground turkey and sausage; cook until meats are browned, stirring until ground turkey crumbles. Drain well. Return mixture to pan. Stir in black beans and next 10 ingredients; bring to a boil. Cover, reduce heat, and simmer 20 to 30 minutes. Stir in cilantro. Yield: 17 cups.

California Sizzles
The Junior League of Pasadena, California

Harvest Stew

Choose a medium pumpkin that is no larger than 10 inches in diameter so that it will fit in a pan and in the oven. Toast the pumpkin seeds, and use them to garnish the stew.

1 medium pumpkin (about
  10 inches in diameter)
2 cups fresh green beans
¼ cup all-purpose flour
1½ teaspoons salt
⅛ teaspoon pepper
⅛ teaspoon ground cloves
2 pounds beef stew meat

3 tablespoons vegetable oil
1 (16-ounce) can whole
  tomatoes, undrained
1 cup beef broth
4 medium baking potatoes,
  peeled and quartered
8 boiling onions, peeled
Toasted Pumpkin Seeds

Cut off pumpkin top; reserve top. Scrape out and discard membranes, removing and reserving pumpkin seeds. Remove 2 cups pumpkin flesh from pumpkin, leaving walls at least ½ inch thick, especially near the bottom of pumpkin. Set shell aside. Cut pumpkin flesh into chunks; set aside. Trim green beans; set aside.

Combine flour, salt, pepper, and cloves in a large heavy-duty, zip-top plastic bag; add meat. Seal bag securely, and shake until meat is coated.

Brown meat in oil in a Dutch oven over high heat. Add tomatoes and broth; bring to a boil. Cover, reduce heat, and simmer 1½ hours. Add reserved pumpkin chunks, reserved green beans, potato, and onions; cover and simmer an additional 1½ hours or until meat and vegetables are tender.

Spoon stew mixture into reserved pumpkin shell; cover with reserved pumpkin top. Place pumpkin in an ungreased 13- x 9- x 2-inch pan. Bake on lowest position of oven rack at 350° for 45 minutes. To serve, ladle stew into individual soup bowls. Sprinkle each serving with Toasted Pumpkin Seeds. Yield: 10½ cups.

Toasted Pumpkin Seeds

Seeds of 1 pumpkin　　　　　　**½ teaspoon salt**
2 tablespoons vegetable oil

Remove membranes from seeds; wash seeds, and drain well. Pat seeds with paper towels to remove moisture. Spread seeds in a single layer on an ungreased baking sheet; let stand at room temperature until dry, stirring occasionally.

Combine seeds, oil, and salt in a bowl; toss to coat. Place seeds in a single layer in an ungreased 15- x 10- x 1-inch jellyroll pan. Bake at 350° for 25 minutes or until golden, stirring every 5 minutes. Let cool completely. Yield: about 1⅓ cups.　　　　　　Ellen Saum

The McClellanville Coast Cookbook
The McClellanville Arts Council
McClellanville, South Carolina

Spicy Malaysian Lamb

Cilantro, turmeric, gingerroot, green chiles, and chili powder give this hearty lamb stew its exotic flavor.

2 tablespoons cider vinegar
2 tablespoons fresh lime juice
1½ teaspoons chili powder
3 pounds boneless lamb, cut into 1-inch pieces
3 tablespoons vegetable oil, divided
2½ cups thinly sliced onion (about 2 medium)
1 (4-ounce) can chopped green chiles, undrained
2 cloves garlic, minced

1½ tablespoons peeled, minced gingerroot
1½ teaspoons salt
½ teaspoon ground turmeric
1 (28-ounce) can whole tomatoes, undrained and chopped
¾ cup water
Salt and freshly ground pepper to taste
Garnish: chopped fresh cilantro

Combine first 3 ingredients; stir well. Place lamb in a large shallow dish. Pour vinegar mixture over lamb; cover and let stand at room temperature 15 minutes.

Brown lamb in 2 tablespoons oil in a large Dutch oven over medium heat. Drain and set aside.

Sauté onion and next 5 ingredients in remaining 1 tablespoon oil in pan over medium heat, stirring constantly, until onion is tender. Add reserved lamb, tomatoes, and water. Bring to a boil; cover, reduce heat, and simmer 1½ hours or until lamb is tender, stirring occasionally. Stir in salt and pepper to taste. To serve, ladle stew into individual soup bowls. Garnish, if desired. Yield: 8 cups.

Culinary Arts, Volume II
Society of the Arts of Allentown Art Museum
Allentown, Pennsylvania

Vegetables

*Celebrate the crunchy textures, fresh flavors,
and bold colors that vegetables bring to the table with the bounty
of recipes in this chapter.*

Steamed Corn with Basil Butter, page 306

Asparagus with Pistachio-Orange Sauce

When sautéing the pistachios in the melted butter, watch them closely because they'll brown very quickly.

1½ pounds fresh asparagus
3 tablespoons pistachios
¼ cup plus 2 tablespoons
   butter or margarinc, melted
1 tablespoon grated orange
   rind

3 tablespoons fresh orange
   juice
Freshly ground pepper to taste

Snap off tough ends of asparagus. Remove scales from stalks with a knife or vegetable peeler, if desired. Set aside.

Sauté pistachios in butter in a small skillet over medium heat, stirring constantly, 3 to 4 minutes or until lightly browned. Add orange rind and orange juice; cook, stirring constantly with a wire whisk, 1 minute or until thoroughly heated. Set aside; keep warm.

Blanch reserved asparagus in boiling water 3 to 5 minutes or until crisp-tender. Drain. Arrange asparagus on a serving platter. Pour reserved sauce over asparagus. Sprinkle with pepper to taste. Serve immediately. Yield: 6 servings.   Doris Gillard

Grazing Across Wisconsin, Book II
Telephone Pioneers of America, Wisconsin Chapter 4
Milwaukee, Wisconsin

Asparagus Pudding

1½ pounds fresh asparagus
¼ cup butter or margarine
¼ cup all-purpose flour
1 cup milk
1 tablespoon fresh lime juice

1½ teaspoons salt
⅛ teaspoon ground red
   pepper
6 large eggs, separated

Snap off tough ends of asparagus. Remove scales from stalks with a knife or vegetable peeler, if desired. Arrange in a vegetable steamer over boiling water. Cover and steam 8 minutes or until crisp-tender. Cut into ½-inch pieces; place in a bowl. Set aside.

Melt butter in a heavy saucepan over low heat; add flour, stirring until smooth. Cook 1 minute, stirring constantly. Gradually add milk; cook over medium heat, stirring constantly, until mixture is thickened and bubbly. Remove from heat; stir in lime juice, salt, and pepper. Beat egg yolks until thick and pale. Gradually stir about one-fourth of hot mixture into yolks with a wire whisk; add to remaining hot mixture, stirring constantly. Pour over reserved asparagus, and stir gently.

Beat egg whites at high speed of an electric mixer until stiff peaks form. Gently fold beaten egg white into asparagus mixture. Spoon into a lightly buttered 3-quart soufflé dish. Place dish in a large shallow pan. Add hot water to pan to depth of 1 inch. Bake, uncovered, at 350° for 1 hour and 10 minutes or until a knife inserted in center comes out clean. Serve immediately. Yield: 8 to 10 servings.   Jackie Bopp

Kitchen Operations
Windham Community Memorial Hospital Auxiliary
Willimantic, Connecticut

Green Beans with Fontina

This green bean dish is served at room temperature, but it can also be served warm. Simply omit rinsing the beans in cold water, and heat the oil mixture in a small saucepan over medium heat until warm.

1 pound fresh green beans   **½ teaspoon Dijon mustard**
8 ounces Fontina cheese, cut   **½ cup olive oil**
  into very thin strips   **¼ cup lemon juice**
1 clove garlic, crushed   **Salt and pepper to taste**

Wash beans and remove strings. Cook beans in a small amount of boiling water 10 to 12 minutes or until crisp-tender; drain. Rinse beans with cold water; drain. Combine beans and cheese in a large bowl. Set aside.

Combine garlic and mustard in a bowl; gradually add olive oil and lemon juice, beating with a wire whisk until blended. Pour over bean mixture; toss. Sprinkle with salt and pepper to taste. Yield: 4 to 6 servings.   Anne Schopick

Cooking Up a Storm
L.Z. Aerobics Class
Lawrenceville, Georgia

Green Beans with Peanut Sauce

Substitute 1 tablespoon peeled, grated gingerroot for ground ginger.

1½ pounds fresh green beans
½ cup water
2 tablespoons creamy peanut butter
1 teaspoon ground ginger

¼ teaspoon ground red pepper
1 large clove garlic, minced
1 teaspoon peanut or sesame oil
½ teaspoon salt

Wash beans and remove strings. Cook in a small amount of boiling water 10 to 12 minutes or until crisp-tender. Drain; set aside.

Combine ½ cup water and next 3 ingredients; set aside.

Sauté garlic in oil in a large skillet over medium heat, stirring constantly, until tender. Add reserved peanut butter mixture and salt; stir well. Add reserved beans; cook over medium heat, stirring constantly, 4 minutes or until beans are tender and mixture is thoroughly heated. Serve immediately. Yield: 4 servings.

From Portland's Palate
The Junior League of Portland, Oregon

Harvest Cinnamon Beans

1½ pounds fresh green beans
¼ cup chopped onion
¼ teaspoon ground cinnamon
1 tablespoon butter or margarine, melted

½ cup chicken broth
2 tablespoons tomato paste
⅛ teaspoon salt
⅛ teaspoon pepper

Wash beans and remove strings; cut into 1-inch pieces. Set aside.

Sauté onion and cinnamon in butter in a large skillet over medium heat, stirring constantly, until tender. Combine chicken broth and tomato paste; stir well, and add to skillet. Add reserved beans, salt, and pepper; bring to a boil. Cover, reduce heat, and simmer 15 to 20 minutes or until beans are tender. Yield: 6 servings.

Ruth Lovell

Reflections of the West
Telephone Pioneers of America, Skyline Chapter No. 67
Helena, Montana

Danish Limas

Danish blue cheese is a mild-flavored variety that's heavily laced with greenish-blue veins.

2 (10-ounce) packages frozen
  lima beans, thawed
½ cup chopped celery
¼ cup chopped onion
1 (8-ounce) carton sour cream

½ cup crumbled blue cheese
¼ cup diced pimiento, drained
4 slices bacon, cooked and
  crumbled

Combine first 3 ingredients in a medium saucepan; add water to cover. Bring to a boil; reduce heat, and simmer, uncovered, 10 minutes or until tender. Drain well.

Return bean mixture to pan. Stir in sour cream and cheese. Cook over medium-low heat, stirring frequently, until cheese melts (do not boil). Stir in pimiento. Sprinkle with bacon. Serve immediately. Yield: 6 to 8 servings. Janet Wesseldine

From the Kitchens of . . . Columbia Employees
Columbia Gas Distribution Companies
Columbus, Ohio

Vagabond Beans

Golden raisins are specially treated to prevent their color from darkening, but you can certainly substitute dark raisins in this recipe if you wish.

2 (28-ounce) cans baked beans
2 Granny Smith apples, peeled
  and chopped
2 small onions, chopped
1 cup golden raisins

1 cup chopped cooked ham
1 cup chili sauce
½ cup sweet pickle relish
1 tablespoon dry mustard

Combine all ingredients in a bowl; stir well. Pour into a greased 3-quart casserole. Cover and bake at 350° for 1 hour or until thoroughly heated. Yield: 10 servings. Carl and Emilie Dubuy

A Taste of Reno
The Food Bank of Northern Nevada
Sparks, Nevada

Broccoli with Zesty Sauce

The sour cream sauce gets its name and zesty flavor from vinegar, poppy seeds, and ground red pepper.

1 pound fresh broccoli	1 teaspoon white vinegar
2 tablespoons minced onion	½ teaspoon poppy seeds
2 tablespoons butter or margarine, melted	½ teaspoon paprika
1½ cups sour cream	¼ teaspoon salt
2 tablespoons sugar	Dash of ground red pepper
	⅓ cup chopped cashews

Trim off large leaves of broccoli, and remove tough ends of stalks. Wash broccoli thoroughly; cook in a small amount of boiling water 8 minutes or until tender. Drain well. Set broccoli aside, and keep warm.

Sauté onion in butter in a medium skillet over medium heat, stirring constantly, until tender. Reduce heat to low. Stir in sour cream and next 6 ingredients; cook, stirring constantly, until thoroughly heated. Pour over reserved broccoli; sprinkle with cashews. Serve immediately. Yield: 4 servings.　　　　　Yvette Goldman

What's Cooking in Nutley!
The Friends of the Nutley Public Library
Nutley, New Jersey

Golden Cheddar-Broccoli Bake

2 tablespoons butter or margarine	¾ cup corn flake crumbs, divided
2 tablespoons all-purpose flour	2 (10-ounce) packages frozen broccoli spears
1½ cups milk	2 tablespoons butter or margarine, melted
¼ teaspoon salt	
1½ cups (6 ounces) shredded sharp Cheddar cheese	
1 (11-ounce) can whole kernel corn, drained	

Melt 2 tablespoons butter in a heavy saucepan over low heat; add flour, stirring until mixture is smooth. Cook 1 minute, stirring constantly. Gradually add milk; cook mixture over medium heat, stirring constantly, until mixture is thickened and bubbly. Stir in salt. Add cheese; cook, stirring constantly, until cheese melts. Remove from heat; stir in corn and ¼ cup corn flake crumbs. Set mixture aside.

Cook broccoli according to package directions; drain. Arrange broccoli in a lightly greased 11- x 7- x 1½-inch baking dish. Pour reserved cheese sauce over broccoli.

Combine remaining ½ cup corn flake crumbs and 2 tablespoons butter in a small bowl; stir well. Sprinkle corn flake crumb mixture evenly over broccoli mixture. Bake, uncovered, at 350° for 25 to 30 minutes or until hot and bubbly. Yield: 8 servings.

Bone Appetite
San Diego Humane Society & SPCA Auxiliary
San Diego, California

Sesame Broccoli

Extracted from sesame seeds, sesame oil is available in either a light or dark form. The dark oil has a stronger sesame flavor. It can be used in this recipe in place of the vegetable oil for a nutty-flavored accent.

1 pound fresh broccoli	**1 tablespoon white vinegar**
1 tablespoon sesame seeds,	**1 tablespoon soy sauce**
toasted	**1½ teaspoons vegetable oil**
1 teaspoon sugar	**1½ teaspoons water**

Trim off large leaves of broccoli, and remove tough ends of stalks. Wash broccoli thoroughly, and cut into spears. Cook in a small amount of boiling water 8 to 10 minutes or until crisp-tender; drain. Place in a serving dish; set aside, and keep warm.

Combine sesame seeds and remaining ingredients in a small saucepan; stir well. Bring to boil; pour over reserved broccoli. Serve immediately. Yield: 8 servings.

A Taste of New England
The Junior League of Worcester, Massachusetts

Best Brussels Sprouts

Brussels sprouts are named for the Belgian city where they were first cultivated during the 16th century.

1 pound fresh brussels sprouts
2 to 3 cloves garlic, minced
1 tablespoon butter or
  margarine, melted
1 tablespoon olive oil
½ cup chicken broth
¼ teaspoon salt

¼ teaspoon pepper
1 tablespoon butter or
  margarine, melted
1 tablespoon chopped fresh
  parsley
1 teaspoon lemon juice
  (optional)

Wash brussels sprouts thoroughly; remove discolored leaves. Cut off stem ends, and slash bottom of each sprout with a shallow X. Set aside.

Sauté garlic in 1 tablespoon butter and olive oil in a medium skillet over medium heat, stirring constantly, until tender. Add reserved brussels sprouts, stirring gently to coat. Add chicken broth, salt, and pepper; bring to a boil. Cover, reduce heat, and simmer 10 to 15 minutes or until tender. Drain.

Return brussels sprouts to skillet. Add 1 tablespoon butter, chopped parsley, and lemon juice, if desired; stir gently. Cook over low heat until mixture is thoroughly heated, stirring frequently. Yield: 4 servings.   Suzanne Townsend

Mitten Bay Gourmet
Mitten Bay Girl Scout Council
Saginaw, Michigan

Braised Red Cabbage

Bacon, apples, vinegar, and caraway seeds flavor this traditional German cabbage dish.

4 slices bacon, diced
¼ cup firmly packed brown
  sugar
1 small onion, thinly sliced
  and separated into rings
  (optional)

4 cups shredded red cabbage
2 Granny Smith apples, peeled
  and thinly sliced
2 tablespoons red wine vinegar
½ teaspoon caraway seeds
¼ teaspoon salt

Cook diced bacon in a Dutch oven until crisp. Add brown sugar and onion, if desired; cook over medium heat, stirring constantly, until sugar melts. Reduce heat to low. Stir in shredded cabbage and remaining ingredients. Cover and cook 30 minutes or until cabbage is tender, stirring occasionally. Serve immediately. Yield: 4 servings. Virginia Cooper Matthews

A Taste of Twin Pines
Twin Pines Alumni of Twin Pines Cooperative House
West Lafayette, Indiana

Chinese Celery

This side dish is quick and easy. It takes less than 15 minutes to cook.

1½ cups sliced celery
1 medium onion, chopped
1 (8-ounce) can sliced water
  chestnuts, drained
1 (4-ounce) can sliced
  mushrooms, drained

2 tablespoons slivered almonds
2 tablespoons butter or
  margarine, melted
2 tablespoons soy sauce

Combine all ingredients in a large skillet; bring to a boil. Cover, reduce heat, and simmer 12 to 14 minutes or until celery is crisp-tender, stirring occasionally. Yield: 4 to 6 servings.

Southwest Seasons Cookbook
Casa Angelica Auxiliary
Albuquerque, New Mexico

Celery Leaf Soufflé

Fresh celery leaves give this side-dish soufflé its subtle flavor. Use celery leaves that are green and crisp for best results.

1 medium onion, grated	1 cup chicken broth
¼ cup butter or margarine, melted	¼ cup whipping cream
	½ teaspoon salt
1½ cups chopped celery leaves	¼ teaspoon pepper
1 cup fine, dry breadcrumbs	4 large eggs, separated

Sauté onion in butter in a large saucepan over medium heat, stirring constantly, until tender. Remove from heat; stir in celery leaves and next 5 ingredients.

Beat egg yolks with a wire whisk until thick and pale. Gradually stir beaten egg yolk into celery mixture.

Beat egg whites at high speed of an electric mixer until stiff peaks form. Gently fold beaten egg white into celery mixture.

Pour into a lightly greased 1½-quart soufflé dish. Bake at 375° for 30 to 35 minutes or until puffed and golden. Serve immediately. Yield: 6 servings.

Family & Company
The Junior League of Binghamton, New York

Steamed Corn with Basil Butter

This zesty herb butter can also be served over English peas. You can substitute your favorite herb for a custom-flavored herb butter.

3 tablespoons chopped fresh basil	1 teaspoon grated orange rind
3 tablespoons butter or margarine, softened	6 ears fresh corn, husks and silks removed
3 tablespoons whipped butter, softened	

Combine first 4 ingredients in a small bowl, stirring until blended. Set aside.

Arrange corn in a vegetable steamer over boiling water. Cover and steam 10 to 15 minutes or until corn is tender. Remove corn from vegetable steamer; spread butter mixture evenly over corn. Serve immediately. Yield: 6 servings.

Heavenly Hosts
Bryn Mawr Presbyterian Church
Bryn Mawr, Pennsylvania

Broiled Basil Eggplant

Select a large eggplant so that the slices will be the right diameter. A smaller eggplant can be used, but you'll need to reduce the broiling time.

¼ cup olive oil	8 (⅓-inch-thick) slices large
2 tablespoons chopped fresh basil	eggplant
	3 tablespoons olive oil
2 tablespoons chopped fresh parsley	¼ teaspoon salt
	¼ teaspoon pepper
2 tablespoons lemon juice	3 ounces mozzarella cheese,
¼ teaspoon salt	cut into ⅛-inch-thick slices
⅛ teaspoon pepper	Garnish: fresh basil sprigs

Combine first 6 ingredients in a small bowl, beating with a wire whisk until blended. Set aside.

Brush both sides of eggplant slices with 3 tablespoons olive oil. Arrange eggplant slices in a single layer on an ungreased baking sheet. Sprinkle with ¼ teaspoon salt and ¼ teaspoon pepper. Broil 5½ inches from heat (with electric oven door partially opened) 5 minutes on each side or until tender and lightly browned.

Arrange eggplant slices on an ovenproof platter, overlapping slices slightly. Arrange cheese slices over eggplant slices. Broil 1 minute or until cheese melts. Whisk reserved olive oil mixture until blended; spoon over eggplant. Garnish, if desired. Serve immediately. Yield: 8 servings.

Blooming Good
National Council of State Garden Clubs
St. Louis, Missouri

Parsnips Puree

Thin Parsnips Puree with milk or chicken broth for a quick and easy soup.

2 pounds parsnips, scraped
   and cut into 1-inch pieces
1 (8-ounce) carton plain yogurt

Dash of ground white pepper
Dash of ground nutmeg
Salt to taste

Cook parsnips in a small amount of boiling water 10 minutes or until tender. Drain well. Position knife blade in food processor bowl; add parsnips. Cover and process 1 minute or until smooth, stopping once to scrape down sides. Add yogurt; cover and process 20 to 30 seconds or until blended, stopping once to scrape down sides. Stir in pepper, nutmeg, and salt to taste. Serve immediately. Yield: 6 servings.

Sharen Benenson

Cooking with Grace
Grace Church School Parents' Association
New York, New York

Black-Eyed Pea Cakes

This recipe offers a new menu twist to the New Year's tradition of serving black-eyed peas for good luck.

¾ cup finely chopped purple
   onion
½ cup finely chopped sweet
   red pepper
1 jalapeño pepper, seeded and
   finely chopped
1 tablespoon butter or
   margarine, melted
2 (16-ounce) cans black-eyed
   peas, drained
½ cup fine, dry breadcrumbs
2 egg yolks, lightly beaten

¼ cup chopped fresh cilantro
3 cloves garlic, crushed
1 teaspoon ground cumin
1 teaspoon dry mustard
1 teaspoon dried oregano
1 teaspoon dried thyme
½ teaspoon salt
⅓ cup yellow cornmeal
¼ cup vegetable oil, divided
¾ cup sour cream
¼ cup chopped green onions
1½ cups commercial salsa

Sauté first 3 ingredients in butter in a large skillet over medium-high heat, stirring constantly, until tender. Remove from heat; set aside, and let cool slightly.

Mash black-eyed peas in a large bowl. Add reserved vegetable mixture, breadcrumbs, and next 8 ingredients; stir well. Shape mixture into 12 (2½-inch) patties. Dredge patties in cornmeal.

Fry half of patties in 2 tablespoons oil in a large skillet over medium-high heat 3 to 4 minutes on each side or until lightly browned. Transfer to a serving platter; set aside, and keep warm. Repeat procedure with remaining patties and 2 tablespoons oil. Top each patty with 1 tablespoon sour cream; sprinkle evenly with green onions. Serve with salsa. Yield: 6 servings.

Virginia Celebrates
The Council of the Virginia Museum of Fine Arts
Richmond, Virginia

Peas with Lemon and Tarragon

You can substitute 2 pounds of fresh unshelled English peas for the frozen peas, but note that the cooking time will take longer—about 15 minutes instead of 6 minutes.

1 (16-ounce) package frozen English peas
1 teaspoon sugar
½ teaspoon salt
3 tablespoons butter or margarine, melted

1 teaspoon minced fresh tarragon
½ teaspoon grated lemon rind
1 teaspoon lemon juice
Salt and freshly ground pepper to taste

Combine peas, sugar, and ½ teaspoon salt in a medium saucepan; add water to cover. Bring to a boil; cover, reduce heat, and simmer 6 minutes or until tender. Drain; place peas in a serving bowl. Add butter and remaining ingredients; toss gently. Serve immediately. Yield: 4 servings.

Kathryn Pusey

The Montauk Lighthouse Cookbook
The Montauk Lighthouse Committee
Montauk, New York

Peas for a Party

½ cup water
¼ cup butter or margarine
2 tablespoons sugar
2 teaspoons salt
¼ teaspoon pepper

2 (10-ounce) packages frozen
  English peas
6 cups shredded iceberg
  lettuce

Combine first 5 ingredients in a large saucepan; bring to a boil. Stir in peas; return to a boil. Cover, reduce heat, and simmer 5 to 6 minutes or until peas are crisp-tender. Remove from heat, and stir in lettuce. Cover and let stand 2 minutes; drain. Serve immediately. Yield: 8 servings.   Nell Long

Culinary Creations
Retired Senior Volunteer Program of Cleveland
and McClain County
Norman, Oklahoma

Corn in Green Peppers

2 large green peppers
2 cups frozen whole kernel
  corn, thawed
1½ cups (6 ounces) shredded
  sharp Cheddar cheese
1 (2-ounce) jar diced pimiento,
  drained

1 small onion, chopped
1 teaspoon celery seeds
1 teaspoon dried marjoram
¼ teaspoon salt
⅛ teaspoon pepper
¼ cup (1 ounce) shredded
  sharp Cheddar cheese

Cut green peppers in half lengthwise, removing stems. Remove and discard seeds and membranes; set peppers aside.

Combine corn and next 7 ingredients in a medium bowl; stir well. Spoon corn mixture evenly into reserved pepper halves. Place in a lightly buttered 11- x 7- x 1½-inch baking dish. Cover and bake at 350° for 1 hour. Uncover; sprinkle evenly with ¼ cup cheese, and bake an additional 5 minutes or until cheese melts. Serve immediately. Yield: 4 servings.

Cooking with Herb Scents
Western Reserve Herb Society
Bay Village, Ohio

Pilaf-Stuffed Peppers

Although sweet red, orange, and yellow peppers are a little more expensive, consider using them, as well as green peppers, for a more colorful side dish.

4 large green peppers
½ cup finely chopped onion
½ cup thinly sliced celery
2 tablespoons butter or
    margarine, melted
½ cup long-grain rice,
    uncooked

¼ cup chopped ripe olives
¼ teaspoon salt (optional)
1 cup vegetable broth or water
¼ cup sunflower kernels
2 cups canned stewed
    tomatoes, undrained and
    chopped

Cut off tops of green peppers 1 inch from top, removing stems. Remove and discard seeds and membranes. Chop tops of peppers, and set aside. Cook peppers in boiling water to cover 5 minutes; drain well, and set aside.

Sauté reserved chopped pepper, onion, and celery in butter in a large saucepan over medium-high heat, stirring constantly, 5 minutes or until tender. Add rice, olives, and, salt, if desired. Cook, stirring constantly, 3 minutes. Add vegetable broth; bring to a boil. Stir in sunflower kernels; cover, reduce heat, and simmer 20 minutes or until rice is tender and liquid is absorbed.

Stuff reserved peppers with rice mixture, and place in an ungreased 8-inch square pan. Spoon stewed tomatoes over stuffed peppers. Cover loosely with aluminum foil. Bake at 350° for 25 to 30 minutes or until peppers are tender and rice mixture is thoroughly heated. Yield: 4 servings.   Elizabeth Forest Tinsley

Rosie's Place Recipes
Rosie's Place
Boston, Massachusetts

Sweet Red Pepper Tart

This vegetable-packed tart makes a hearty meatless meal.

1 unbaked 10-inch pastry shell
1 tablespoon Dijon mustard
2 cups finely chopped onion
1 clove garlic, minced
3 tablespoons unsalted butter
  or margarine, melted
3 large sweet red peppers,
  diced
1 large green pepper, diced
1 cup (4 ounces) shredded
  Swiss cheese

2 tablespoons chopped fresh
  parsley or basil
4 large eggs
1 cup whipping cream
½ cup sour cream
1 teaspoon salt
¼ teaspoon freshly ground
  pepper
⅛ teaspoon ground red
  pepper
⅛ teaspoon ground nutmeg

Prick bottom of pastry with a fork. Bake at 450° for 10 minutes; remove from oven. Brush bottom of pastry with mustard; set aside. Reduce oven temperature to 350°.

Sauté onion and garlic in butter in a large skillet over medium-high heat, stirring constantly, until tender. Add diced red and green pepper, and sauté, stirring constantly, until pepper is tender. Remove from heat; let cool.

Spoon vegetable mixture into prepared pastry shell; sprinkle with cheese and parsley.

Combine eggs, whipping cream, and sour cream in a large bowl; beat with a wire whisk until blended. Stir in salt and remaining ingredients. Pour egg mixture over vegetable mixture in pastry shell. Bake, uncovered, at 350° for 30 to 40 minutes or until golden and knife inserted in center comes out clean. Let stand 10 minutes before serving. Yield: 8 servings.

A Taste of New England
The Junior League of Worcester, Massachusetts

Rosemary Cheese-Crusted Potatoes

1 medium onion, thinly sliced
3 cloves garlic, minced
1 tablespoon olive oil
4 cups peeled, chopped baking
  potatoes
1 teaspoon seasoned salt
⅛ teaspoon coarsely ground
  pepper
⅛ teaspoon grated lemon rind
2 cups (8 ounces) shredded
  Cheddar cheese, divided
¼ cup fine, dry breadcrumbs
1 tablespoon butter or
  margarine, melted
1 teaspoon chopped fresh
  rosemary

Sauté onion and garlic in oil in a large skillet over medium heat, stirring constantly, until tender. Stir in potato, seasoned salt, pepper, and lemon rind. Layer half of potato mixture in a greased 1½-quart casserole. Sprinkle with 1 cup cheese. Repeat layers once.

Combine breadcrumbs, butter, and rosemary; stir well. Sprinkle breadcrumb mixture evenly over potato mixture. Cover and bake at 400° for 40 minutes. Uncover and bake an additional 20 minutes or until potato is tender. Yield: 6 servings. Shirley Kilgore

Golden Goodies: Favorite Recipes from Positive Maturity
Positive Maturity
Birmingham, Alabama

Savory Roast Potatoes

4 large baking potatoes (about
  3 pounds)
¼ cup butter or margarine,
  melted
1½ teaspoons seasoned salt
¼ cup chicken broth

Peel potatoes; cut into 1-inch cubes. Combine potato and butter in a bowl; toss. Place in an ungreased 15- x 10- x 1-inch jellyroll pan; sprinkle with seasoned salt. Bake, uncovered, at 350° for 45 minutes. Pour broth over potato; stir. Bake, uncovered, an additional 45 minutes or until tender, stirring occasionally. Yield: 6 to 8 servings. Jeanne Roehl

Cross-Town Cooking
Women's Group of Assumption and Sacred Heart Parishes
Bellingham, Washington

Spiced Sweet Potato Balls

3 large sweet potatoes (about
  3 pounds)
1 cup chopped pecans
2 tablespoons butter, softened
1 teaspoon salt

⅛ teaspoon ground allspice
⅛ teaspoon ground cinnamon
⅛ teaspoon ground nutmeg
All-purpose flour
Vegetable oil

Cook sweet potatoes in boiling water to cover 30 to 35 minutes or until tender; drain. Let cool slightly. Peel sweet potatoes; mash in a mixing bowl. Add pecans and next 5 ingredients; beat at medium speed of an electric mixer until smooth. Drop mixture, by rounded tablespoonfuls, into flour; gently roll into balls.

Pour oil to depth of 2 inches into a Dutch oven; heat to 380°. Fry balls, a few at a time, 2 to 3 minutes or until golden. Drain on paper towels. Serve immediately. Yield: 8 servings.

New England Pioneer Pantry
The Merrimack Valley Future Pioneers
North Andover, Massachusetts

Maple Sweet Potato Soufflé

1½ pounds sweet potatoes
½ cup maple syrup
¼ cup butter or margarine,
  softened

¼ teaspoon ground nutmeg
¼ teaspoon grated orange rind
4 large eggs, separated

Cook sweet potatoes in boiling water to cover 30 to 35 minutes or until tender; drain. Let cool slightly. Peel sweet potatoes; mash in a large mixing bowl. Add syrup and next 3 ingredients; beat at medium speed of an electric mixer until smooth. Add egg yolks; beat well.

Beat egg whites at high speed until stiff peaks form; gently fold into mixture. Spoon into a buttered 1½-quart soufflé dish. Bake at 350° for 50 to 55 minutes or until puffed and set. Serve immediately. Yield: 4 to 6 servings.

Frances Artigliere

The Best of Friends
Friends of Waterloo Village
Bernardsville, New Jersey

Spaghetti Squash with Tomato Sauce

To turn this recipe into a main dish, omit the vegetable oil, and brown 1 pound of lean ground beef with the onion, celery, carrot, and garlic. Drain the mixture, and proceed with the recipe.

½ cup chopped onion
½ cup chopped celery
½ cup finely chopped carrot
1 clove garlic, minced
2 tablespoons vegetable oil
1 (28-ounce) can whole tomatoes, undrained and chopped
¼ cup Burgundy or other dry red wine

2 tablespoons minced fresh parsley
1 bay leaf
1 teaspoon chicken-flavored bouillon granules
1 teaspoon dried marjoram
½ teaspoon sugar
⅛ teaspoon pepper
1 (3-pound) spaghetti squash

Sauté first 4 ingredients in oil in a large saucepan over medium-high heat, stirring constantly, until tender. Add tomatoes and next 7 ingredients; bring to a boil. Reduce heat, and simmer, uncovered, 45 minutes, stirring occasionally. Remove and discard bay leaf. Set sauce aside, and keep warm.

Wash squash; cut in half lengthwise. Remove and discard seeds and membranes. Place squash, cut side down, in a large Dutch oven. Add water to pan to depth of 2 inches. Bring to a boil; cover, reduce heat, and simmer 25 to 30 minutes or until squash is tender. Drain and let cool 5 minutes.

Remove spaghetti-like strands with a fork, and place on a serving platter. Spoon reserved sauce over squash. Serve immediately. Yield: 6 servings.

Andrea McGeorge

Country Store's 20th Anniversary Cookbook
John Gomes Elementary School PTA
Fremont, California

Turnips Filled with Spinach

Small turnips have a delicate, sweet taste. Choose small turnips that feel heavy for their size to ensure the best flavor and texture.

8 small turnips, peeled
1 (10-ounce) package fresh
  spinach
1 tablespoon butter or
  margarine, melted
¼ cup whipping cream
Salt and pepper to taste
1 tablespoon butter or
  margarine, melted

Arrange turnips in a vegetable steamer over boiling water. Cover and steam 30 minutes or until turnips are tender. Remove turnips from pan, and let cool. Remove centers from turnips, leaving ½-inch-thick shells and bottoms intact. Set aside.

Remove and discard stems from spinach. Wash spinach thoroughly, and pat dry with paper towels. Finely chop spinach. Sauté spinach in 1 tablespoon butter in a large skillet over high heat, stirring constantly, until wilted. Reduce heat to medium; add whipping cream, and cook 5 to 10 minutes or until liquid evaporates. Remove from heat; stir in salt and pepper to taste.

Spoon spinach mixture evenly into reserved turnip shells. Place in a lightly greased 11- x 7- x 1½-inch baking dish; drizzle remaining 1 tablespoon butter over stuffed turnips. Bake, uncovered, at 350° for 15 minutes or until thoroughly heated. Yield: 8 servings.

Georgia Land
Medical Association of Georgia Alliance
Atlanta, Georgia

Mushroom-Stuffed Yellow Squash

4 medium-size yellow squash
½ pound fresh mushrooms,
  finely chopped
1 small onion, chopped
1 clove garlic, minced
¼ cup butter, melted
1 cup soft breadcrumbs
½ teaspoon salt
¼ teaspoon pepper
Garnish: sliced radishes

Cook squash in boiling water to cover 10 minutes or until tender. Drain and let cool slightly. Trim off stems. Cut each squash in half lengthwise; scoop out pulp, leaving a ¼-inch-thick shell. Set squash pulp and shells aside, and keep warm.

Sauté mushrooms, onion, and garlic in butter in a large skillet over medium heat, stirring constantly, until tender. Remove from heat; stir in reserved squash pulp, breadcrumbs, salt, and pepper. Spoon mixture evenly into reserved squash shells. Bake, uncovered, at 350° for 15 minutes. Garnish, if desired. Serve immediately. Yield: 4 servings.

Plain & Elegant: A Georgia Heritage
West Georgia Medical Center Auxiliary
LaGrange, Georgia

Veggie Bake

Four veggies—carrot, rutabaga, potato, and onion—team up with rice in this easy side-dish casserole.

½ cup water	1 cup (4 ounces) shredded
1 cup shredded carrot	Monterey Jack cheese,
½ cup peeled, shredded	divided
rutabaga	¼ cup milk
¼ cup peeled, shredded sweet	½ teaspoon salt
potato	¼ teaspoon lemon-pepper
2 tablespoons chopped onion	seasoning
1½ cups cooked long-grain	⅛ teaspoon ground nutmeg
rice	

Bring water to a boil in a medium saucepan; add carrot and next 3 ingredients. Cover and cook 5 minutes. Drain, reserving liquid. Add water to reserved liquid to equal ¼ cup.

Combine vegetable mixture, ¼ cup liquid, rice, ¾ cup cheese, and remaining ingredients. Pour mixture into a greased 1-quart casserole. Cover and bake at 350° for 20 to 25 minutes. Uncover and sprinkle with remaining ¼ cup cheese; bake 2 to 3 minutes or until cheese melts. Yield: 4 servings. Jan Balserak

Starlight and Moonbeams
Babies' Alumni of Hilton Head Hospital
Hilton Head Island, South Carolina

Vegetable Curry with Yogurt Sauce

Use a large skillet to stir-fry this vegetable curry if you don't have a wok.

1 tablespoon olive oil
1 large onion, finely chopped
2 cloves garlic, minced
2 teaspoons curry powder
½ teaspoon ground cinnamon
2 cups boiling water
2 vegetable-flavored bouillon
  cubes
2 medium tomatoes, chopped
2 carrots, scraped and sliced
1 (15-ounce) can garbanzo
  beans (chick-peas), drained
1½ cups fresh cauliflower
  flowerets

1 cup frozen English peas
½ cup long-grain rice,
  uncooked
½ cup raisins
2 teaspoons lemon juice
¼ teaspoon salt
1 cup plain nonfat yogurt
½ cup grated cucumber
⅛ teaspoon pepper
2 tablespoons minced fresh
  parsley

Pour oil around top of preheated wok, coating sides; heat at medium-high (375°) for 2 minutes. Add onion, and stir-fry 2 to 3 minutes or until tender. Add garlic, curry powder, and cinnamon, and stir-fry 2 minutes.

Combine boiling water and bouillon cubes, stirring until bouillon dissolves. Add bouillon, tomato, and next 8 ingredients to mixture in wok. Bring to a boil, cover, reduce heat, and simmer 20 minutes or until rice is tender and liquid is absorbed.

Combine yogurt, cucumber, and pepper; stir well. To serve, sprinkle parsley over vegetable mixture, and serve immediately with yogurt mixture. Yield: 4 to 6 servings.   Janet Beer Jacobs

A Jewish Family Cookbook
Valley Beth Shalom Nursery School
Encino, California

Ybor City Vegetable Paella

This Spanish-style vegetable mixture makes a great meatless entrée for 8, but it can also be served as a side dish for 12 to 14.

1 medium eggplant
1 medium onion, diced
⅓ cup olive oil
½ pound fresh mushrooms, cut in half
2 small zucchini, cut into ¾-inch pieces
3 (14½-ounce) cans ready-to-serve chicken broth
1 (16-ounce) package converted rice
1 (9-ounce) package frozen artichoke hearts, thawed
2 medium tomatoes, cut into ¾-inch pieces
¾ teaspoon salt
½ teaspoon threads of saffron, crushed
¼ teaspoon pepper
1 (15-ounce) can garbanzo beans (chick-peas), drained
1 (10-ounce) package frozen English peas
1 (3-ounce) jar pimiento-stuffed olives, drained

Cut eggplant in half lengthwise; cut each half crosswise into ½-inch-thick slices. Set aside.

Sauté onion in oil in a large ovenproof Dutch oven over medium-high heat, stirring constantly, 3 minutes or until tender. Add mushrooms and zucchini, and cook 4 minutes, stirring occasionally. Add reserved eggplant, and cook 3 minutes or until eggplant is crisp-tender, stirring frequently. Add chicken broth and next 6 ingredients; stir well. Bring to a boil; place pan in oven.

Bake, uncovered, at 350° for 50 minutes or until rice is tender and liquid is absorbed. Stir in garbanzo beans, peas, and olives. Cover and bake an additional 15 minutes or until thoroughly heated. Serve immediately. Yield: 8 servings.

Tampa Treasures
The Junior League of Tampa, Florida

Acknowledgments

Each of the cookbooks listed is represented by recipes appearing in *America's Best Recipes: A 1994 Hometown Collection.* Unless otherwise noted, the copyright is held by the sponsoring organization whose mailing address is included.

Above & Beyond Parsley, Junior League of Kansas City, Inc., 9215 Ward Pkwy., Kansas City, MO 64114

ACORD Cookbook I, Avonworth Municipal Authority, P.O. Box 4135, Pittsburgh, PA 15202

All Saints' Cookbook, All Saints' Episcopal Churchwomen, 601 W. Main St., Morristown, TN 37814

American Heritage Cookbook, Brownsville General Hospital Auxiliary, 125 Simpson Rd., Brownsville, PA 15417

Angels & Friends Favorite Recipes II, Angels of Easter Seal, 299 Edwards St., Youngstown, OH 44502

Attaché . . . A Decade of Delicacies, Attaché Booster Club, Inc., of Clinton High School, 711 Lakeview Dr., Clinton, MS 39056

Augusta Cooks for Company, Past and Present, Augusta Council of the Georgia Association for Children and Adults with Learning Disabilities, P.O. Box 3231, Hill Station, Augusta, GA 30904

Batter's Up!, Rembrandt Area Craft Club, 101 E. Main, Rembrandt, IA 50576

The Best of Friends, Friends of Waterloo Village, 30 Mountain Top Rd., Bernardsville, NJ 07924

The Best of Sunset Boulevard, University Synagogue Sisterhood, 11960 Sunset Blvd., Los Angeles, CA 90049

Big Brutus: Treasured Recipes from Coal Mining Families, Big Brutus, Inc., P.O. Box 25, West Mineral, KS 66782

Blooming Good, National Council of State Garden Clubs, Inc., 4401 Magnolia Ave., St. Louis, MO 63110

Bone Appetite, San Diego Humane Society & SPCA Auxiliary, 887 Sherman St., San Diego, CA 92110

California Kosher, Women's League of Adat Ari El Synagogue, 12020 Burbank Blvd., North Hollywood, CA 91607

California Sizzles, Junior League of Pasadena, Inc., 149 S. Madison Ave., Pasadena, CA 91104

Carol & Friends, A Taste of North County, Carol & Friends Steering Committee of the Carol Cox Re-Entry Women's Scholarship Fund at CSU-San Marcos, California State University, San Marcos, San Marcos, CA 92096

Catawba Seasons, Catawba Memorial Hospital Auxiliary, 810 Fairgrove Church Rd., Hickory, NC 28602

Celebrate!, Junior League of Sacramento, Inc., 778 University Ave., Sacramento, CA 95825

Celebration: Saint Andrew's School 30th Anniversary of Celebrated Recipes, Saint Andrew's School Parents' Association, 3900 Jog Rd., Boca Raton, FL 33434

A Centennial Sampler, American Association of University Women, Elkins Branch, P.O. Box 650, Elkins, WV 26241

The Charlotte Central Cooks' Book, Charlotte Central School PTO, R.R. 1, Box 1027, Charlotte, VT 05445

"City" Dining, City of Hope National Medical Center and Beckman Research Institute, 30 W. 26th St., Ste. 301, New York, NY 10010

Classics of the American Midwest, Lancaster County Medical Auxiliary Foundation, Inc., 2966 O St., Lincoln, NE 68510

A Cleveland Collection, Junior League of Cleveland, Inc., 10819 Magnolia Dr., Cleveland, OH 44106

A Collection of Excellent Recipes, Olathe Medical Center, Inc., 20333 W. 151st St., Olathe, KS 66061

A *Collection of Favorite Recipes,* Po'okela Church, P.O. Box 365, Makawao, HI 96768

The Complete Book of Greek Cooking, Recipe Club of St. Paul's Greek Orthodox Cathedral, 110 Cathedral Ave., Hempstead, NY 11550

Concordia Seminary Cookbook 1992-1993, Concordia Seminary Women's Association, 801 DeMun, Clayton, MO 63105

Cookin' for the Kids, WalMart Distribution Center #6011, 2200 Manufacturers Blvd., Brookhaven, MS 39601

Cookin' with C.L.A.S.S., Citizens League for Adult Special Services, 1 Parker St., Lawrence, MA 01843

Cooking Good Eating Better, Sisterhood Israel Center of Hillcrest Manor, 167-11 73rd Ave., Flushing, NY 11366

Cooking in Cade, Episcopal School of Acadiana, Hwy. 92, P.O. Box 380, Cade, LA 70503

Cooking in Ohio, The Heart of It All, 41st National Square Dance Convention, Inc., 2701 Maitland Ave., Cuyahoga Falls, OH 44223

Cooking in Paradise, Key West Power Squadron, 3910 S. Roosevelt Blvd., Apt. 107W, Key West, FL 33040

Cooking Up a Storm, L.Z. Aerobics Class, 630 Rosa Dr., Lawrenceville, GA 30244

Cooking with Class, A Second Helping, Charlotte Latin School, Inc., 9502 Providence Rd., Charlotte, NC 28207

Cooking with Diplomacy, Association of American Foreign Service Women, P.O. Box 70051, Washington, DC 20024

Cooking with Grace, Grace Church School Parents' Association, 86 4th Ave., New York, NY 10014

Cooking with Grace, Grace Episcopal Church, 514 E. Argonne, Kirkwood, MO 63122

Cooking with Herb Scents, Western Reserve Herb Society, 30531 Timber Ln., Bay Village, OH 44140

Cooking with Love, Second Edition, Brevard Hospice, Inc., 866 Westport Dr., Rockledge, FL 32955

Cooking with PRIDE, Volume 2, Alton Community PRIDE, 2628 W. 49th Dr., Alton, KS 67623

Cooking with the Congregation . . . Our Best to You, First Congregational Church, 24 Angela Ln., Billerica, MA 01821

A Cook's Tour of the Bayou Country, Churchwomen of the Southwest Deanery of the Episcopal Diocese of Louisiana, 214 Circle Dr., Franklin, LA 70538

Country Church Favorites, St. John's United Church of Christ, 1213 Washington St., Genoa, OH 43430

Country Cookbook, Our Lady's Guild of St. Christopher's Parish, 102 W. Market St., Red Hook, NY 12571

Country Store's 20th Anniversary Cookbook, John Gomes Elementary School PTA, 555 Lemos Ln., Fremont, CA 94539

The Cradle of Aviation Cookbook, Glenn H. Curtiss Museum, P.O. Box 326, Hammondsport, NY 14840

Cranbrook Reflections: A Culinary Collection, Cranbrook House and Gardens Auxiliary, 380 Lone Pine Rd., Box 801, Bloomfield Hills, MI 48303

Cross-Town Cooking, Women's Group of Assumption and Sacred Heart Parishes, 2116 Cornwall Ave., Bellingham, WA 98225

Culinary Arts, Volume II, Society of the Arts of Allentown Art Museum, 5th and Court Sts., Allentown, PA 18105

Culinary Creations, Retired Senior Volunteer Program of Cleveland and McClain County, 601 N. Porter, Norman, OK 73071

Culinary Masterpieces, Birmingham Museum of Art, 2000 8th Ave. N, Birmingham, AL 35203

Desert Treasures, Junior League of Phoenix, Inc., P.O. Box 10377, Phoenix, AZ 85064

A Dessert A-Fare, Anderson Area Chamber of Commerce, 8072-B Beechmont Ave., Cincinnati, OH 45255

Different, But Still Special!, Service Association for the Retarded, 8th and Locust Sts., Philadelphia, PA 19107

Dining Al Fresco, Wolf Trap Associates, 1551 Trap Rd., Vienna, VA 22182

Edgewood Cooks, Edgewood Auxiliary, 1801 Vicente St., San Francisco, CA 94116

Enon's Best Kept Secret II, Enon Baptist Church, Rt. 3, Box 344, Jayess, MS 39641

Exclusively Pumpkin Cookbook, Coventry Historical Society, Box 534, Coventry, CT 06238

Fabulous Fare, Women's Fellowship of Center Harbor Congregational Church, P.O. Box 229, Center Harbor, NH 03226

Fairfax Heritage Cookbook, Fairfax Community Betterment, P.O. Box 22, Fairfax, MO 64446

Family & Company, Junior League of Binghamton, Inc., 55 Main St., Binghamton, NY 13904

Family Cookbook: A Collection of Favorite Recipes, Women's Ministries of Trinity Assembly of God, 53 N. Main St., Derry, NH 03038

Family Style Cookbook, Northern Door Child Care Center, 340 Hwy. 57, Sister Bay, WI 54234

A Fanfare of Flavors, Stanton Buffalo Bands, 200 N. College St., Stanton, TX 79782

Favorite Recipes by the Students and Staff of St. John's School, St. John's Home and School Association, 100 S. Sturgis, Beloit, KS 67420

Favorite Recipes from Our Best Cooks, Daniel Electric Generating Plant, Hwy. 63 N, P.O. Box 950, Escatawpa, MS 39552

Favorites from First, First Lutheran Churchwomen, 6th Ave. S, Box 268, St. James, MN 56081

A Feast for All Seasons, Junior Women's Club of Mt. Lebanon, 337 Broadmoor Ave., Pittsburgh, PA 15228

Feeding Our Flock, Cross of Christ Lutheran Church, 99 S. County Line Rd., Crown Point, IN 46307

Feeding the Flock, Ellsborough Lutheran Church, R.R. 1, Box 75, Lake Wilson, MN 56151

Fellowship Family Favorites Cookbook, Word of Life Fellowship, Inc., Rt. 9, Schroon Lake, NY 12870

Fiddlers Canyon Ward Cookbook, Fiddlers Canyon Ward Relief Society, 760 E. Cobble Creek Dr., Cedar City, UT 84720

First United Methodist Church Centennial Cookbook, 1993, United Methodist Women of First United Methodist Church, 302 E. 2nd St., Casper, WY 82601

Five Star Sensations, Auxiliary of University Hospitals of Cleveland, 20979 Shaker Blvd., Shaker Heights, OH 44122

The Flavor of Mathews, Mathews County Junior and Senior Woman's Club, P.O. Box 1324, Mathews, VA 23109

Flavors of Cape Henlopen, Village Improvement Association, P.O. Box 144, Rehoboth Beach, DE 19971

Food for Family, Friends and Fellowship, Covenant Women Ministries of Forest Park Covenant Church, 3815 Henry St., Muskegon, MI 49441

Food for Thought: "A Seasoned Celebration," Unitarian-Universalist Fellowship of Athens, 834 Prince Ave., Athens, GA 30606

For Goodness Taste, Junior League of Rochester, Inc., 110 Linden Oaks, Ste. A, Rochester, NY 14625

Franciscan Centennial Cookbook, Franciscan Sisters, 116 8th Ave. SE, Little Falls, MN 56345

From Portland's Palate, Junior League of Portland, 4838 S.W. Scholls Ferry Rd., Portland, OR 97225

From the Heart Classic Recipes, Sacred Heart Hospital Auxiliary, 1314 Cherry Ln., Bluebell, PA 19422

From the Hearts and Homes of Bellingham Covenant Church, Covenant Women's Ministries of Bellingham Covenant Church, 920 E. Sunset Dr., Bellingham, WA 98226

From the Kitchens of . . . Columbia Employees, Columbia Gas Distribution Companies, 200 Civic Center Dr., Columbus, OH 43215

From the Prince's Pantry, Friends of Prince Memorial Library, P.O. Box 158, Cumberland, ME 04021

From Your Neighbor's Kitchen, Friends of Riverton Park, P.O. Box 47, Riverton, NJ 08077

From Zion's Kitchen, Semper Fidelis Sunday School Class of Zion Lutheran Evangelical Church, 10608 Honeyfield Rd., Williamsport, MD 21795

A Full Measure, Long Beach League for John Tracy Clinic, P.O. Box 3565, Long Beach, CA 90803

The Garden Club Cooks, Garden Club of Palm Beach, Inc., P.O. Box 2791, Palm Beach, FL 33480

Gateways, Auxiliary-Twigs . . . Friends of St. Louis Children's Hospital, 400 S. Kingshighway, St. Louis, MO 63110

George Westinghouse Museum Cookbook, George Westinghouse Museum Foundation, Castle Main, Wilmerding, PA 15148

Georgia Land, Medical Association of Georgia Alliance, 938 Peachtree St., Atlanta, GA 30309

German Heritage Recipes, American/Schleswig-Holstein Heritage Society, P.O. Box 313, Davenport, IA 52805

Gethsemane Lutheran Church Centennial Cookbook, Gethsemane Churchwomen, 715 Minnetonka Mills Rd., Hopkins, MN 55343

The Global Gourmet, Multicultural Awareness Council of Nova University, 3301 College Ave., Ft. Lauderdale, FL 33314

Golden Goodies: Favorite Recipes from Positive Maturity, Positive Maturity, Inc., 3600 8th Ave. S, Ste. 301, Birmingham, AL 35222

Golden Valley Women of Today Cookbook, Golden Valley Women of Today, 3312 Quail Ave. N, Golden Valley, MN 55422

Gourmet Wonders of the World, Sixth Grade Class of Savage Elementary School, P.O. Box 399, Ft. Benton, MT 59442

Gracious Goodness, Charleston!, Bishop England High School Endowment Fund, 203 Calhoun St., Charleston, SC 29401

Grazing Across Wisconsin, Book II, Telephone Pioneers of America, Wisconsin Chapter 4, 722 N. Broadway, Rm. 401, Milwaukee, WI 53202

Great Beginnings: The Art of Hors d'Oeuvres, Friends of the Arts of the Tampa Museum of Art, 601 Doyle Carlton Dr., Tampa, FL 33602

The Happy Cooker, Safeway, Inc., 201 4th St., Oakland, CA 94607

Heart & Soul, Junior League of Memphis, Inc., 3475 Central Ave., Memphis, TN 38111

Heavenly Hosts, Bryn Mawr Presbyterian Church, 625 Montgomery Ave., Bryn Mawr, PA 19010

Heavenly Morsels from Hell's Kitchen, Metro Baptist Church, 410 W. 40th St., New York, NY 10018

The Heritage Collection, Western Kentucky University Home Economics Alumni Association, 3341 Cemetery Rd., Bowling Green, KY 42103

Home at the Range with Wyoming B.I.L.'s, Chapter Y of P.E.O. Sisterhood, 1558 Westridge Ct., Casper, WY 82604

Home Cooking with SMRMC, Southwest Mississippi Regional Medical Center Auxiliary, 215 Marion Dr., McComb, MS 39648

Hopewell Heritage, Presbyterian Women of Hopewell Presbyterian Church, 10500 Beatties Ford Rd., Huntersville, NC 28078

Hospitality: A Cookbook Celebrating Boston's North Shore, Salem Hospital Aid Association, 81 Highland Ave., Salem, MA 01970

Idalia Community Cookbook, Women's Fellowship of St. John United Church of Christ, 28439 Co. Rd. 7, Idalia, CO 80735

I'm at the Ballpark, No Time to Cook, Jupiter-Tequesta Athletic Association, 5905 River Club Cir., Jupiter, FL 33458

Impressions: A Palette of Fine Memphis Dining, Auxiliary to the Memphis Dental Society, 6514 Kirby Woods Dr., Memphis, TN 38119

Incredible Edibles, Salvation Army Women's Auxiliary, 2602 Huntingdon Ave., Baltimore, MD 21211

A Jewish Family Cookbook, Valley Beth Shalom Nursery School, 4722 Noeline Ave., Encino, CA 91436

June Fete Fare, Women's Board of Abington Memorial Hospital, Old York Rd., Abington, PA 19001

Kailua Cooks, Le Jardin Academy, 1110-A Kailua Rd., Kailua, HI 96734

Kitchen Operations, Windham Community Memorial Hospital Auxiliary, 55 Northwood Rd., Storrs, CT 06268

Lambda Chi Alpha Brothers', Mothers' Christmas Recipes, Lambda Chi Alpha, Hanover College, P.O. Box 130, Hanover, IN 47243

Landon Legends: Memories and Recipes, Landon School, 10915 Martingale Ct., Potomac, MD 20854

Let Us Break Bread Together, St. Michael's Episcopal Churchwomen, 647 Dundee Ave., Barrington, IL 60010

The Library Cookbook, Friends of the Kent Library, Inc., 42 Smadbeck Ave., Carmel, NY 10512

The McClellanville Coast Cookbook, McClellanville Arts Council, 733 Pinckney St., P.O. Box 594, McClellanville, SC 29458

McMahan Fire Department and Ladies Auxiliary Cookbook, McMahan Fire Department Ladies Auxiliary, Rt. 2, Box 321, Dale, TX 78616

M.D. Anderson Volunteers Cooking for Fun, University of Texas M.D. Anderson Cancer Center, Volunteer Services, 1515 Holcombe, Houston, TX 77030

Mifflinburg Bicentennial Cookbook, Mifflinburg Heritage and Revitalization Association, 300 Chestnut St., Mifflinburg, PA 17844

Mitten Bay Gourmet, Mitten Bay Girl Scout Council, 5470 Davis Rd., Saginaw, MI 48604

The Montauk Lighthouse Cookbook, Montauk Lighthouse Committee, R.F.D. #2, Box 112, Montauk, NY 11954

More, Please!, St. Thomas More Catholic School, 11400 Sherbrook Dr., Baton Rouge, LA 70815

Newcomers' Favorites, International and Regional Recipes, Aiken Newcomers' Club, 712 Winged Foot Dr., Aiken, SC 29803

New England Pioneer Pantry, Merrimack Valley Future Pioneers, 1600 Osgood St., North Andover, MA 01845

The Nineteenth Century Woman's Club Historical Centennial Cookbook, Nineteenth Century Woman's Club, 178 Forest Ave., Oak Park, IL 60301

Now We're Cookin', Presbyterian Women of Northwood Presbyterian Church, 3174 Sandy Ridge Dr., Clearwater, FL 34621

Now You're Cookin', Our Lady of Perpetual Help Church, 1241 Swainwood Dr., Glenview, IL 60025

Our Cherished Recipes, Second Edition, First Presbyterian Church, P.O. Box 513, Skagway, AK 99840

Our Daily Bread, Women's Club of Our Lady of Mt. Carmel, 1045 W. 146th St., Carmel, IN 46032

Our Favorite Recipes, Unity Truth Center, 5844 Pine Hill Rd., Port Richey, FL 34668

Overtures and Encores, Gainesville Chamber Orchestra, 2074 N.W. 11th Rd., Gainesville, FL 32605

Palate Pleasers, Women's Auxiliary of the Hebrew Rehabilitation Center for Aged, 1200 Centre St., Boston, MA 02131

Palmetto Palate Cookbook, American Cancer Society, South Carolina Division, 128 Stonemark Ln., Columbia, SC 29210

The Pasquotank Plate, Christ Episcopal Churchwomen, 200 McMorrine St., Elizabeth City, NC 27909

Plain & Elegant: A Georgia Heritage, West Georgia Medical Center Auxiliary, 1514 Vernon Rd., LaGrange, GA 30240

Pride of Gaithersburg, Gaithersburg Lioness Club, P.O. Box 612, Gaithersburg, MD 20884

Quilted Quisine, Paoli Memorial Hospital Auxiliary, 255 W. Lancaster Ave., Paoli, PA 19301

Recipes from Historic Hotels, National Trust for Historic Preservation, 1785 Massachusetts Ave. NW, Washington, DC 20036

Recipes Worth Begging For, Friends of the Gastineau Humane Society, 7705 Glacier Highway, Juneau, AK 99801

Reflections of the West, Telephone Pioneers of America, Skyline Chapter No. 67, 441 N. Park Ave., Rm. 100, Helena, MT 59624

Rhapsody of Recipes, Chattanooga Symphony Youth Orchestra, 630 Chestnut St., Chattanooga, TN 37402

Rhode Island Cooks, American Cancer Society, Rhode Island Division, Inc., 400 Main St., Pawtucket, RI 02860

Ritzy Rhubarb Secrets Cookbook, Litchville Committee 2,000, P.O. Box 11-A, Litchville, ND 58461

RiverFeast: Still Celebrating Cincinnati, Junior League of Cincinnati, 3500 Columbia Pkwy., Cincinnati, OH 45226

Roaring Springs Recipes & Memories, Roaring Springs Volunteer Organization, 204 Broadway, Box 360, Roaring Springs, TX 79256

Rockingham County Cooks, Rockingham County Arts Council, P.O. Box 83, Eden, NC 27288

Rogue River Rendezvous, Junior Service League of Jackson County, 526 E. Main St., Medford, OR 97504

Roll'n the Dough, Meals on Wheels of Central Arkansas, P.O. Box 5988, North Little Rock, AR 72119

Rosie's Place Recipes, Rosie's Place, 889 Harrison Ave., Boston, MA 02118

Settings: From Our Past to Your Presentation, Junior League of Philadelphia, Inc., P.O. Box 492, Bryn Mawr, PA 19010

"Show-me" Fine Dining, United Guardsman Foundation, Missouri Air National Guard, Rosecrans MAP, St. Joseph, MO 64503

Simply Heavenly, Woman's Synodical Union of the Associate Reformed Presbyterian Church, 1 Cleveland St., Greenville, SC 29601

Sisseton Centennial Cookbook, Sisseton Centennial Committee, 305 E. Walnut, Sisseton, SD 57262

Some Like It Hot, Bement School, Main St., Deerfield, MA 01342

Some Like It Hot, Junior League of McAllen, Inc., 2212 Primrose E, McAllen, TX 78504

Southern Savoir Faire, Altamont School, 4801 Altamont Rd., Birmingham, AL 35213

Southwest Cooks! The Tradition of Native American Cuisines, Southwest Museum, P.O. Box 41558, Los Angeles, CA 90041

Southwest Seasons Cookbook, Casa Angelica Auxiliary, Inc., 5629 Isleta Blvd. SW, Albuquerque, NM 87105

Specialties of the House, Kenmore Association, Inc., 1201 Washington Ave., Fredericksburg, VA 22401

St. Gregory the Great Parish Jubilee Cookbook, St. Gregory the Great Parish, 405 Meadowview Dr., Lebanon, PA 17042

Starlight and Moonbeams, Babies' Alumni of Hilton Head Hospital, 2 Long Brow Rd., Hilton Head Island, SC 29928

Steamboat Entertains, Steamboat Springs Winter Sports Club, 2155 Resort Dr., Ste. 207, Steamboat Springs, CO 80487

Still Gathering: A Centennial Celebration, Auxiliary to the American Osteopathic Association, 142 E. Ontario St., Chicago, IL 60611

Sugar Snips & Asparagus Tips, Woman's Auxiliary of Infant Welfare Society of Chicago, 1931 N. Halsted, Chicago, IL 60614

The Summerhouse Sampler, Wynnton Elementary School PTA, 2303 Wynnton Rd., Columbus, GA 31906

Tampa Treasures, Junior League of Tampa, Inc., P.O. Box 10189, Tampa, FL 33679

Taste & Share the Goodness of Door County, St. Rosalia's Ladies Sodality of St. Rosalia's Catholic Church, 220 Hwy. 42, Ellison Bay, WI 54210

A Taste of History, University of North Alabama Women's Club, UNA, Box 5366, Florence, AL 35632

A Taste of Honey, Cranston-Warwick Hadassah, 15 Nakomis Dr., Warwick, RI 02888

A Taste of New England, Junior League of Worcester, Inc., 71 Pleasant St., Worcester, MA 01609

A Taste of Paradise, Anna Maria Island Community Center, P.O. Box 253, Magnolia St., Anna Maria, FL 34216

A Taste of Reno, Food Bank of Northern Nevada, 994 Packer Way, Sparks, NV 89431

The Taste of St. Louis, St. Louis Catholic Church, 7270 S.W. 120 St., Miami, FL 33156

A Taste of Twin Pines, Twin Pines Alumni of Twin Pines Cooperative House, 321 Highland Dr., West Lafayette, IN 47906

Taste the Magic!, Junior Club of Twin Falls, 624 Blue Lakes Blvd. N, P.O. Box 127, Twin Falls, ID 83301

The Tasty Palette Cookbook, South County Art Association, 5115 Annette Ave., St. Louis, MO 63119

Texas Cookin' Lone Star Style, Telephone Pioneers of America, Lone Star Chapter 22, 208 S. Akard, Rm. 924, Dallas, TX 75202

Thymely Treasures, Hubbard Historical Society, 269 Hager St., Hubbard, OH 44425

Tiger Favorites, American School for the Deaf Alumni Association, 139 N. Main St., West Hartford, CT 06107

Treasured Recipes, Morton County Hospital Auxiliary, P.O. Box 675, Elkhart, KS 67950

Tropical Seasons, A Taste of Life in South Florida, Beaux Arts, Inc., of the Lowe Art Museum of the University of Miami, 1301 Stanford Ave., Coral Gables, FL 33146

Under the Crabapple Tree, Northwestern Elementary School PTA, 13000 Freemanville Rd., Alpharetta, GA 30201

Under the Mulberry Tree, United Methodist Women of Mulberry Street United Methodist Church, 719 Mulberry St., Macon, GA 31202

United Methodist Church Cookbook, Haxtun United Methodist Church, 106 S. Washington, Haxtun, CO 80731

Virginia Celebrates, Council of the Virginia Museum of Fine Arts, 2800 Grove Ave., Richmond, VA 23221

The Virginia Hostess, Junior Woman's Club of Manassas, Inc., P.O. Box 166, Manassas, VA 22110

We're Really Cookin' Now!, Epsilon Sigma Alpha of Oklahoma, 1517 Pineywood Dr., McAlester, OK 74501

We the People . . . have the right to eat Good Food!, Fifth Grade Classes of Milwaukie Elementary School, 11250 S.E. 27th, Milwaukie, OR 97222

What's Cooking in Nutley!, Friends of the Nutley Public Library, 93 Booth Dr., Nutley, NJ 07110

When the Master Gardener Cooks, Seminole County Master Gardeners, 250 W. County Home Rd., Sanford, FL 32773

The Wild Wild West, Junior League of Odessa, Inc., P.O. Box 13675, Odessa, TX 79768

Windows: Reflections of Taste, Brenau University Alumnae Association, 1 Centennial Cir., Gainesville, GA 30501

A World of Good Taste, St. Bernadette's Home and School Guild, 6813 18th Century Ct., Springfield, VA 22150

YUMMM . . . Delicious & Fun Recipes, YWCA of Ridgewood Children's Educational Services, 112 Oak St., Ridgewood, NJ 07450

National Community Cookbook Award Winners

The editors salute the three national and six regional winners of the 1993 Tabasco® Community Cookbook Awards competition sponsored by McIlhenny Company, Avery Island, Louisiana.

- **First Place Winner:** *Heart & Soul*, Junior League of Memphis, Inc., Memphis, Tennessee
- **Second Place Winner:** *From Generation to Generation*, Sisterhood of Temple Emanu-El, Dallas, Texas
- **Third Place Winner:** *California Sizzles*, Junior League of Pasadena, Inc., Pasadena, California
- **New England:** *As You Like It*, Williamstown Theatre Festival Guild, Williamstown, Massachusetts
- **Mid-Atlantic:** *Dining Al Fresco*, Wolf Trap Associates, Vienna, Virginia
- **South:** *The McClellanville Coast Cookbook*, McClellanville Arts Council, McClellanville, South Carolina
- **Midwest:** *Women Cook for a Cause*, Women's Resource Center of Schoolcraft College, Livonia, Michigan
- **Southwest:** *Some Like It Hot*, Junior League of McAllen, Inc., McAllen, Texas
- **West:** *From Portland's Palate*, Junior League of Portland, Oregon

Index